ANGLO-
AMERICAN
FOLKSONG
STYLE

ANGLO-AMERICAN FOLKSONG STYLE

ROGER D. ABRAHAMS

University of Texas

GEORGE FOSS

Louisiana State University

Prentice-Hall, Inc., Englewood Cliffs, New Jersey

© 1968 by PRENTICE-HALL, Inc.
Englewood Cliffs, New Jersey

Library of Congress Catalog Card No.: 68–11288

Current printing (last digit):
10   9   8   7   6   5   4   3   2   1

PRENTICE-HALL INTERNATIONAL, INC., *London*
PRENTICE-HALL OF AUSTRALIA, PTY. LTD., *Sydney*
PRENTICE-HALL OF CANADA, LTD., *Toronto*
PRENTICE-HALL OF INDIA PRIVATE LTD., *New Delhi*
PRENTICE-HALL OF JAPAN, INC., *Tokyo*

To the Singers

And to the Memory of MacEdward Leach

CONTENTS

INTRODUCTION   1

THE ART OF FOLKSONG   4

Folk, Popular, and Sophisticated Art, 5   Public and Private
Expression, 7

THE CYCLE OF ORAL TRANSMISSION
AND COMPOSITION   12

Oral Change, 13   Degenerative Causes of Change, 17   Rationalization and Conventionalization, 18   Forgetting and Emotional Core, 19   Forgetting and Negative Tropisms, 24   Universalization and Localization, 29   Conventional Elements, 31
Composition and Recomposition of Folksongs, 33   The Question
of Literacy and Record, 35

FROM BALLAD TO LYRIC   37

Story-Songs, 37   Changing Styles in the Ballad, 48   Ballad
and Oral Change, 49

THE TRADITIONAL SHAPES OF CONTENT   61

Verse Forms, 62   Form and Repetition, 65   Form and Formula, 69

vii

STYLE AND THE
ORGANIZATION OF MEANING   77

Story-Songs-The Ballad, 78   Blues Ballads, Coronachs, Last
Goodnights, 83   Dialog Songs, 85   Lyric Songs, 87   Legendary Songs, 89   Other Song Types, 89

THE CONTENT OF THE SONGS:
LOVE AND DEATH   92

Once More, The Child Ballads, 92   Father's Opposition to
Lovers, 110   Separation of Lovers by Their Own Devices, 114
American Songs of Death, 120   Men Away from Women: The
Occupational Ballads, 126

THE METRICAL ASPECT OF FOLKSONG   132

Rhythm and Meter, 132   Meter in Traditional Verse and Song,
133   Meter in Traditional Music, 134   The Interdependence
of Text and Tune, 139   Metrical Rigidity, 140   Story-Song,
142   The Influence of Instruments, 148   Motion Songs, 149

THE NATURE OF FOLK TUNES   151

What Is a Folk Tune?, 151   Melody, 152   Common Characteristics in Folk Tunes, 153   Scale, 153   Melodic Progression, 159   Contour, 160   Variety of Contour, 162

THE MUSICAL FORM OF FOLKSONG   165

Musical Stability in Oral Tradition, 170   Same Song, Different
Tunes, 172   Same Tune, Different Songs, 177

AFTERWORD   186

CHAPTER REFERENCES   190

REFERENCES   195

SOURCES OF SONGS   199

APPENDIX I   203

APPENDIX II   206

APPENDIX III   210

SELECTED BIBLIOGRAPHY   225

DISCOGRAPHY   231

INDEX   233

INDEX OF TITLES AND FIRST LINES   240

ANGLO-AMERICAN FOLKSONG STYLE

INTRODUCTION

This book attempts an objective description of the dominant song tradition of English speaking America. We will examine those characteristics of a group of folksongs which when taken together make up a distinct Anglo-American song style. By style, we mean the observable patterns of expression found consistently throughout this group of songs. We will focus on various aspects of these songs; we will study characteristics of verse, song type, rhythm, meter, melody, and dramatic organization.

Previous scholarship meaningfully approached aspects of folksong style; we have attempted to incorporate and build upon this work in our discussions. However, in much work on folksong, both in matters of verse and music, students have depended on the theories, techniques, and vocabularies of fine art. This is all too often unsatisfactory in describing the folk idiom. When it seemed necessary, we adopted different vocabularies and techniques of analysis in order to describe more accurately those characteristics of folksong which have no direct correlation in fine art.

The origins of an English language folksong tradition in America began with the first immigrations of British settlers around 1600. Of subsequent and perhaps even greater importance was the arrival of the Scotch-Irish settlers later in the same century. Their spread throughout North America established the dominant language, song style, and repertoire for white rural America. It is this tradition we will describe and refer to as "Anglo-American folksong." This term is more limiting than "American folksong" because we do not include folksong idioms and styles which exhibit significant influence from other language and ethnic groups—most notably

1

songs of the American Negro. To include such songs of disparate style and esthetic would require the adoption of additional vocabulary and analytical techniques. Negro song really demands a separate study of its own, a need answered in part by Harold Courlander's *Negro Folk Music USA*. Therefore, our study is not based solely on either geographic or linguistic considerations but rather on a specific ethnocultural style.

The geographical confines of the songs under discussion are broad and non-regional. We refer to the British tradition wherever it is found in North America. Our examples are drawn primarily from the Southern Appalachians and the Ozark Plateau. This permits us to draw upon our own field collections and to speak in a firsthand manner about areas with which we are intimately acquainted. In selecting our examples in this way we nevertheless feel that we maintain an accurate representation of the entire Anglo-American folksong tradition. This opinion is based on a comparative study of our material with other regional collections. When specific song types or examples are not adequately represented in our own regional collections, we have used suitable material from other regions. With regard to regional differences in folksong style in the area covered here, it can be demonstrated that differences exist from song to song, version to version, and singer to singer within a small geographical area which are as great or greater in significance and degree as the differences found between cross sections of songs from different geographical areas. However, where a regional bias does seem to exist, we will mention it.

Although this book has been written as an introductory text to the study of one specific folksong style, it is hoped that the techniques of objective observation and analysis evolved for this particular purpose may lead the student to new insights when attacking other problems in the discipline of folklore.

In keeping with usual practice, when we use examples which are versions of songs included in F. J. Child's *The English and Scottish Popular Ballads* we will follow the title of the song with the number assigned by Child. Local titles, if different from the Child designation, will be given also. Songs followed by a letter and a number are those discussed in G. Malcolm Laws' bibliographical studies *Native American Balladry* and *American Ballads from Broadside*.

To facilitate comparison of various elements such as scale, range, etc., all musical examples have been transposed to share the tone g^1 as a common final. The actual pitch level of recorded performances or the printed tonality of published sources is indicated by the small notes preceding each example. The final of the recorded performance or published source is represented by a whole note and the extremes of range by black notes. The printing of tunes in this text has been arranged to demonstrate graphically the relationship of the tune to its text and of the various segments of the tune to one another. These examples do not represent a detailed or stylistic realization of actual performance but rather an attempt to project the unembellished core of the melody. For this reason, as the number of syllables may vary from verse to verse in the text, rhythm and numbers of notes must vary within the general melodic contour presented.

chapter 1

THE ART
OF FOLKSONG

Since this book will be devoted to a description of the folksong style of white rural cultures in America, it is important to begin by discussing what kind of artistic materials we will be investigating. One of the most popular ideas held by the public and by some folklorists is that there is no "art" involved in the creation and dissemination of traditional songs. As one critic put it, folksongs only occasionally "drift" into art. What such writers mean is that if one weighs folk composition by the standards of sophisticated art, folk art must come out second best, and in this comparison seem "artless." Such evaluation, however, is not illuminating to either sophisticated art or folk art.

There is indeed an art of folksong, and in addition there is a distinction between the creative and presentational techniques of folksong and art song. It is true that a contrast is observable between the two, but the difference is one of degree rather than kind. Both are creations blending individual experience and traditional form. Sophisticated art makes the process of composition into something quite conscious and stresses the innovations brought to form and subject by the individual artist. Folk composition, on the other hand, is oriented more strongly toward the continuity of a tradition and is created by those who are much less conscious of the esthetic principles under which the folk performer or creator is working (Gerould: 1932, 13–14; Leach: 1961, 35). This introduction will explore the differences between sophisticated art (*belles lettres*) and folk art in their presentation, their audience, and their concepts of expectation.

4

Folk, Popular, and Sophisticated Art

Though we have been referring to folk art and *belles lettres* as if a dichotomy exists between the two, this only is true of their *tendencies.* Actually there has been a great deal of interplay between them and there are a number of characteristics which under certain circumstances they share. Many songs have come from written literature and entered tradition with few changes. Similarly, creative artists in sophisticated culture have frequently turned to folksong for forms, subjects, and melodies. This practice was especially prevalent among the Romantics such as Keats, Burns, Coleridge, Brahms, and Tschaikowsky, though it was not absent from Shakespeare, Auden, Bach, and Bartók. In the United States, some of the most characteristically native artists have worked in this way: Aaron Copland, Virgil Thompson, Carl Sandburg, and William Faulkner.

There is good reason to believe that the relationship between the two strata of sophisticated and folk art are totally symbiotic and circular. Sophisticated societies isolated from other cultures, folk or foreign, seem to fall into devitalized, self-conscious artistic expressions. Likewise, peasant communities which become totally isolated seem to lose their own traditional expressions through a similar loss of energy. (We are speaking of peasant or rural communities and not of primitive cultures, though the same may be true there as well.)

In most matters, urban influence upon rural cultures is much stronger than rural influence upon urban cultures. But in regard to art the imbalance is much less severe:

> ... the direction of culture flow is not alone outward and downward, from city to country and from upper to lower classes. Rather we are facing a circular phenomenon in which folk culture draws on and is continually replenished by contact with the products of intellectual and scientific social strata, but in which folk culture continually, though perhaps in lesser degree, contributes. . . . The dance is illustrative of this process. In the 17th and 18th centuries Western European dance masters introduced folk dances to social dancing, adapting them to the needs of the courts. English country square dances played a part in the development of the French quadrille, which was then introduced back to London. . . . Not all aspects of culture, obviously, participated in this circular flow. In the case of religion, government, education, economics and the like, most of the flow is one way, outward and downward. The arts appear best to typify the circular relationship between folk and sophisticated.

(Foster: 1953, 169, 172)

Such "social dancing" could not be considered sophisticated art and yet neither is it folk expression. There is a considerable body of artistic

creation lying between folk art and sophisticated art, which has a life of
its own and yet serves a transitional function between folk and sophisticated art. Most material printed in magazines would fit into this category,
and so would most movies, stage plays, and songs on phonograph records.
These are the production of popular culture and as such are generally
called "popular art."

Popular art, like sophisticated art, is printed, recorded and found in
fixed forms. In other matters popular expression is closer to folk art, especially in regard to values. Although one must class popular art as written
literature, it is in feeling and intent more often like folk than sophisticated art. Both popular and folk expression deal primarily in sentiment;
they both try to be understandable to all and to express community
values; and they are both more closely related to conventional expression
than is sophisticated art. However, popular and sophisticated art are
related in that many popular forms are conventionalizations of sophisticated inventions.

The interrelationship of folk expression and the creations of high culture has already been pointed out; popular expression shares much with
both. The novel, basically a popular form in origin and execution, has
been adopted and enlivened by the most consciously sophisticated artists.
The popular broadside ballad, written by paid "hacks" and sold in printed
form on the streets, is derived from the folk ballad; it in turn has produced many songs which have subsequently been learned by traditional
singers and achieved an oral currency. When Joseph Addison in his *Spec-
tator* was trying to bring the lesson of sophisticated values to the new
reading class, he chose a folk ballad in a broadside text (that is, not taken
directly from oral tradition but rewritten by a "hack") in order to best
convey his message.

Thus it seems important to recognize the interrelationships of *three*
levels of art: folk, popular, and sophisticated, with popular art often representing the midground between folk and sophisticated art.

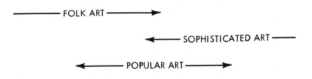

However, in attempting to understand esthetic values, we shall emphasize the extremes of contrast between folk and sophisticated expression, bearing in mind that popular art shares some attributes of both.

Public and Private Expression

There are certain characteristics which seem to be universal in folk expression. These are:

1. understatement and overstatement,
2. concrete and specific language,
3. the translation of idea and emotion into action or public symbol,
4. the use of conventional expression, often in a highly repetitive manner.

(Leach: 1961, 40; Friedman: 1956, xviii)

All of these are readily observable in Anglo-American folksongs, though one characteristic may be more fully felt in one type of song than another. Understatement and its by-product, underplay of emotion, is most evident in ballads. Typical is "Earl Brand." *

Example 1-1. Earl Brand

1. "Rise ye up, rise up my seven sons bold,
   Put on your armour bright,
   That it may not be said that a daughter of mine,
   Can stay with Lord Thomas overnight."

2. "Lady Margaret, my love, be brave," cried he,
   "Hold this rein in your white hand,
   That I may fight your seven brothers bold,
   As in yonders green meadow they stand."

* See *Index of Songs* for a listing of examples by title and by first line. See "Sources of the Songs" for data about informants in printed sources.

3. Lady Margaret did watch the battle so grim,
   She never shed one tear,
   Until she saw her seven brothers fall,
   And the father she loved so dear.

4. "Lady Margaret, my love, will you go, will you go?
   Or will you here abide?"
   "Oh I must go, Lord Thomas, you know,
   You have left me now without a guide."

5. He placed Lady Margaret on the milk white steed,
   Himself upon the bay,
   Drew his buckler down by his side,
   And then rode bleeding away.

6. Lord Thomas died of his bloody, bloody wounds,
   Lady Margaret died of grief,
   Lady Thomas died from the loss of her son,
   The eleventh one that must be.

7. They buried Lord Thomas on the church's right side,
   Lady Margaret they laid upon the left,
   They would not be parted before they died,
   And they were united in death.

8. Out of one grave grew a climbing rose,
   Out of the other grew a briar,
   They grew till they met at the top of the church,
   And they did grow no higher.

Overstatement, or hyperbole, is most often found in the most humorous songs. Children's nonsense songs abound with it, as we find in such fanciful pieces as "Nottalin Town."

Example 1-2. Nottamun Town

1. As I went down to fair Nottalin Town,
   They all were so mad not a soul would look down,
   They all were so mad not a soul would look down,
   To show me the way to fair Nottalin Town.

2. I sat down on a red hot, cold frozen stone,
   Ten thousand was 'round me but yet I were alone,
   Ten thousand was 'round me, no one could I see,
   Ten thousand was 'round me a'gazing at me.

3. I rode the old grey horse they call a grey mare,
   With a white mane and tail and a green lick down her back,
   With a white mane and tail and a green lick down her back,
   There weren't a hair on her be what was coal black.

4. I met a king and a queen and a company more,
   Riding behind and walking before,
   A stark naked drummer came beating his drum,
   With his heels in his bosom came marching along.

5. I bought me a quart to drive sadness away,
   To stifle the dust for it rained the whole day,
   My hat in my hand to keep my head warm,
   Ten thousand was drowned that never was born.

As we may observe from "Earl Brand," in the narrative stanzas, idea and emotion are translated into action, while the final stanza substitutes public symbol and symbolic action for emotion. These characteristics of folk expression all emphasize the public nature of folklore; its inclinations are toward the simple and immediately comprehensible. Herein lies the basic cleavage between oral literature and *belles lettres,* a division which exists because one is written down and the other is not. The intent, means, and effects of folk and sophisticated literature differ because they are aimed at different audiences from whom they demand different kinds of perception. Sophisticated literature, with the exception of drama, is written in full knowledge that it will be read under conditions which will allow for reflection. Works are put into a tangible form and can be returned to repeatedly. The creative artist can, and often does, rely on this. The oral creator or performer, on the other hand, is obliged to use expression which is immediately understandable because of the oral nature of his presentation and the limitations which this places upon his audience. He must present pieces that can be understood almost as a reflex action. And as he repeats the piece on other occasions the reflex action is even more immediate. Furthermore, in orally oriented environments, pieces must also be memorable, for the group relies upon oral transmission to embody its knowledge and entertainment. Oral composition will gravitate toward conventional expression and repetitive expression because they are more immediately understandable and retainable.

The difference between folk and sophisticated art can then be characterized as the difference between *reflexive* (oral) and *reflective* (written).

The ability of the sophisticated artist to rely upon repeated perusal of
his work both by his audience and by himself has made him increasingly
conscious of his techniques. This consciousness has given him the ability
to abstract technical means and thus to control them more individually
and effectively. He is capable of evolving theories of form and composition and of allowing these to affect his future work. In a sense, he can
never get away from his theory as long as he is creating reflective works.
This is a capacity that the traditional performer does not have.

This contrast is clear when viewing the different ways in which the
folk performer/creator with his reflexive techniques and the writer with
his cerebral and reflective devices manipulate their audiences. The traditional performer is synthesizing the group, reaffirming its values, giving
it a feeling of community. His aim is a normative one, and his arguments
will thus be conservative, in favor of the status quo. For the performance
to function the whole group must understand and react to it. Thus the
performer must utilize expression which is similar to that used in the
past and with a vocabulary common to all. On the other hand, the creative artist sees his mission as one of revealing life freshly, individually;
he implicitly assumes that life is deadened by excessive repetition. He
attempts to speak as a perceptive individual to the individuals in his
audience. His ties with the past are more to enrich the present experience than to unite the audience with the past, and in matters of expression he must in some way give the impression of going beyond the past.
The emphasis is not on the artist's role as representative of the group
who sees group values as right and who therefore ratifies them in his
creations, but as an individual who sees what is wrong or limited in
present values and modes of experience and who therefore seeks to lead,
as an individual, through the expression of his insights. With such a point
of view, his creation naturally emphasizes newness and reinterpretation.
But newness brings with it shock and disorientation, and therefore demands reflection for its understanding.

This *belletristic* emphasis upon change is a natural by-product of city
life. Urban values approve and ratify change, and literature of record
echoes and emphasizes this. On the other hand, the conventionality of
folklore emphasizes existent experience and does not attempt to induce
change. Conventions such as sentiment or melodrama which folklore
utilizes do exactly this—they applaud the audience for feeling the way
it does. Sophisticated works militate against this in favor of change.

Both sophisticated artists and folk creators/performers are attempting
to induce the members of their audience to enter into a state in which
connections can be made on a non-literal level through the power of

language. Both try to remove the listener to a state of suspended judgment, of temporary acceptance of his world and his values. Both create an imaginary world which is like life but wholly apart from it. Any anxieties which exist in the real world can be abstracted, played out, and perhaps alleviated.

The primary anxieties of folk societies seem to arise from the conflict between man's social and asocial tendencies. Folklore emphasizes in a highly formalistic and traditional manner the necessity for man to live together in order to master external forces which are potentially destructive. In other words, the anxiety created by the existence of threatening outside forces causes man in folk communities to insist upon banding together, but in doing so creates the further conflict generated by man's asocial tendencies. Consequently, when invoking the imaginary world, folklore argues in the name of community. The traditional performer's weapon of control is tradition itself; that is, the uses of the past that are familiar and comfortable and understandable, evoking the response of commonality and sympathy on a group basis.

Although the anxieties of urban man are not substantially different from the folk, he attacks them in a significantly different way in his fictional expression. Written literature, existing primarily in urban societies, assumes that man is basically social, thus taking for granted a premise which, to the contrary, the folk seem to need to prove. Urban man's major anxieties arise from his lack of tradition, from his restlessness, and from his constant state of change. His solution may be a clinging to vestiges of peasant or primitive values, for example, pastoralism (with its by-product suburbanism) or escapist heroism. On the other hand, some kind of personal mystique may arise in which urban man sees himself as master of his own fate in achieving a state of earthly grace.

Belles lettres emphasize the isolation and individuality of the reader by forcing him to think about the ideas he encounters and to interpret them as a personal experience. The artist has become one of the heroes of urban culture. Along with the scientist, the artist in his most important role attempts to teach us about ourselves, making us capable of controlling our own lives more fully and therefore capable of changing ourselves and our destinies "to the better." To progress one must change, and philosophy, art, and science all interpret reality in terms of change to make progress possible. Art in the modern world expresses a universe in constant flux and thus capable of maintaining only relative, temporary truths based on the insight of individuals speaking to other individuals. Folk society and folk art do not accept, reflect, or value change.

chapter

THE CYCLE
OF ORAL TRANSMISSION
AND COMPOSITION

The creator/performer in a folk community works in a much more restricted manner than his sophisticated counterpart in the city. Even in those groups where he is called on to improvise as he is performing, he does so within a severely restricted form, using traditional verse patterns, tunes, subjects, and compositional techniques. In such traditions of improvising, the performer often in some way manages to center his composition on himself, for he is trying to impress the audience with his creative powers.

Improvisation of this sort is nearly totally absent from Anglo-American song traditions. Commonly here, the singer views himself as a voice for whatever piece he is performing; he places himself in the background, letting the piece speak for itself. He attempts to reproduce the song exactly as he has heard and learned it. His range of expression is considerably more limited than that of the improvisor. The improvisor relies more heavily on his own creative techniques than upon his memory of songs from the past. The performer who cannot improvise must rely wholly on memory. Consequently, his pieces tend to be filled with devices which will aid memory, and these songs must of necessity be brief. *Stichic* or line-by-line composition, generally employed by epic singers, is impossible in such a tradition; rather, one finds *strophic* or stanzaic composition, with an emphasis on repeated verbal, metrical, and melodic patterns.

Anglo-American folksong tradition is very firmly of the latter type: strongly strophic, restrictive, song-oriented rather than performer-oriented. Such a tradition relies primarily on oral transmission in contrast to oral re-creation as the mode by which its songs persist.

Oral Change

It is generally supposed that the process of change in the oral transmission of folksong is one of slow decay. One commentator, Tristram P. Coffin, referring specifically to ballads, has broken this process down into three stages: (1) the original piece is created; (2) unneeded action and subliterary frills are lost, the song is made into a folksong; and (3) unessential details drop off until lyric or meaningless jumble of undirected dramatic action results (Coffin: 1957, 210–211).

However, this is by no means the whole story of folksong in oral transmission. It is true that most of the changes that occur in traditional songs are a result of oral transmission, and that often these changes are at the expense of the song, but the process is by no means one of inevitable and unilateral degeneration. As a song is transmitted by word of mouth, the compositional integrity of the piece is the strongest operating force. Under the stimulus of altered needs, functions, or attitudes, this integrity will often be preserved by conscious or unconscious changes. In a favorable cultural situation a folksong tradition will constantly renew itself.

There is a curious disagreement in the logic of scholarship in regard to oral transmission. One pervading idea is that a folksong is valuable simply because it has been orally conveyed throughout its life. Any suspicion of influence on the song from a printed source and the value of the song itself becomes suspect. On the other hand, to many scholars oral transmission is seen as producing degenerative change (Macmillan: 1964, passim).

It is incontestable that certain changes which occur in oral transmission are degenerative. If you have ever played the parlor game, "Whispering Down the Lane," you have been involved in a situation which epitomizes all the decaying forces of the folk process. In this game the participants sit in a line and someone gives the first player a long sentence which he must memorize. He must then whisper the sentence to the player next to him, and he in turn must do the same. The game continues until the last player is reached. The last player then reveals the sentence as it was relayed to him. Invariably there is considerable change and comparing the original sentence with the final player's version is often humorous.

The premise of the game—that each player will try his best to hear what is whispered to him and to convey it to the next player in exactly the same form—is very close to the attitude of most singers in the Anglo-American tradition. It is this reliance upon past performance which provides both a standard of preservation and a tendency toward decay. If a performer attempts to sing a piece exactly as he has heard it, this guarantees continuity. When this attitude is instilled into the singer and yet something happens to mar his perception of the song, the same kind of bizarre changes seen in "Whispering Down the Lane" may result.

Change is an integral part of the process of oral dissemination. Even though the individual singer may be conscientious in his effort to re-create a song exactly as he has heard it, changes would still occur. "Singers of ballads are quite unconscious of changing them, and yet never sing them, line by line and musical phrase by musical phrase, quite like their neighbors" (Gerould: 1932, 163). Within every tradition there will be stylistic conventions common to all performers. There will also be stylistic variables, permitted by the audience, but not necessarily found in all performers. In many cases, these variables will exist below the threshold of perception for both the singer and his audience; that is, he may not be conscious of his variance. The extent of variation possible without the singer's awareness seems fairly high.

Here are four examples of a song collected from one restricted area. The song (sung in each instance to almost the same tune) was probably originated in the area from which it was collected, the eastern slope of the Blue Ridge mountains in central Virginia. As the song indicates, the Allegheny mountains can be seen from the first crest of the Blue Ridge.

Example 2-1. Across the Blue Mountain

1. Good morning, good morning, good morning in May
   I heard a married man to a single lady say,
   "Pick you up pretty Katy and go along with me
   And across the Blue Mountain to the Allegheny."

2. "I'll buy you a horse, love, a saddle for to ride
   I'll buy me another one to ride by your side,
   We'll stop at every tavernter and drink when we are dry
   And across the Blue Mountain goes Katy and I."

3. For up steps her mother and angry was she
   "Oh daughter, oh daughter he is a married man,
   Besides there are plenty more young handsome than him
   And let him take his own wife to the Allegheny."

4. "Oh Mother, oh Mother, he's the man of my heart
   And wouldn't hit be hard for me and my love to part,
   I valley not his own wife, as anyone can see
   And along with him I'm a'going to go to the Allegheny."

5. She traveled, she traveled till she became lame
   She turned back home which she thought it was a shame,
   "A'living with a Dutchman, he thought me to maintain
   And if I were back with my kin I would never come here again."

6. He left me, he left me, he left me alone
   He left me no house nor no money nor no home,
   He left me no friend nor no relation a'nigh
   And when I think on my Mother, I sit down and cry.

Example 2 - 2.

1. One morning, one morning, one morning in May
   I heard a married man to a single lady say,
   "Fix you up, fix you up pretty Katy and go along with me,
   'Cross the Blue Mountain to the Allegheny."

2. "I'll buy you a horse and a saddle to ride
   I'll buy myself another one to ride by your side,
   We'll stop at all taverns and drink when we get dry
   And across the Blue Mountain goes Katy and I."

3. "Oh Mother, oh Mother he's the man of my own heart
   And won't it be hard for me and my love to part,
   Besides there are other ones no handsomer than he
   And along with him I intend to go to the Allegheny."

4. They traveled, they traveled 'til they became lame
   They turned back home and they found it was a shame,
   She was living with a Dutchman, no fortune to maintain
   "And if I was back with my own kin I'd never come here again."

Example 2 - 3.

1. One morning, one morning, one morning in May
   I heard a married man to a single lady say,
   "Wake up my pretty Polly and come and go with me
   Across the Blue Mountain to the Allegheny."

2. I'll furnish you a horse and a saddle for to ride
   I'll furnish you another one to ride by your side,
   We'll stay at every tavernt and drink when we're dry
   And across the Blue Mountain goes Katy and I."

3. Oh, up stepped her Mother and angry was she
   "My daughter, oh daughter a married man is he,
   I'll valley not his own wife can anyone can see
   Let him take his own wife to the Allegheny."

4. "Mother, oh Mother he's the man of my own heart
   Would it be fair for me and my love to part?
   I'll valley not his own wife can anyone can see
   And with him I'm a'going to the Allegheny."

Example 2 - 4.

1. One morning, one morning, one morning in May
   I heard a married man to a young girl did say,
   "Oh rise you up pretty Katy and go along with me,
   Across the Blue Mountain to the Allegheny."

2. "I'll buy you a horse, love, and a saddle to ride,
   I'll buy me another to ride by your side,
   We'll stop at every tavernt and drink when we dry
   Across the Blue Mountain goes Katy and I."

3. It's up steps her mother and angry was she then,
   "Dear daughter, dear daughter he is a married man,
   Besides there's young men plenty more handsome than he
   And let him take his own wife to the Allegheny."

4. "Dear Mother, dear Mother he's the man of my own heart
   And wouldn't that be an awful thing for me and my love to part?
   I'd valley all the women that ever I did see
   'At crossed the Blue Mountain to the Allegheny."

Here we have one song whose existence in oral currency is limited to what appears to be a relatively brief period and a rather small area. Despite these reasons and despite the strong unity the song maintains, there is an abundance of variation ranging from the incidental to the meaningful. There is not one line which does not exhibit some degree of change within these four examples. Even the relatively stable line, "Across the Blue Mountain to the Allegheny," has a variance of pronunciation in the long "e" in Allēgheny of Example 2–3. Such changes evident in details such as line 3; Pick you up/Fix you up/Wake up/Rise you up, are probably below the threshold of awareness of both singers and audiences. Other changes are more likely to have occurred not unconsciously but from misunderstanding or trouble with words like "tavern" and "valley." When asked about the meaning of the latter, informants demonstrated no common understanding of the word. The responses ranged from statements that it meant "to value" (Example 2–1) to it meant to "fight" or "whup em" (Example 2–4). The appearance of "pretty Polly," the conventional folksong heroine, seems to have been a temporary memory lapse and substitution which is corrected later in the same stanza (Example 2–3). The singers of Examples 2–3 and 2–4 both mention that they believe there is more to the song than they can remember. It is of interest to note the extent to which their forgetting alters the flavor of the song. In these last two examples, the piece has become a lyric love song with only a hint of possible tragedy: "he is a married man." Katy and her love might well ride to the Allegheny to live happily ever after. Gone are the stanzas of disappointment and remorse found in the other versions. It should be noted that the loss of the final stanzas in these two examples could hardly be called "degenerative change," for the song seems to benefit from the rejection of the "Dutchman" references.

Degenerative Causes of Change

The causes of change in both the whispering game and conservative oral tradition of the songs are patent:

1. mishearing,
2. forgetting,
3. lack of understanding of a word or of word relationships.

Mishearing is much more common in the whispering game than in tradition because, in the game, the expression to be remembered is repeated only once, is whispered and must be transmitted in haste. Misunderstanding of terms is more likely to occur in folksongs' words, since constructions and terms can become outmoded or change meaning as a song is transmitted over a period of time.

This misunderstanding is clearly seen in many forms of the refrain (or "burden"), "Savory (or Parsley), sage, rosemary and thyme." This refrain, found in various old ballads, has been changed by singers who did not know the meaning of these herbs or the formulaic incantation from which the refrain probably came.

> Save rosemary and thyme.
> Rosemary in time.
> Every rose grows merry in time.
> Rose de Marian Time.
> Rozz marrow and time.
> May every rose bloom merry in time.
> Let every rose grow merry and fine.
> Every leaf grows many a time.
> Sing Ivy leaf, Sweet William and thyme.
> Every rose grows bonny in time.
> Every globe grows merry in time.
> Green grows the merry antine.
> Whilst every grove rings with a merry antine.
> So sav'ry was said, come marry in time.

Perhaps an even clearer case is one pointed out by Reed Smith. He takes the common phrase from Scottish ballads, "twirl at the pin" and the analogous one from England, "tinkle at the ring," both being outmoded ways of announcing one's arrival at the door, and shows what has happened to these phrases in songs in the United States.

> He dingled so loudly with the ring.
> Dingled so low at the ring.
> Dingled at the ring and it rung.
> She knocked so loud upon the ring.
> And he knocked at the ring.
> So clearly he knocked at the ring.
> He knocked till he made things ring.
> Who knocks so loud and don't come in?
> He knocked thereat, therein.
> All jingling in the rings.
> She went till she came to the gate, she tingled.
> How boldly she rang the bell.
> And then he rang the bell.
> He knocked so loud on the door.
>
> (Smith: 1928, 62)

Rationalization and Conventionalization

When an element of a song is misheard, misunderstood, or forgotten, as the examples above illustrate, gibberish may result. More commonly, however, the singer consciously tries to make sense out of nonsense. Most of the refrains stemming from the sources above show an attempt toward rationalization (Gerould: 1932, 187).

Another positive result is change toward conventional expression of objects or situations. When forgetting or any other destructive force operates on a song, the singer will tend to fill in the missing parts with the appropriate conventional element (Moore: 1916, 407; Coffin: 1963, 16–17). Thus a hand when mentioned in folksong tends to become a "lily-white hand," and many other similar instances could be offered (Gerould: 1932, 114–115). Such conventions will be discussed extensively later.

Forgetting and Emotional Core

It is clear that most of the mistakes made in transmission are due to either mishearing or misunderstanding or both. As such, the changes which occur are smaller textual ones. With forgetting, larger elements of a song can be lost, causing more extensive changes to occur. While mishearing or misunderstanding can attack almost any element of a song, forgetting tends to work in more clearly discernible patterns.

As Freud and many psychologists since have shown, we remember or forget things for very specific reasons. Memory can be stimulated by striking an emotional response in the portrayal of a subject; it can also occur because of the artful phrasing of such a portrayal. Forgetting occurs because of an inability to distinguish an object from other similar objects, or because of lack of emotional importance of a line or stanza, or because some inner force or taboo causes one to block the expression of a certain subject from memory. All of these forces have meaning in relation to the oral process of transmission.

One cannot doubt that certain songs and drifting stanzas have persisted in tradition not only because they portray a situation or a sentiment with which the singers and their audiences agree, but because they are well expressed. The ubiquity of stanzas like:

> The longest train I ever did see
> Was a hundred coaches long,
> The only woman I ever did love
> Was on that train and gone.

or

> Don't you see that little dove
> Flying from pine to pine?
> She's mourning for her own true love
> Just like I mourn for mine.

is accounted for by their congenial construction as much as for the feeling they convey.

Even more important in the distillation of what in a song is remembered or forgotten is what the singer sees as the "message" or importance of the song. Coffin has termed this attention-center of the song its "emotional core" (Coffin: 1950). As a song is transmitted those stanzas will be retained which are closest to this emotional core, and conversely the ones which are forgotten are those which are farthest from it, i.e., those stanzas having less importance in imparting the action or situation which the singer emphasizes. Although most singers in a homogeneous community will view a song in the same way, what one singer sees as the emotional core may, in certain instances, seem incidental to another. These two singers would consequently tend to remember different parts of the same song. In this way songs develop divergent paths in their history.

Here are two American versions of "The Two Sisters." In the earliest recorded versions of this song, the story is quite complex—being one re-telling of an international folktale. Two daughters of noble birth, the eldest dark and the youngest fair, are courted by a young man. As is common in Northern European tradition, the fair daughter is chosen. The elder sister in jealousy lures her sister to the edge of the sea and pushes her in to drown. The young sister floats until she enters a mill dam. She is taken from the water by the miller, sometimes alive, sometimes already drowned. Often the miller robs the girl of her valuables and pushes her again into the water. The body ultimately is found by a harper or fiddler who fashions an instrument from it (the hair is used to make the strings and the finger bones to make the pins, etc.). The instrument then sings and relates the whole story, accusing the sister and sometimes the miller of her death. The murderer(s) are punished.

This ballad is widely found throughout America in approximately the following form:

> 1. There lived an old lord by the Northern Sea,
>   Bow down,
>   There lived an old lord by the Northern Sea,
>   The boughs they bend to me.
>   There lived an old lord by the Northern Sea,
>   And he had daughters one, two, three.
>   I will be true, true to my love,
>   Love and my love will be true to me.

> 2. A young man came a-courting there,
>   Bow down,
>   A young man came a-courting there,
>   The boughs they bend to me.

A young man came a-courting there,
And he took choice of the youngest there.
    I will be true, true to my love,
    Love and my love will be true to me.

3. He gave the youngest a gay gold ring,
    Bow down,
He gave the youngest a gay gold ring,
    The boughs they bend to me.
He gave the youngest a gay gold ring,
But never the oldest a single thing.
    I will be true, true to my love,
    Love and my love will be true to me.

4. He gave the youngest a beaver hat,
    Bow down,
He gave the youngest a beaver hat,
    The boughs they bend to me.
He gave the youngest a beaver hat,
The oldest she thought much of that.
    I will be true, true to my love,
    Love and my love will be true to me.

5. "Oh sister, oh sister let us walk out,"
    Bow down,
"Oh sister, oh sister let us walk out,"
    The boughs they bend to me.
"Oh sister, oh sister let us walk out,
And see the ships a'sailing about."
    I will be true, true to my love,
    Love and my love will be true to me.

6. On they walked down by the salty brim,
    Bow down,
They walked down by the salty brim,
    The boughs they bend to me.
On they walked down by the salty brim,
The oldest pushed the youngest in.
    I will be true, true to my love,
    Love and my love will be true to me.

7. "Oh sister, oh sister lend me your hand,"
    Bow down,
"Oh sister, oh sister lend me your hand,"
    The boughs they bend to me.
"Oh sister, oh sister lend me your hand,
And I will give you my house and land."
    I will be true, true to my love,
    Love and my love will be true to me.

Example 2-5. The Two Sisters

8. "I'll lend you neither my hand nor glove,"
   Bow down,
   "I'll lend you neither my hand nor glove,"
   The boughs they bend to me.
   "I'll lend you neither my hand nor glove,
   But I will have your own true love."
   I will be true, true to my love,
   Love and my love will be true to me.

9. Oh, down she sank and away she swam,
   Bow down,
   Oh, down she sank and away she swam,
   The boughs they bend to me.
   Oh, down she sank and away she swam,
   And into the miller's fish pond she ran.
   I will be true, true to my love,
   Love and my love will be true to me.

10. The miller came out with his fish hook,
    Bow down,
    The miller came out with his fish hook,
    The boughs they bend to me.
    The miller came out with his fish hook,
    And fished the fair maid out of the brook.
    I will be true, true to my love,
    Love and my love will be true to me.

11. He robbed her of her gay gold ring,
        Bow down,
   He robbed her of her gay gold ring,
        The boughs they bend to me.
   He robbed her of her gay gold ring,
   And into the sea he pushed her again.
        I will be true, true to my love,
        Love and my love will be true to me.

12. The miller was hung at his mill gate,
        Bow down,
   The miller was hung at his mill gate,
        The boughs they bend to me.
   The miller was hung at his mill gate,
   The oldest daughter was burned at the stake.
        I will be true, true to my love,
        Love and my love will be true to me.

As can be seen, this tradition has fastened upon the murder and the miller's complicity in the crime as the emotional core of this piece. Lost completely is the supernatural element of the magical instrument made of hair and bones. However, there exists a minor and probably local tradition which illustrates a quite different emphasis (Foss: 1964).

Example 2-6. The Two Sisters (Wind and Rain)

1. Two loving sisters was a–walking side by side,
        Oh the wind and rain.
   One pushed the other off in the waters, waters deep,
        And she cried, "The dreadful wind and rain."

2. She swum down, down to the miller's pond,
        Oh the wind and rain.
   She swum down, down to the miller's, miller's pond,
        And she cried, "The dreadful wind and rain."

3. Out run the miller with his long hook and line,
    Oh the wind and rain.
  Out run the miller with his long hook and line,
    And she cried, "The dreadful wind and rain."

4. He hooked her up by the tail of the gown,
    Oh the wind and rain.
  He hooked her up by the tail of the gown,
    And she cried, "The dreadful wind and rain."

5. They made fiddle strings of her long black hair,
    Oh the wind and rain.
  They made fiddle strings of her long black hair,
    And she cried, "The dreadful wind and rain."

6. They made fiddle screws of her long finger bones,
    Oh the wind and rain.
  They made fiddle screws of her long finger bones,
    And she cried, "The dreadful wind and rain."

7. The only tune that my fiddle would play, was
    Oh the wind and rain.
  The only tune that my fiddle would play, was
    And she cried, "The dreadful wind and rain."

Clearly this represents a separate tradition instituted by some singer who saw the emotional core of the piece in the song of the instrument rather than in the cruel murder. This difference is explainable in part by the refrain which emphasizes the plaintive nature of the song and even becomes a functional part of the story as the tune which the instrument plays.

These two variants of the same song point out the direction which songs can take when certain parts of them are forgotten and only those parts associated with the emotional core are remembered. In the "Bow down" version the core of the story is the action relating to the murder; parts of the story are eliminated, compressing the total movement of action. In most ballads, the story is paramount and this kind of compression generally results. On the other hand, as in the "Wind and rain" version, certain ballads have uncommonly interesting lyric elements and the attraction is toward retaining the lyric passages and forgetting the narrative portions.

Forgetting and Negative Tropisms

In dealing with songs from the point of view of their emotional core, forgetting is a passive phenomenon; verses are lost because of their distance from the major focus of the song. There are, however, ways in which certain elements in a song are not only *not* remembered, they are consciously or unconsciously rejected. These changes occur because of negative tropisms; some individual or group attitude causes certain aspects of a song to appear ridiculous or morally repulsive, or to hit some psychological "sore spot." As a result of such forces, whole sections of a song may be dropped, either consciously or unconsciously. In some cases these changes may occur because of individual idiosyncrasy; but more often they reflect group or community attitudes. We do know a number of changes occur in those British ballads which survive the ocean voyage to become established in American tradition. Stanley Edgar Hyman catalogues some of these:

> Magic and supernatural slough off readily, even where they seem the ballad's basic point, and demons, ghosts, elves, and mermaids rationalize and humanize. . . . sex, incest, and kin-murder tend to disappear or diminish, in a folk process very like individual repression. . . . another type of acclimatization is a Christianizing at best and a vague pietizing at worst.
>
> (Hyman: 1957, 237–238)

These are changes which have influenced only *some* of the songs which have persisted in tradition, and in not a great many versions of those. But such change occurs and must be accounted for.

It is not surprising that in the midst of our highly rational culture, songs which contain magic and supernatural occurrences should either change or lose some of their currency. Certainly the rural areas in which traditional songs have remained in most active tradition sustain superstitious belief more than do urban areas. Just as certainly, however, the influence of reason has been felt in these rural areas and has slowly made an imprint on its songs.

We have already seen in "The Two Sisters" how in most versions collected in America, the supernatural motif of the singing instrument is missing. Similarly, in its older versions, "James Harris or The Daemon Lover" (commonly called "The House Carpenter" in the New World) tells of a revenant (a visitor from the dead) or of the devil coming to carry off a woman. American tradition has modified this; the ballad now simply describes a love triangle.

Example 2-7. The House Carpenter

1. "Well met, well met my old true love
   Well met, well met," cried he
   "I have just returned from the great salt sea
   To take thee away with me."

2. "I once could have married a king's daughter fair
   She wanted to marry me
   But a crown of gold I have refused
   Because of my love for thee."

3. "If you could have married a king's daughter, sir,
   I'm sure you are to blame,
   For I am married to a house carpenter
   And he is a nice young man."

4. "Will you forsake your house carpenter
   To sail away with me?
   I will take you where the grass grows green
   On the banks of the low country."

5. "How can I leave my house carpenter
   Oh, how can I leave I say?
   How could I leave my three little babes
   To sail so far away?"

6. "I have sailing ships upon the sea
   All sailing for this land
   And a hundred and ten brave, jolly, bold men
   Shall be at your command."

7. She picked up her three little babes
   She gave them kisses three
   Saying, "Stay here with your papa, my dear,
   To keep him company."

8. She arrayed herself in rich attire
   Most glorious to behold
   And every hamlet they rode through
   She shown and glittered like gold.

9. They had been on the sea about two weeks
   I'm sure it was not three
   When this fair maiden began for to weep
   And she wept most bitterly.

10. "Is it for the gold you weep
    Or is it for the store?
    Or can it be for your house carpenter
    You'll never see anymore?"

11. "It is not for the gold that I weep
    And neither for the store
    But I am grieving for my three little babes
    I never shall see anymore."

12. They had been on the sea about three weeks
    I'm sure it was not four
    When there sprang a leak in the bottom of the ship,
    And it sank to rise no more.

13. "What is it that looms so black,
    As black as the feathers of a crow?"
    "That is the smoke from the fires of Hell
    Where you and I must go."

14. "What is it that shines so bright
    As white as driven snow?"
    "That is the gate of Heaven itself
    Where we can never go."

While there has been a drift away from the supernatural in many songs, some of the most popular ballads are concerned with ghosts and revenants. For instance, "The Wife of Usher's Well," (commonly called "The Lady Gay") has been collected throughout America and is concerned with the belief that excess grief will cause the dead to return. Furthermore, one song, "Lost Jimmy Whalan," apparently written in North America, is concerned with the same idea and attained a fairly wide circulation among lumberjacks:

Example 2-8. Lost Jimmy Walen

By permission of Dr. Helen Creighton.

1. As slowly I roamed by the banks of the river,
   Watching the sunbeams as evening drew nigh,
   As onward I rambled I spied a fair damsel,
   Oh weeping and wailing with many a sigh.

2. Crying for one who was now lying lowly,
   Weeping for one that no mortal could save,
   The dark morning waters flow swiftly around her,
   And green grows the grass o'er her young lover's grave.

3. "O Jimmy," she cried, "Won't you come to me darling?
   Come to me here from your cold silent tomb,
   You promised to meet me this evening, my darling,
   E'er death's cruel angel had sealed your sad doom.

4. "You promised we'd meet by the banks of the river,
   And you'd give me sweet kisses as oftimes before,
   And fold me again in your strong loving arrums,
   O come to me Jimmy dear, come as of yore."

5. Then slowly he rose from the banks of the river
   A vision of beauty more bright than the sun,
   With bright rows of crimson around him a'flowing,
   And unto this maiden to speak he begun.

6. "Dear, why did you call me from realms of glory
   Back to this world which again I must leave,
   To hold you again in my fond loving arrums?
   To see you once more, love, I've come from my grave.

7. "Once more embrace, love, before I must leave you,
   One more fond kiss before we must part,"
   Cold were the arrums that did her encircle,
   And cold was the bosom he pressed to her heart.

8. "Adieu," then he whispered, and vanished before her,
   Back to the waters his form seemed to go,
   A'leaving the maiden forlorn and distracted
   A'weeping and wailing in sorrow and woe.

9. And throwing herself on the ground she wept sorely,
   With wild words of torment this maiden did rave,
   Crying, "Jimmy my darling, my lost Jimmy Whalan,
   I sighed till I died by the side of your grave."

In a similar fashion, the incest theme has been dropped from some older songs such as, "The Cruel Brother," "The Two Brothers," and "Lizzie Wan" (Coffin: 1963, 18). Moralization, sentimentalization and jocularity have crept into many songs which in earlier forms were quite somber (Cf. Chapter 8, the versions of "The Three Ravens").

Occasionally a song will be rejected or relegated to a special and less-performed position because it is considered too outlandish, childish, or bawdy. Informants will frequently decline to sing songs containing a high degree of nonsense words or will do so with obvious embarrassment. The same singers will most likely sing the same songs unhesitatingly to children.

Universalization and Localization

One of the most mutable features of songs are names of individuals and locales. Both are of local interest except in quasi-historical ballads where the persons and places are known in a broader area ("Mary Hamilton," "Death of Queen Jane"). Such topical references are easily forgotten, being peripheral to the emotional core of the piece.

When such details are forgotten, two directions can be taken by a song: localization or universalization. Localization substitutes local names for the originals. For example, in the United States the "Oxford Girl" easily mutates to the "Knoxville Girl" and in Texas becomes the "Waco Girl" (Laws: 1957, 104–120, 267). In certain cases, a local event will closely parallel one told in a previous song and the piece will be rewritten to conform to the new situation by adding a few details and changing names. The widely collected murder ballad, "Fair Florella" (F1) or "The Tragic Romance" became "Pearl Bryan" in Southern Indiana after a resident of Greencastle by that name was murdered in a way that paralleled the earlier song. The rewritten song has achieved a provenience nearly as wide as the source song, "Fair Florella."

Example 2 - 9. Fair Florella

> Down in the lovely meadow
> Where the violets they bloom and fade
> There lies my Sweet Florella
> A—mouldering in the clay.
> (*Etc.*)

Sung to the same tune and consciously changed in names and details is the song "Pearl Bryan" (F1B).

Example 2 - 10. Pearl Bryan

1. Deep, deep in a lonely valley
   Where violets fade and bloom,
   There sleeps my own Pearl Bryant
   So silent in the tomb.

2. She died not broken hearted
   Nor from sickness did she fall,
   But in one moment parted
   From the home she loved so well.

3. Last night the moon shown brightly,
   The stars were shining too,
   When to this maiden's cottage
   Her jealous lover drew.

4. "Come love, and let us wander
   Down to the meadow gate,
   And we will wander and ponder
   About our wedding date."

5. The way was cold and dreary;
   The night was coming on.
   Into that lonely valley
   He lead this maiden on.

6. "Scott Jackson, I am tired
   Of wand'ring here so long.
   The way is cold and dreary,
   I pray you take me home."

7. "You have not the wings of an eagle,
   Nor from me can you fly.
   No human hand can save you;
   You instantly must die."

8. "What have I done, Scott Jackson,
   That you should take my life?
   You know I've always loved you
   And promised to be your wife."

9. Down on her knees before him
   She pleaded for her life,
   And into that snowy bosom
   He plunged a gleaming knife.

10. "Scott Jackson, I'll forgive you
    With my last and dying breath.
    I never have deceived you—
    As I close my eyes in death."

11. Down on his knees he bended
    Saying, "O, what have I done!
    I've murdered my Pearl Bryant
    As pure as the rising sun."

12. Now in this lonesome valley
    Where the willows weep o'er her grave
    Pearl Bryant lies forgotten
    Where the merry sunbeams play.

Universalization is the other alternative when specific names and places are forgotten. Here, when a local place name is lost, either no specific locale is substituted or a well-known place name is inserted: "London Town" or "Baltimore." Similarly, specific or historical personal names may change to conventional ones: "Pretty Polly," "Fair Margaret," or "Sweet William."

Conventional Elements

Up to this point the chapter has dealt with changes which occur in folksongs as they are orally transmitted. The assumption throughout has been that the force of Anglo-American tradition in song is opposed to such change and thus it occurs only as a consequence of a malfunction in transmission. This assumption we will have to modify later, but for now it will stand. In order for songs *not* to change there must be elements in them which are memorable enough to create the continuity we expect.

We have already mentioned one of these factors, the emotional or dramatic core which causes the singer to focus on his song in a special way, thus aiding the memory process. The beauty or conciseness of certain lines or stanzas causes them to be aurally memorable and further helps in the process of retention. When such memorable expressions begin to filter into other similar songs, we see them becoming conventions. It is these conventions and the fact that folksongs are in the main conventional, which create an idiom that is easily retained. And it becomes evident that songs often *are* remembered in this way when one recalls that songs tend to become more conventional the more they are transmitted.

Convention and conventional elements provide an important part of the vocabulary used in the creation/transmission of traditional songs. This vocabulary is difficult to describe accurately because to do so one must utilize a terminology which is vague and overused. Such terms as "cliche," "commonplace," "formula," and even "convention" have been used in approximately synonymous ways by folklorists. Yet convention acts in many different ways and on many levels in the construction of folksong. Some of these are:

> *Conventional diction.* Songs will use special language not ordinarily found in conversational speech. A song about lords and ladies will use certain archaisms ("steed," "heed," "morrow," etc.) not found in either common parlance or in other kind of songs.

> *Conventional epithet.* A name or object often found in songs always with the same modifiers ("milk-white steed," "lily-white hand," "wee pen knife," "rank robber," "Sweet William," "Fair Margaret," etc.).

> *Conventional phrase.* An action, describable alone, but which always includes the result of the action. Tears, for instance, have a tendency not to be merely shed but to "blind the eye." Similarly, when someone is stabbed the "heart's blood" often comes "trinkling down the knee."

> *Commonplace.* A conventional description of a prescribed situation. These are found frequently in ballads, but are the stock-in-trade of the lyric. This is a larger unit than the conventional epithet or phrase, and may include either or both. We find the following commonplace stanza in both "Mattie Groves" and "Lord Thomas and Fair Ellender":

> > He's taken her by the *lily-white hand* (epithet)
> > And *led her through the hall* (phrase)
> > He's cut her head off from her shoulder
> > And kicked it against the wall.

Another familiar commonplace from the older ballads is the rose-briar stanza found at the end of many tragic love ballads:

> > They buried her in the *old churchyard* (epithet)
> > They buried him in the choir.
> > Out of her grave grew a *red, red rose* (epithet)
> > And out of his a green briar.

> > They grew and they grew to the top of the wall
> > Till they could grow no higher.
> > And there they *twined in a true lover's knot* (phrase)
> > The red rose and the green briar.

Formulaic opening or ending, or *framing device,* closely related to the commonplace, this announces the commencement and conclusion of the song in a conventional manner. The rose-briar stanzas could be considered a formulaic close for the many songs in which they are found. Common openings are "It fell upon a Martinmas (or "Christmas" or "high holiday"), "One morning, one morning, one morning in May (or "Spring")," and "Come all you young fellows and listen to me."

These are all formal conventional devices which, through their use in various songs, have contributed to the songs' retention. Repetition is a facet of the style of folksongs and when used structurally within a song is generally called "incremental repetition." This is simply the repetition of phrases or stanzas (usually conventional ones) within the song, varying them only slightly to fit the changed dramatic situation. The supposition has been that this repetition has been a device to build dramatic tension but this theory seems somewhat alien to the traditional singer's esthetic; such repetition is more likely a technical aid in construction. Incremental repetition usually occurs when two or more scenes of similar setting and situation are found in the same song. It therefore seems natural that these situations would be expressed similarly considering the tendency towards conventional expression in folksong. There are certain songs in which this kind of repetition is so widespread that it controls the entire movement of the song. In cases of such extreme use of repetition we call this device *formulaic patterning* (See Chapter Four for a fuller consideration of formula).

There is one further conventional device which demands attention: the conventional story pattern or conventional situation which controls the movement of action, emphasis, moral stance and response to an entire piece. Conventional patterns function formally in creating stereotype situations which lead to a repetitive story mold or lyric stance (the bereft pregnant girl, the man whose girl was left behind, the wandering pilgrim-stranger, the dying or rejected lover, etc.).

Some combination of these devices is what is generally meant when it is said that folksongs are conventional. Within the compass of folksong in English, there are a number of different types of songs which are definable in terms of the conventional elements which they use. Each type contains a conventional stance and begins with certain conventional openings, and by their use creates an expectation of what other conventional elements may follow.

Composition and Recomposition of Folksongs

We have examined two aspects of the cycle of oral transmission, the ways in which songs are remembered and passed on as they are heard, and the ways in which they change in the process of transmission. It is left now to describe the ways in which songs among the orally-oriented are created and re-created.

We have already mentioned a number of places in which rewriting may occur. Rationalization, localization and conventionalization all call for a kind of minor recasting, usually after an element of a song has been forgotten. Further, unconscious censorship can cause a similar kind of rewriting. When such moral or esthetic rejections occur to an individual, the rewriting process becomes a more deliberate one.

It is clear that a great deal of such composition must have occurred without the event being recorded. The creativity of the orally-oriented songster is not to be denied. It is common throughout rural America, even today, to celebrate any catastrophic event, local or not, in song. This is a tradition which has been capitalized upon by the country-music recording industry as well as continued on the strictly local level. Some of these topical songs excite the interest of the traditional singer and achieve the same kind of oral circulation associated with older traditional songs. For instance, the ballad of "Floyd Collins," which related the futile attempts to rescue Collins from a cave-in in Kentucky in 1925, has already achieved wide currency in the Eastern and Mid-western United States (Wilgus: 1959, 196).

Especially hard to perceive is the dividing line between local songs and imitations and parodies. Should we regard "Pearl Bryan" as a local-ization or a parody of "Fair Florella"? Whatever the answer, it is clear that parody and imitation cause many new songs to arise within the con-ventions of the old. Such a song as "Casey Jones" is a conscious imitation of an earlier homiletic song, "The Ship that Never Returned."

It is difficult to comprehend fully the amount of influence such parody has had on the total picture of the traditional song in English. Parodies seem to have infused new life into the otherwise moribund tradition of such songs as "Springfield Mountain," "Bangum and the Boar," and per-haps "Lord Lovel." A fine case in point is "The Three Ravens" or its Scottish counterpart, "The Twa Corbies," which now are virtually un-known among traditional singers in their earlier (and highly literary) forms, but are still widely sung in various comic versions.

It is certain that the folksongs (most of them of limited currency and duration) of many part-time folk groups are in the main, parodies of this sort. Most political songs, union songs, songs of sitters-in, skiers, fliers, Army, Navy, Marine Corps, highwiremen, and many others, have origins in humorous or militant imitation.

With notice of such conscious creation and recasting, it should now be clear that the tradition of songs being orally transmitted is, under proper conditions, a regenerative one. Folksongs are under the influence of creative and uncreative singers and are subject to disastrously decadent and wonderfully creative influences.

The Question of Literacy and Record

A common misconception concerning the folk process is that there is an equation between illiteracy and "good" folklore, and that any suspicion that a piece or a community have been influenced by print renders it unworthy of further consideration. Such thinking sees literacy as the sole cause of the decline of folklore: "As literacy waxes, oral tradition wanes" (Smith: 1928, 56). On the other hand, some have argued quite the opposite: "... the favorable results in tradition are in direct ratio to the intelligence and literacy of the singers" (Eckstorm and Barry: 1930, 2).

Those who argue for illiteracy are simply indulging in wishful thinking. It is considerably easier to observe and analyze a tradition which is "uncontaminated" by print, but there is a real question whether any such tradition has ever existed.

The problem is really a moot one, because the crucial element in the worth of a tradition is not one of literacy but of intelligence and creativity. Literacy is only one reflection of intelligence. Certainly there have been many nonliterate societies. On the other hand, there have been highly literate communities which have also been productive of folklore of great value.

Scotland is a good case in point. Here is a country in which literacy is nearly total, and has been for some time, because the Presbyterian Church has insisted upon the ability of all members to read the Bible. And it is in parts of this country that some of the richest sources of folksong have been uncovered—riches which include not only a large number of traditional songs but also texts of great fullness and complexity and tunes of rare beauty.

Field experience indicates that intelligent and sensitive informants are more totally concerned with the songs they sing, are more hesitant to sing fragments, and construct fuller and better texts than others with perhaps larger and more varied repertoires.

Finally, the cycle of the transmission process would not be complete without noting the actual influence of print on repertoire. As pointed out in Chapter 1, there is a constant exchange of materials on the levels of folk, popular, and sophisticated culture. This can mean that certain pieces are written and purveyed in recorded form for popular audiences which strike the fancy of the traditional singer and therefore enter into oral circulation. This is true, for instance, of certain broadside ballads and "hillbilly" songs. Most of the important stylistic trends in Anglo-

American folksong have been dictated by popular song styles, though not all popular song types have influenced the course of traditional song. As W. Edson Richmond has pointed out, certain scribal errors can affect a song's traditional life in much the same way that errors in oral transmission do (Richmond: 1951). Furthermore, many traditional singers write down their own songs so that they can better remember them, putting them into what they call "ballet books." Thus, the recording of songs may influence the traditional singer in many ways.

chapter 3

FROM BALLAD TO LYRIC

It is a truism of literary criticism that since the Renaissance, Western European poetry has been dominated by the lyric expression. Lyric, in this sense, refers to artistic creations emphasizing the *emotions* of an individual rather than the actions of a group of characters. Lyric arrests time in order to investigate the moment in terms of prevalent emotion. The artist's preoccupations in this mode come to be of primary importance, emphasizing the dominance of the artist over the audience during this period.

As far back as our records take us, folk lyrics have been an important part of the folksong repertoire in English. But until comparatively recent times, the lyric has not provided the significant part of the folksinger's repertoire which it now seems to do. Our early records of collection, however, may be tremendously overbalanced by the song collectors' interest in balladry. For this reason, it is not possible to assess accurately the character of the repertoire in the past, but we may say with accuracy that lyric now dominates folk expression as well as poetic *belles lettres*. Ballads and lyrics are united in that they both describe dramatic occasions—that is, they are both types of story-songs.

Story-Songs

In fact, most of the songs in the Anglo-American tradition tell a story. In these the listener is placed into the midst of a dramatic occurrence through the agency of the song. Designations for story-song genres arise from the predominant mood and techniques for presenting the drama. If the private experience, the emotional dimension of a story, is stressed in a song, then it has been called a *lyric;* if action predominates then the term *ballad* has been used. This dichotomy ignores a third type, the *dialog song,* in which neither action nor emotion, but the dramatic confrontation of characters is underscored.

This tripartite distinction arises, in a large extent, out of the limited compositional techniques available for focusing a dramatic situation. Songs may be composed from the fixed first person or the roving third person point of view or they may use dialog to reveal the drama. Each of these techniques, when qualitatively predominant, will provide a good index for the type of story-song being presented. In the case of a lyric, emotion has conventionally been expressed best through a first person point of view: action can be stopped and situation explored at length in terms of the emotional reactions of the parties involved, either directly or through metaphor.

> If I had known before I courted
> Your love would be so hard to win,
> I'd have locked my heart in a box of golden
> And fastened it over with a silver pin.

In the ballad, which emphasizes action, the third person point of view predominates, a technique by which action can be described dispassionately from an observer's vantage.

> It fell upon a high holiday
> And the very first day of the year
> Little Mattie Groves to church did go
> God's holy words to hear.
> God's holy words to hear.
>
> The first came by was a gay lady
> The second come by was a girl.
> The third came by was Lord Darnel's wife
> The flower 'mongst them all.
> The flower 'mongst them all.

The dialog song has a shifting first person point of view, the shift corresponding to the change in speakers.

> Oh, will you wear red,
> Oh, my dear, oh, my dear?
> Oh, will you wear red, Jennie Jenkins
> I won't wear red, it's the color of my head
> I'll buy me a foldy roldy, tiddly toldy
> Seek a double roll,
> Jennie Jenkins, roll.

Oh will you wear green,
Oh, my dear, oh my dear?
Oh, will you wear blue, Jennie Jenkins
I won't wear blue, the color isn't true
I'll buy me a foldy roldy, tiddly toldy
Seek a double roll,
Jennie Jenkins, roll.

If third person narrative is generally the most active song expression, and first person lyric the least, dialog song is somewhere between them. Pure narrative (if such a song existed) would be emotionless, filled only with action; pure lyric would stop action totally in order to explore the emotions. Dialog has elements of both action and emotion. Thus it seems convenient to see the three in terms of a spectrum, the poles of which would be action and emotion, a spectrum on which any song could be placed.

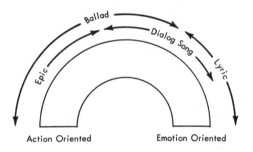

Action Oriented   Emotion Oriented

Most Anglo-American folksongs use more than one narrative technique to present their drama, and therefore to classify such songs is to refer to the predominance of one above the others, and even then classification may be arbitrary. Here, for instance, is a song often called a ballad that could be considered either a lyric or a dialog song because of an equal emphasis upon first person and dialog techniques.

Wagonner's Lad

1. I am a poor girl, my fortune is sad
   I've always been courted by a wagonner's lad,
   He courted me gaily, by night and by day
   And now he is loaded and going away.

2. Your horses are hungry, go feed them some hay.
   Come sit down here by me as long as you stay.
   My horses ain't hungry, they won't eat your hay,
   So fare you well, darling, I'll be on my way.

3. Your wagon needs greasin', your whip needs to mend.
   Come sit down here by me as long as you can.
   My wagon is greasy, my whip's in my hand,
   So fare you well darling, I'll no longer stand.

Of all the types of song, the ballad is most eclectic in its use of techniques, and the "ballad problem" has been considerably complicated by certain songs being called ballads which clearly have little action. A song like "The Unquiet Grave" (77), which is always listed as a ballad, has almost no action and uses only lyric and dialog stanzas.

Example 3-1. The Unquiet Grave

Reprinted by permission of the publishers from Elisabeth Bristol Greenleaf and Grace Yarrow Mansfield, *Ballads and Sea Songs of Newfoundland,* Cambridge, Mass.: Harvard University Press. Copyright 1933 by the President and Fellows of Harvard College, 1961 by Elisabeth Bristol Greenleaf and Grace Yarrow Mansfield.

1. There been falling drops of dew, sweetheart,
     And heavy falls the rain;
   I've only had but one sweetheart,
     On the green fields he was slain.

2. I would do so much for my sweetheart
     As any young maid may;
   I'll sit and mourn upon his grave,
     For a twelvemonth and a day.

3. When the twelvemonth and a day been up,
     This young man rose and spoke;
   What keeps you mourning upon my grave?
     You will not let me sleep.

4. Why do you weep, why do you mourn?
       What do you want of me?
   One kiss, one kiss from your lily-white lips,
       That's all I want of thee.

5. My lily-white lips are cold as clay,
       And my breath smells vile and strong;
   If you takes one kiss from my lily-white lips,
       Your time it won't be long.

6. Down yonder meadow where the grass grows green,
       Where you and I used to walk,
   The prettiest flowers that ever we had seen
       It is withered unto the stalk.

7. It is withered unto the stalk sweetheart,
       And the leaves will never return;
   But since I have lost my own sweetheart,
       What shall I do but mourn?

8. Mourn not for me, my own truelove,
       Mourn not for me I pray,
   So I must leave you and all the whole world,
       And go into my grave.

Furthermore, a number of the most anthologized "ballads" not only have little action, but use dialog technique exclusively.

Example 3-2. Hangman, Hangman

1. "Hangman, hangman hold your rope,
       Hold it for awhile,
   I think I see my Father comin',
       A many and a many long mile."

2. "Father, father have you gold,
   Gold to set me free,
   Or have you come to see me hang,
   Upon the gallows tree?"

3. "No, my son, I have no gold,
   Gold to set you free,
   I will have to see you hang,
   Upon the gallows tree."

4. "Hangman, hangman hold your rope,
   Hold it for awhile,
   I think I see my Mother comin',
   A many and a many long mile."

5. "Mother, mother have you gold?
   Gold to set me free,
   Or have you come to see me hang,
   Upon the gallows tree?"

6. "No, my son, I have no gold,
   Gold to set you free,
   And I will have to see you hang,
   Upon the gallows tree."

7. "Hangman, hangman hold your rope,
   Hold it for awhile,
   I think I see my sweetheart comin',
   A many and a many long mile."

8. "Oh my love, do you have gold?
   Gold to set me free,
   Or have you come to see me hang,
   Upon the gallows tree?"

9. "Yes, my love, I have brought gold,
   Gold to set you free,
   I did not come to see you hang,
   Upon the gallows tree."

However, there are no Anglo-American songs which rely completely on narrated action, and few which even use it heavily. One might see a correlation here between the lack of songs relying on descriptions of action and the dearth of truly heroic songs, for such compositions naturally emphasize heroic action. The ballad is more imbued with romantic and sentimental than with heroic values, and thus stands somewhere between the totally narrative and the lyric; justifiably, the ballad has been described as "lyrical narrative." The closest one comes to an heroic, totally narrative expression, is in a ballad such as "Chevy Chase" (162) rarely collected in America. A Maine example is given here for illustrative purposes.

Example 3-3. Chevy Chase

1. God prosper long our noble king,
     Our lives and safety all;
   A woeful hunting once there did
     At Shiver Chase befall.

2. To drive the deers with hound and horn
     Earl Percy went his way.
   The child may rue that is unborn
     The hunting of that day.

3. The gird Lord of Northumberland
     A vow to God did make
   His pleasure in the Scottish woods
     Three summer days to take,

4. The chiefest harts at Shiver Chase
     To kill and bear away.
   These tidings to Earl Douglas sped
     In Scotland where he lay.

5. He sent Earl Percy of his word—
     He would prevent that sport.
   But England's earl, no fear of that,
     Did to those woods resort.

6. His fifteen hundred bowmen bold,
     All chosen men of might,
   Who knew full well in time of need
     To aim their shafts aright.

7. His gallant grayhounds swiftly ran
     To chase the fallow deer.
   On Monday they began to hunt
     Ere daylight did appear.

8. Year, long before high noon they had
     A hundred fat bucks slain.
   They having dined, the drove-years went
     To rouse the deers again.

9. Lo! yonder doth Lord Douglas come,
     With men in armor bright;
   Full twenty hundred Scottish spears
     A-marching into sight.

---

* From Barry, Eckstorm, and Smyth, *British Ballads from Maine*. Used by permission of Houghton Mifflin Company, publisher.

10. Oh, cease your sports, Earl Percy said,
      And take your bows with speed;
    Ye men of pleasant Tivetdale,
      Fast by the river Tweed.

11. And now with me, my countrymen,
      With courage, never fear;
    I durst encounter any man
      With him to break a spear.

12. Earl Douglas on his milk-white steed
      Wast like a baron bold;
    Rode foremost of his companee
      Whose armor shawn like gold.

13. Show me, he said, whose men ye be
      Was noble Percy he,
    Who said, We list not to declare
      Nor tell what men we be.

14. The first man that did answer make
      Was noble Percy he,
    Who said, we list not declare
      Nor tell what men we be.

15. Yet we will spend our dearest blood
      Thy chiefest harts to slay.
    Then Douglas swore a mighty oath
      And thus in rage did say:

16. Ere thus I will out-braved be,
      One of us twain shall die;
    I know thee well, thou art an earl,
      Lord Percy. So am I.

17. Let thou and I the battle try,
      And save our men aside.
    Cursed be he, Earl Percy said,
      By whom this is denied.

18. Then stepped a gal-yant squire a-forth,
      Withrington was his name,
    Who said, I would not have it told
      To our King Henry's shame,

19. That e'er my captain fought on foot
      And I stood looking on.
    You be two earls, said Withrington,
      And I a squire alone,

20. But I'll do all that do I may,
      While I have strength to stand,
    While I keep power to wield my sword,
      I'll fight with heart and hand.

21. The fight did last from high noonday
      Till setting of the sun;
    For when they rung the evening bell
      The battle scarce was done.

22. Oh! God! it was a grief to see,
      And likewise for to hear,
    The cries of men fast in their gore
      And scattered there and here.

23. With stout Earl Percy there was slain
      Sir John of Edgerton,
    Sir Robert Ratscliff, and Sir John,
      Sir James the bold baron.

24. Likewise Sir George and stout Sir James,
      Both knights of good account;
    And Sir Ralph Rabby there was slain
      Whose courage none surmount.

25. For Withrington all hearts were sad
      And lost in doleful dumps,
    Yet when both legs were smitten off
      He fought upon the stumps.

26. Of fifteen hundred Englishmen
      Went home but fifty-three,
    The rest were dead at Shiver Chase
      Beneath the greenwood tree.

27. Next day did many widows came
      Their husbands to bewail;
    To wash the wounds and shed salt tears,
      But all without avail.

28. The bodies stiff in purple gore
      They bare with them away;
    They kissed them dead a thousand times
      Ere they were wrapped in clay.

29. God save our king and bless our land
      With plenty, joy, and peace;
    And grant that henceforth fool debate
      Twixt noble lords may cease.

Even such a ballad uses dialog technique occasionally. More common is a song like "Lord Thomas and Fair Eleanor" (73) which is more romantic in subject and tone, and which uses a blend of dialog and narrative stanzas in telling its story.

Example 3-4. Three Lovers

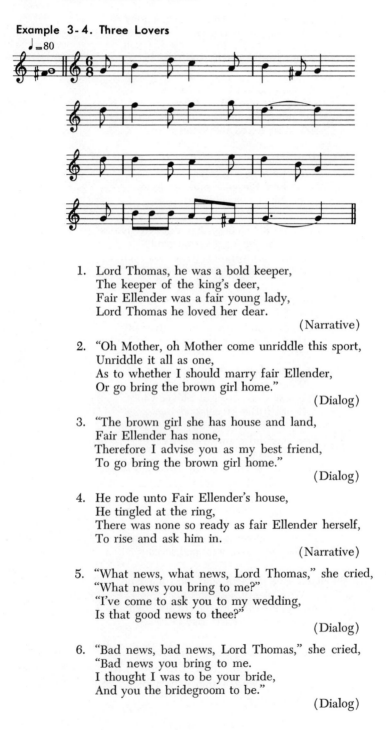

1. Lord Thomas, he was a bold keeper,
   The keeper of the king's deer,
   Fair Ellender was a fair young lady,
   Lord Thomas he loved her dear.
                                    (Narrative)

2. "Oh Mother, oh Mother come unriddle this sport,
   Unriddle it all as one,
   As to whether I should marry fair Ellender,
   Or go bring the brown girl home."
                                    (Dialog)

3. "The brown girl she has house and land,
   Fair Ellender has none,
   Therefore I advise you as my best friend,
   To go bring the brown girl home."
                                    (Dialog)

4. He rode unto Fair Ellender's house,
   He tingled at the ring,
   There was none so ready as fair Ellender herself,
   To rise and ask him in.
                                    (Narrative)

5. "What news, what news, Lord Thomas," she cried,
   "What news you bring to me?"
   "I've come to ask you to my wedding,
   Is that good news to thee?"
                                    (Dialog)

6. "Bad news, bad news, Lord Thomas," she cried,
   "Bad news you bring to me.
   I thought I was to be your bride,
   And you the bridegroom to be."
                                    (Dialog)

7. "Go saddle me up the milk-white horse,
    Go saddle me up the brown,
    Go saddle me up the swiftest horse,
    That ever walked on ground."

                                    (Dialog)

8. She rode unto Lord Thomas' house,
    She tingled at the ring,
    There's none so ready as Lord Thomas himself,
    To rise and ask her in.

                                    (Narrative)

9. He took her by the lily white hand,
    He led her through the hall,
    He led her to the head of the table,
    Among the gentries all.

                                    (Narrative)

10. "Is this your bride, Lord Thomas?" she cried,
    "She looks most wonderful brown,
    When you could 'a' married as fair a young lady,
    That ever the sun shone on."

                                    (Dialog)

11. The brown girl had a pen knife in her hand,
    It looked most keen and sharp,
    She pierced it through fair Ellender's side,
    And it entered near her heart.

                                    (Narrative)

12. "What is the matter?" Lord Thomas, he cried,
    "What is the matter?" cried he,
    "Why don't you see my own heart's blood,
    Come trinkling down by me?"

                                    (Dialog)

13. He took the brown girl by the hand,
    He led her through the hall,
    He took a sword and cut her head off,
    And stoved it against the wall.

                                    (Narrative)

14. "Oh Mother, oh Mother, go make my grave,
    Go make it wide and deep,
    And bury fair Ellender in my arms,
    And the brown girl at my feet."

                                    (Dialog)

15. He placed the sword against the ground,
    The point against his breast,
    Saying, "Here's the end of three young lovers,
    God send them all to rest."

                                (Narrative and Monolog)

Changing Styles in the Ballad

The history of balladry in English is characterized by a succession of ballad styles (or substyles). As each developed and was accepted, the element of sentiment and its attendant emotions became progressively more prominent until one finds a ballad style which is totally sentimental in its approach. The changes generally occur in direct relation to how much a ballad subtype has introduced the personal voice, or how closely the subject is related to a discussion of bereavement, dying, and death.

One must begin any ballad study of this sort with those songs contained in the volumes edited by Francis James Child, *The English and Scottish Popular Ballads* (1882–1898), because his work contains most of the oldest traditional ballads in English. These are, in the main, characterized by the total qualitative dominance of the impersonal (though not unemotional) voice. The broadside ballads which succeeded the Child ballads in popularity, were in many cases equally impersonal, and in fact rendered as much action as most of the older songs, though more diffusely. One special kind of broadside ballad introduced a framing element which was in the familiar voice; the story is reported by an observer of the scene who announces himself to have been there. Such personal introductions seldom consume more than one or two stanzas, but the observer sometimes becomes an actor in the ensuing drama. These songs often begin with expressions such as "As I roved out" or "One morning in spring." In another important ballad style, the "Come-all-ye," the singer is often one of the principals in the action, telling the story in the first person, and emphasizing matters which happened to him as well as how he felt about them. This was succeeded by the sentimental ballad which took two directions; the first was the story told from the first person, highly emotional point of view, generally in the form of a confessional (a tradition arising as much out of the coronach [lament] and "last goodnight" convention as out of the ballad proper); and the third person or first person narrative which tells such a pathetic story (generally concerned with the death of an orphan, of a mother, or of a poor child) that its effect is totally emotional and completely centered on the situation rather than the events which led up to it. The emotional concern of many of these songs is underlined by the inclusion of a refrain or chorus.

Ballad and Oral Change

The distinguishing feature of the ballad is its *predominant interest in action,* with only subsidiary use of other story-telling techniques.

A ballad does *tell* its story and thus has a recognizable beginning, middle, and end, making it relatively stable in its travels in oral circulation. Because the action of the ballad story is told consecutively, if the ballad is to make sense it tends to remain in approximately the same form, the elements of the plot providing internal cues for remembering.

However, as we pointed out in the last chapter, ballads do change, and in recognizable patterns. In America, these changes emphasize a growing emotional orientation both in the mutations affecting individual songs and in the content of the repertoire. This is seen in the drift toward lyric, toward a greater compression of action, and toward increasing use of repetition and conventionalized expression. All three in some way cause action to be slowed down or eliminated. Thus all three drifts of change are illustrative of the increasing domination of the more emotional (and sentimental) element in folksong.

The direct change from ballad to lyric is naturally the most extreme example of this shifting emphasis, but it is seldom encountered in the history of individual ballads. A striking example of this type of change is what has generally happened to "Mary Hamilton" (173) in America. The story concerns an illicit relationship and the resultant offspring of a member of Mary, Queen of Scots' court, the murder of the infant, the Queen's anger and final punishment of the mother, Mary Hamilton. Child's A text, which comes from Charles Kilpatrick Sharpe's Scottish collection, *The Ballad Book* (1823) is one of the fullest renderings of the story.

Example 3-5. Mary Hamilton

1. Word's gane to the kitchen,
   And word's gane to the ha',
   That Marie Hamilton gangs wi bairn
   To the richest Stewart of a'.

2. He's courted her in the kitchen,
   He's courted her in the ha',
   He's courted her in the laigh (low) cellar,
   And that was warst of a'."

3. She's tyed it in her apron
   And she's thrown it in the sea;
   Says, "Sink ye, swim ye, bonny wee babe,
   You'l ne'er get mair o' me."

4. Down then cam the auld queen,
   Goud tassels tying her hair:
   "O Marie, where's the bonny wee babe
   That I heard greet (weep) sae sair?"

5. "There was never a babe intill my room,
   As little designs to be;
   It was but a touch o' my sair side,
   Come o'er my fair bodie."

6. "O Marie, put on your robes o'black,
   Or else your robes o'brown,
   Fe ye maun gang wi' me the night,
   To see fair Edinbro' town."

7. I winna put on my robes o'black,
   Nor yet my robes o'brown;
   But I'll put on my robes o'white,
   To shine through Edinbro' town."

8. When she gaed up the Cannogate,
   She laugh'd laud laughters three;
   But whan she cam down the Cannogate
   The tear blinded her ee.

9. When she gaed up the Parliament stair,
   The heel cam aff her shee;
   And lang or she cam down again
   She was condemend to dee.

10. When she cam down the Cannogate,
    The Cannogate sae free,
    Many a ladie look'd o'er her window,
    Weeping for his ladie.

11. "Ye need nae weep for me," she says,
    "Ye need nae weep for me;
    For had I not slain mine own sweet babe,
    This death I wadna dee.

12. "Bring me a bottle of wine," she says,
    "The best that e'er ye hae,
    That I may drink to my well-wishers,
    And they may drink to me.

13. "Here's a health to the jolly sailors,
    That sail upon the main;
    Let them never let on to my father and mother
    But what I'm coming home.

14. "Here's a health to the jolly sailors,
    That sail upon the sea;
    Let them never let on to my father and mother
    That I cam here to dee.

15. "Oh, little did my mother think,
    The day she cradled me,
    What land I was to travel through,
    What death I was to dee.

16. "Oh, little did my father think,
    The day he held up me,
    What lands I was to travel through,
    What death I was to dee.

17. "Last nicht I wash'd the queen's feet,
    And gently laid her down;
    And a' the thanks I've gotten the nicht
    To be hang'd in Edinbro' town!

18. "Last nicht there was four Maries,
    The nicht there'll be but three;
    There was Marie Seton, and Marie Beton,
    And Marie Carmichael, and me."

But in North America most of the story is generally forgotten and only the lyric lament featured at the end is retained. Almost certainly this portion survives because it is associated so strongly with the magnificent "Last night" stanza.

Example 3 - 6. Mary Hamilton

Reprinted by permission of the publishers from Arthur Kyle Davis, Jr., *Traditional Ballads of Virginia*, Cambridge, Mass.: Harvard University Press, copyright 1929, by the President and Fellows of Harvard College, 1957 by Arthur Kyle Davis, Jr.

1. "Little did my mother think
    When first she cradled me,
    That I should die so far from home,
    So far o'er the salt, salt sea.

2. "Last night there were four Maries,
   Tonight there'll be but three;
   There was Mary Seaton, Mary Beaton,
   And Mary Carmichael and me.

3. "Last night I washed Queen Mary's feet
   And carried her to her bed;
   Today she'll give me my reward,
   The gallows hard to tread.

4. "They'll tie a napkin 'round my eyes,
   They'll ne'er let me see to die;
   They'll ne'er let on to my father and mother
   That I'm far away over the sea."

The shift from ballad to lyric emphasis is seen more readily in a group of songs which share certain commonplaces. For instance, the commonplace stanzas found most notably in "The Lass of Loch Royal" (76) which asks "who will shoe your feet?" are seldom collected in North America connected to the ballad, but are widely found as part of a number of lyric songs:

Example 3-7. Time Draws Near

1. Oh, time draws near my dearest dear,
   When you and I must part,
   How little did you know of the grief and the woe,
   That lays on my poor broken heart.

2. Everyday it seems like two,
   And every hour like ten,
   You caused me to weep when I might 'a been asleep,
   And say you had lost a friend.

3. So I went a roving one cold winter night,
   While drinking on sweet wine,
   When I fell in love with this pretty little miss,
   She stole this heart of mine.

4. For she looked like some pink colored rose,
   Which blossomed in the month of June,
   Or some other musical instrument,
   Just newly put in tune.

5. So I would to the Lord that I'd never been born,
   Or died when I was young,
   So I never could have kissed your sweet ruby lips,
   Nor heard your lying tongue.

6. So I'll put my foot in the bottom of the ship,
   I'll sail it on the sea,
   I would not have treated you, my love,
   Like you have treated me.

7. "Now who will shoe your pretty little feet,
   And who will glove your hand,
   And who will kiss your sweet ruby lips,
   When I'm in some far off land?"

8. "Oh Papa will shoe my pretty little feet,
   And Mama will glove my hand,
   And you can kiss my sweet ruby lips,
   When returned from a far off land."

9. And the blackest crow that ever flew,
   I surely will turn white,
   Whenever I prove false to you,
   Bright day shall turn to night.

10. And the time'll roll on when the sea shall run dry,
    And the rocks melt down with the sun,
    I never will prove false to you,
    Till all this work is done.

A similar situation can be observed in relation to the riddles traditionally connected with the ballad "Captain Wedderburn's Courtship" (46).

1. As I walked out one evening down by a strawberry lane,
   It was there I saw Bold Robbington, the keeper of the game.
   It is true I loved that handsome maid, and if it was not for the law,
   I would take that fair maid round the waist and roll her away from the wall.

2. "Oh, hold your tongue, you silly man, and do not me perplex,
   Before that you can lie with me, you must answer questions six;
   Six questions you must answer me, and I will put them all,
   Then you and I in one bed shall lie, and you lie next to the wall.

Example 3-8. Captain Wedderburn's Courtship

From Barry, Eckstorm and Smyth, *British Ballads from Maine*. Used by permission of Houghton Mifflin Company, publisher.

3. "O what is rounder than a ring? What is higher than a tree?
   What is worse than a woman's tongue? What is deeper than the sea?
   What bird flies far the broad sea across? And where does the first dew fall?
   Then you and I in one bed shall lie, and you lie next to the wall."

4. "This world is rounder than a ring; Heaven is higher than a tree;
   The devil is worse than a woman's tongue; Hell is deeper than the sea;
   The gull flies far the wide sea across, and there is where the first dew falls,
   So you and I in the bed shall lie, and you lie next to the wall."

5. "O hold your tongue, you silly man, and do not bother me,
   Before that you with me can lie, you must answer questions three;
   Three questions you must answer me, and I will put them all,
   Then you and I in the bed shall lie, and you lie next to the wall.

6. "You must get for me a winter fruit that in September grew,
   You must get for me a silk mantle that never web went through,
   A sparrow's thorn, and priest unborn, that shall make us one and all,
   Then you and I in the bed shall lie, and you lie next to the wall.

7. "My father has a winter fruit that in September grew,
   My mother has a silk mantle that never web went through;
   A sparrow's thorn is easily found, for there is one on every scroll,
   Belshazzar was a priest unborn, so you lie next to the wall.

8. "For my breakfast you must get me a cherry without any stone,
   And for my dinner you must get me a chicken without any bone,
   And for my supper you must get me a bird without any gall,
   Then you and I in one bed shall lie, and you lie next to the wall."

9. "Oh, when the cherry is in the bloom I am sure it has no stone,
   And when the chicken is in the egg, I am sure it has no bone;
   The dove it is a gentle bird, and it flies without a gall,
   So you and I in the bed shall lie, and you lie next to the wall."

10. She found her Willy so manfully did Mary's heart enthrall,
    He took this young girl by the waist; but—she didn't lie next to the wall.

These riddles are much more commonly found in the much less active context of such well-known pieces as "The Riddle Song" and "Peri Meri Dixie Dominie."

Example 3-9. Peri Meri Dixie Dominie

1. I had four brothers over the sea,
       Perry merry dinctum dominee;
   And each one sent a present unto me;
       Partum, quartum, perry dee centum,
       Perry merry dinctum dominee.

2. One sent a cherry that hadn't any stone,
       Perry merry dinctum dominee;
   One sent a chicken without any bone,
       Partum, quartum, perry dee centum,
       Perry merry dinctum dominee.

3. The next sent a blanket without any thread,
       Perry merry dinctum dominee;
   And the next send a book that couldn't be read.
       Partum, quartum, perry dee centum,
       Perry merry dinctum dominee.

4. When the cherry's in the blossom, it has no stone,
  Perry merry dinctum dominee;
When the chicken's in the egg, it has no bone.
  Partum, quartum, perry dee centum,
  Perry merry dinctum dominee.

5. When the wool's on the sheep, it has no thread,
  Perry merry dinctum dominee;
When the book's on the press, it can't be read.
  Partum, quartum, perry dee centum,
  Perry merry dinctum dominee.

"The Death of Queen Jane" (170) is another ballad, one variant of which is often pointed to as an example of a shift to lyric emphasis.

This song, however, does not illustrate a complete changeover to a lyric stance but rather a step toward an intermediate position in a reliance upon formulaic repetition. The "Queen Jane" text involves a simple state-

Example 3-10. Queen Jane

From Dorothy Scarborough, *A Song Catcher in the Southern Mountains* (New York: Columbia University Press); used by permission.

ment of the Queen's problems in the delivery of her child and her calling for solace:

1. Well, Jane was in labor
       For three days or more.
   She grieved and she grieved
       And she grieved her heart sore.
   She sent for her mother
       And her mother came o'er,
   Said, "The Red Rose of England
       Shall flourish no more."

2. Well, Jane was in labor
       For three days or more.
   She grieved and she grieved
       And she grieved her heart sore.
   She sent for her Father,
       Her father came o'er.
   Said, "The Red Rose of England
       Shall flourish no more."

3. Well, Jane was in labor
       For three days or more.
   She grieved and she grieved
       And she grieved her heart sore.
   She sent for Prince Henry,
       Prince Henry came o'er.
   Said, "The Red Rose of England
       Shall flourish no more."

This is hardly a lyric, but it does do something which lyric also does: it arrests time—or at least slows it down. And it does this through simple formulaic repetition. Such change toward formula points up the tendency toward progressive conventionalization of ballad texts in oral transmission (the falling back on conventional methods of description and on commonplace situations). This formulaic expression in ballads is seldom found, as here, divorced from dialog. Dialog is, as mentioned, an intermediate point between narrative and lyric, for it slows action down in centering upon character relationships. When dialog becomes formulaic, action is further slowed down because of repetition. Although there are few examples of ballads mutating from narrative to pure lyric, there *are* many which do add formulaic dialog, and these songs are perhaps better illustrations of the tendency away from action *toward* lyric.

Repetition then, in addition to formula, de–emphasizes action. This is seen not only in those individual songs which change formulaically, but also in the change in repertoire. Perhaps because of an influence from Negro tradition, a progressively large number of traditional songs are

either in simple repetition formula (especially religious songs) or use
the techniques of the blues of repeating the first line of a stanza two or
three times.

> I used to be a rambler, I rambled around
> I used to be a rambler, I rambled around.
> I courted Pretty Polly, the prettiest girl in town.
>
> Pretty Polly, Pretty Polly, come and go with me.
> Polly, Pretty Polly, come and go with me.
> Before we get married some pleasure to see.

This kind of repetition is not unknown in older ballads, but becomes
increasingly evident in more recent compositions. Another repetition technique of growing importance is the use of a refrain. Though found in
burden (interlineal) form in certain old songs like "The Two Sisters,"
more and more recent songs use the complete repetition of a verse after
each stanza as a chorus.

> My heart is sad and I'm in sorrow
> Thinking on the one I love.
> When shall I see her? Oh, no never,
> Till we meet in heaven above.
>
> (Chorus)
> So bury me beneath the willow
> Under the weeping willow tree
> So she may know where I am sleeping
> And perhaps she'll weep for me.
>
> Tomorrow was to be our wedding
> Where, oh where, where is she?
> She's gone, she's gone to wed another,
> She no longer cares for me.
>
> (Chorus)
> So bury me beneath the willow
> Under the weeping willow tree
> So she may know where I am sleeping
> And perhaps she'll weep for me.

More difficult to understand in relation to the movement toward lyric
is the tendency toward compression of action. Of all the forces acting
on ballads remarked upon here, compression of action is most widely
observable. Almost any ballad if it has been in oral circulation for long
will drop off the inessentials of the action (those elements farthest from

the "emotional core"). We have seen one good example of this already with regard to the usual American version of "The Two Sisters" where the incident concerning the singing instrument has been lost. Another example is the changes wrought in "Sir Lionel" (18) in America, where it has become "Bangum and the Boar." The original ballad is clearly in the genre of medieval romance. It involves the progression of a number of incidents between the statement of an original circumstance of duress (the virtuous lady under attack by a boar, the agent of a giant) and the resolution of the problem (the killing of the giant). Child's description of the ballad story is:

A knight finds a lady sitting in (or under) a tree, who tells him that a wild boar has slain (or worried) her lord and killed (or wounded) thirty of his men. The Knight kills the boar, and seems to have received bad wounds in the process. The boar belonged to a giant, or to a wild woman. The knight is required to forfeit his hawks and leash and the little finger of his right hand (or his horse, his hound, and his lady). He refuses to submit to such disgrace, though in no condition to resist. The giant allows him time to heal his wounds, and he is to leave his lady as security for his return. At the end of the time the knight comes back sound and well, and kills the giant as he has killed the boar ... the last quarter of the Percy copy would, no doubt, reveal what became of the lady who was sitting in the tree, as to which the traditional copies give no light.

(Child: I, 208–209).

American variants are considerably shorter and often describe only the killing of the boar (See Example 3–11 on page 60). Lost to the song is the giant. Typically, the boar is reported or sighted, regarded as a danger, and killed. Sometimes Bangum blows a horn to attract the beast. The whole story is told in two incidents with a minimum of description. The effect is like a comic tableau. Most important, the elimination of the action does not sharpen the remaining movement, but simply impresses us with its brevity. Lost is the expectation pattern of the narrative. Lost is the audience's relish for the delayed resolution and the embellishment of the story. The effect of telling a good story in song is considerably lessened by this compression of action.

Change toward dialog, formula, and lyric and this compression all serve the same function then: to slow down or eliminate the action of a narrative. The lyric interest not only reigns in regard to percentage of repertoire, but is seen in effects on ballad transmission. These matters will be illustrated in greater detail in respect to specific song types in the next two chapters.

Example 3-11. Old Bangum

1. There is a wild boar in these woods,
       Dillom dom dillom.
   He eats our flesh and drinks our blood,
       Tum a qui quiddle quo qum.

2. How shall I this wild boar see?
       Dillom dom dillom.
   "Blow your horn and he'll come to thee."
       Tum a qui quiddle quo qum.

3. Bangum blew his horn a blast,
       Dillom dom dillom.
   The wild boar came cutting oak and ash.
       Tum a qui quiddle quo qum.

4. Bangum drew his wooden knife,
       Dillom dom dillom.
   And he worried the wild boar out of his life.
       Tum a qui quiddle quo qum.

5. Bangum rode to the wild boar's den,
       Dillom dom dillom.
   And he found the bones of a thousand men.
       Tum a qui quiddle quo qum.

chapter 4

THE TRADITIONAL
SHAPES OF CONTENT

In describing folksongs as expressions of culture being transmitted in time and space, we have been assuming the artistic nature of these expressive materials. Folksongs are esthetic entities capable of producing pleasure by organizing materials and projecting life situations. But their esthetic effect is different from that of high art in that it is not only more simple and reflexive but its sense of organization is always insistently clear. This is evident in the presentation of themes and values, in dramatic presentation, and most notably in the conventional forms.

> Formal patterns are also found in sophisticated literature, but rarely are they as prominent as in folklore. Whereas the sophisticated poet may disguise his structure, folk poetry works toward very evident patterns that stand out even more starkly because the lack of vivid imagery emphasizes them. This is necessary to give a sense of form to an oral performance. Sophisticated poetry is primarily written poetry; a good part of its formal effect is visual, the arrangement of black marks upon a sheet of a paper. Oral poetry on the other hand, must achieve similar effects in other ways—with the end-stopped line, for example, which is the only line possible in folk poetry because there is no other way to show that one has come to the end of a "line" except by stopping.

> (Paredes: 1964, 217)

One characteristic of folk poetry is extreme regularity and balance. In oral performance, this kind of effect provides the reminder of ordering that is needed for a hearing audience (but which is regarded as monotonous to a reader). Given the principles of regularity and balance, each tradition voices itself in different conventional forms, and none more indicative of these severe limitations than Anglo-American folksong.

Verse Forms

The essential formal unit of Anglo-American folksong is the stanza. Each stanza fully states the melody, and each generally is a full grammatical statement, a sentence. The constituent parts of the stanza are the lines, and the parts making up the lines are stressed and un-stressed syllables, which generally group themselves in pairs (dipods).

Anglo-American folksong, as with all folk verse in English, is primarily cast in lines of four stresses, generally with a marked break in the middle of the line (between the dipods). Developing on this binary pattern, the lines generally group themselves in couplets (not necessarily rhymed), with an even stronger caesura between the lines. Furthermore, the most common stanzaic pattern is one of two couplets. The binary nature of the stanza is further amplified by the rhyming arrangement, rhymes occurring either at the end of each line or at the end of the second and fourth lines. The number of unstressed syllables coming between the stresses varies and is commonly irregular, an arrangement called *isochronic.* Thus, we might typify Anglo-American folksongs as binary, dipodic, and isochronic in verse composition. (These terms and their meaning in regard to both words and music will be discussed more fully in Chapter 8.)

It is commonly assumed that the basic meter for folksongs is the alter-nation of lines of four stresses with ones of three, an arrangement often called *ballad meter.* That this is simply a variation of the regular four-stress pattern is immediately perceivable, however, insofar as the musical dimension of metrical composition insists on a pause after the three-stress line so that the fourth stress can be implied. But the ballad meter is, in-deed, a common formal arrangement for English language songs.

In its simplest, and most characteristic statement, ballad meter appears as lines which are rhymed at the end of the second and fourth lines: *abcb.* This arrangement can be visualized in print as a couplet of two lines, each with seven stresses, though the four-line form is the more common in printed collections. The effect of this line can be varied con-siderably. For instance, though a masculine rhyme scheme can give a more powerful effect:

> An old knight rode one summer's day,
> Down by the greenwood side;
> And there he spied a fair young maid,
> And all alone she cried.

a greater fluidity is achieved by using feminine rhyme:

> Last night I dreamed of my true love
> All in my arms I had her;
> When I awoke there was no such there;
> I was forced to lie without her.

The stanzaic pattern is varied considerably when the second and fourth lines are in *burden* form, causing the rhyme to be thrown to the first and third lines:

> If you can't answer my questions nine,
> Sing ninety-nine and ninety,
> Oh, you're not God's, you're one of mine,
> And you're not the weaver's bonny.

Even more commonly the stanzaic form is varied by line repetitions, the most usual being a reiteration of the last line: *abcbb.*

> Lord Lovel he sat at his castle gate,
> Combining his milk-white steed,
> When along there came Lady Nancy Bell,
> Wishing her lover good speed, good speed,
> Wishing her lover good speed.

Ballad meter is by no means the only metrical pattern in Anglo-American folksongs; an equally prevalent stanzaic form is one which conforms more closely to the four-stress norm of folk verse in construction stanzas of four lines of four stresses each.

> Lord Bateman was a noble lord,
> And held himself in high degree.
> He would not rest nor be contented
> 'Til he had voyaged across the sea.

This lengthened second and fourth line is perhaps more characteristic of broadside verse than the earlier traditions, but it is by no means absent in the older songs. For instance, in "The Two Sisters" (20) the four-stressed line is used in combination with repetitions and a burden to achieve an uncommon stanzaic form:

> There was an old lord by the northern sea,
> Bow down, bow down.
> There was an old lord by the northern sea,
> Bow and balance to me.*

---

* This one line uses the three–stress pattern with a strong pause implied.

/ / / /
There was an old lord by the northern sea,
/ / / /
And he had daughters, one, two, three.
/ / / /
I shall be true, true to my love,
/ / / /
Love and my love shall be true to me.

Though ballad meter, and the closely related lines of four-stress, in four–line stanzas are the most common forms in English language folk-song, it would be foolish to imagine that they are the only ones. This is evident just from the "Two Sisters" pattern. There are many other verse forms which can be observed in Anglo-American tradition which vary in line-length, number of lines in the stanza, and in rhyme scheme. To take one of the most extreme examples, a complex form found in songs as diverse as "Wondrous Love," "Sam Hall," and "Captain Kidd" has three rhyming lines of three stresses in the center of a rather long stanza:

Oh! my name was Robert Kidd,
As I sailed, as I sailed.
Oh, my name was Robert Kidd,
As I sailed.
My name was Robert Kidd,
God's laws I did forbid,
And most wickedly I did,
As I sailed, as I sailed,
And most wickedly I did,
As I sailed.

(Bronson: 1940)

Songs of broadside origin were a great deal more self-consciously literary than their purely traditional forebears, and this is reflected not only in the creation of sentimental and democratic situations with appropriate diction, but also in new and slightly more complex verse forms. Most broadside ballads which went into tradition conformed to the meter and stanzaic form of traditional song, but in certain cases changes were wrought. The most common of these was to take the stanza of four lines, each with four stresses, and to turn it into two rhyming couplets.

Monday morning I married me a wife,
A'thinking I'd live a happy life.
Oh, fiddle invention was all that I craved,
To think how happy I were made.

An equally modest modification, but an important one, was that of doubling stanza length, yoking together in one stanza the elements of two, thus allowing for an expansion of detail and moment. This was accompanied by an equivalent expansion in tunes. It is especially characteristic of the "come-all-ye" style of broadside composition.

> Come all of you bold shanty boys,
> And list while I relate.
> Concerning a young shanty boy
> And his untimely fate:
> Concerning a young river man,
> So manly, true and brave:
> 'Twas on the jam at Gerry's Rock
> He met a watery grave.

(The stanza is often printed in four expanded lines, rather than the eight given here, especially when printed on broadsheets or in chapbooks.)

Another change which occurred, and a very self-consciously literary one, was the introduction of rhyme into the midpoint of the line, causing an additional emphasis on the regularity of the rhythm. Thus, the broadside hack recast "The Gypsy Laddie" (200):

> Oh, saddle with speed my milk-white steed,
> Quickly make him ready.
> I will ride this night till the broad daylight,
> Till I overtake my lady.

Form and Repetition

The most important characteristic of formal style of Anglo-American folksong is its reliance on repetition to achieve artistic coherence. Repetition is the primary organizing principle of folk art in general: "In literature, there are many means of producing emphasis ... For example, the dimensions or significance of something can be depicted by the degree and detail of the description of that particular object or event. In contrast, folk narrative lacks this full-bodied detail, for the most part, and its spare descriptions are all too brief to serve as an effective means of emphasis ... there is but one alternative: repetition" (Olrik: 1909, 132–133). But each tradition is characterized by the matters it chooses to repeat and the patterns etched by these repeated elements. It should never be forgotten that repetition performs many functions in regard to composition: it establishes a sense of familiarity within a specific piece that enables the audience to follow and sympathize; it provides points in a composition which aid memory; and in many cases it helps establish the incantatory feeling which encourages vicarious identification and the consequent enjoyment of the pleasure in the simultaneous contemplation of and involvement with the work of art.

As mentioned in the discussion of the importance of convention, the major repeated element in Anglo-American folksong is the melody. Because of the stanzaic arrangement, the tune is constantly restated. But there are a number of other devices intensifying the repetitive quality of the strophic organization—specifically, incremental repetition, burdens, refrains, and choruses.

Burdens do not always contribute to the meaning of a song; they often simply function as an additional incantatory device. This is especially evident in the songs which use flower and herb burdens like "Savory, sage, rosemary and thyme," and ones in which the repeated lines are nonsensical, introduced mainly for the sound patterns which they establish. (This seems to be the function of the "Ninety-nine and ninety" line, for instance.) In such cases, a burden helps establish a mood or intensify the tone already created. This is carried one step further in burdens which introduce the place in which the action is supposed to occur: "Down by the greenwood side" or "Down by the green, by the burnie-o." Burdens are as conventional as other folksong elements and consequently often crop up in places in which their effect is nullified by a *non sequitur* feeling, or by one of lack of appropriateness. (For instance, look at the tension between the horrifying story of "The Two Sisters" (20) and the usual burden in North America of "Bow and balance to me.") In such cases, the incantatory effect must take precedence over meaning, for the song to "make sense."

Closely allied in technique and function to the burden is the refrain, the lines repeated at the end of each stanza. Once again, these often work merely as incantation, but they often become more highly integrated into the dramatic or lyric movement of a song. This is true of the refrain in most versions of "The Golden Vanity."

> There was a little ship that sailed upon the sea,
> And the name of that ship was the *Golden Willow Tree*,
> Sailing on the low and lonesome low,
> Sailing on the lonesome sea.

In songs of this sort, the actual content of the refrain can be varied somewhat to conform to and comment upon dramatic developments.

The extension of this technique is observable in the use of choruses. As pointed out in Chapter 3, one of the devices used to slow down a song and to emphasize emotional situation is the addition of a chorus, a tendency discernible in sentimental songs. Commonly, a song which has a chorus-verse arrangement uses the chorus as the most extreme expression of the emotional involvement of the situation, and the verses fill in the dramatic details somewhat. Consequently, each time the chorus is restated it tends to take on a slightly different, amplified significance. This is played upon by song-writers who are completely at home with the verse-chorus alternation, so that the chorus can function in the same song as an extension of the story in one place and later as an ironic commentary on what has transpired.

Example 4-1. Jack and Joe

1. Three years ago both Jack and Joe
   Set sail across the foam.
   Each vowed a fortune they would earn
   Before returning home.
   In one short year Jack gained his wealth
   And set for home that day,
   And as the boys shook hands to part,
   Poor Joe could only say:

Chorus:
   "Give my love to Nellie, Jack,
   And tell her I am well.
   Sweetest girl in all this world,
   I'm sure you'll say 'tis she.
   Treat her kindly, Jack old pal
   And tell her I am well;
   And don't forget the parting words—
   Jack, give my love to Nell."

2. Three years had passed when Joe at last
Gained wealth enough for life.
He started home across the foam
To make sweet Nell his wife.
But on his way he heard them say
That Jack and Nell had wed;
And deeply he regretted then
That he had ever said:

Chorus:

"Give my love to Nellie, Jack,
And kiss her once for me.
Sweetest girl in all this world,
I'm sure you'll say 'tis she.
Treat her kindly, Jack old pal
And tell her I am well;
And don't forget these parting words—
Jack, give my love to Nell."

3. Upon the street they chanced to meet
Joe said, "You selfish elf;
The very next girl I learn to love
I'll kiss her for myself.
But all is fair in love, they say,
And since you're truly wed,
And don't forget the parting words,
Jack, give my love to Nell."

Chorus:

"Give my love to Nellie, Jack,
And kiss her once for me.
Sweetest girl in all this world,
I'm sure you'll say 'tis she.
Treat her kindly, Jack old pal
And tell her I am well;
And don't forget these parting words—
Jack, give my love to Nell."

Such sentimental compositions utilize to their fullest extent the poten-
tialities of the verse-chorus alternation to emphasize the pathos inherent
in the dramatic situation being presented. The addition of the chorus to
the stanzaic form changes the feeling of a song tradition as much as
the breaking up of stories into stanzaic form did—a changeover the impact of which is underlined by the use of one tune for the chorus and
another for the verses. This is clearly seen in those songs which are found
in variants both with and without choruses. Choruses were often added
to traditional songs by early hillbilly performers such as the Carter
Family. (See, for instance, their "Storms Are On the Ocean" and compare
it to any traditional version of "Ten Thousand Miles" or "Who's Gonna

Shoe Your Pretty Little Feet?") In doing so, such performers were developing on a tendency already present in American country tradition.

Form and Formula

Because of their conventional nature there is a certain amount of predictability to the songs in Anglo-American tradition. This predictability is heightened in proportion to the amount of conventional form or phrasing used in a specific song, and how often the conventional expressions are repeated. Further, certain songs set up a formal pattern which permits even greater predictability; this is especially evident in dialog songs in which the conversation is in question-and-answer or offer-and-rejection form, for the phrasing of the conversation gravitates toward a repeated pattern. The most extreme expression of this formal predictability is found in formulaic repetition—that is, in formalistic control on the level of phrasing which is repeated throughout the entire composition. There are a limited number of formulaic patterns observable in Anglo-American song:

> *Simple repetition*—one phrase, sentence, stanza or series of stanzas is repeated with only slight alterations caused by the progression of events or introduction of new situations. When a narrative is involved the variance may become more pronounced as the song progresses to allow for the necessary conclusion. This is what is most commonly called "incremental repetition."

Example 4-2. Who Killed Cock Robin?

1. Oh, who killed Cock Robin?
   Oh, who killed Cock Robin?
   It's I said the sparrow,
   With my little bow and arrow.
   It was I, it was I killed Cock Robin.

2. Oh, who dug his grave?
   Oh, who dug his grave?
   It's I said the crow,
   With my little crooked toe.
   It was I, it was I dug his grave.

3. Oh, who made his coffin?
   Oh, who made his coffin?
   It's I said the snail,
   With my little hammer nail.
   It was I, it was I that made his coffin.

4. Oh, who preached his funeral?
   Oh, who preached his funeral?
   It's I said the owl,
   Just as hard as I could growl.
   It was I, it was I preached his funeral.

Circular—repetition of material without change; the composition provides, in its ending, an introduction leading back to the beginning. This process is most often found in children's songs, like the endless "Found a Peanut" and the chant:

My name is Yon Yonson,
I come from Visconsin,
I vork in the lumberyards there.
Oh, the people I meet,
As I valk on the street,
They say "Hello"
I say "Hello"
They say, "What's your name?"
I say,
My name is Yon Yonson
I come from Visconsin
Etc.

Causal chain—actions which cause a further happening, which in turn cause a further happening, and so on.

1. Sold my cow and bought me a calf,
   I never made a bargain but what I lost half.
   Wing wang waddle, Jack straw straddle,
   Little boy bridle sewing with a broom.

2. I sold my calf and bought me a goose,
   Lord, what a pretty thing I had for the roost.
   Wing wang waddle, Jack straw straddle,
   Little boy bridle sewing with a broom.

Example 4-3. Foolish Boy

3. I sold my goose and bought me a drake,
    Durned little thing always kept me awake.
    Wing wang waddle, Jack straw straddle,
    Little boy bridle sewing with a broom.

4. I sold my drake and bought me a hen,
    Lord, what a pretty thing I had for to lay.
    Wing wang waddle, Jack straw straddle,
    Little boy bridle sewing with a broom.

5. I sold my hen and bought me a mouse,
    Blamed little thing stuck fire to my house.
    Wing wang waddle, Jack straw straddle,
    Little boy bridle sewing with a broom.

6. I sold my mouse and bought me a mole,
    Durned little thing climbed down in a hole.
    Wing wang waddle, Jack straw straddle,
    Little boy bridle sewing with a broom.

7. I sold my mole and bought me a fly,
    Durned little thing got sick and died.
    Wing wang waddle, Jack straw straddle,
    Little boy bridle sewing with a broom.

Progressive recitation—changes (often narrative movements) are related
to numbers or letters in progression, days of the week or some other
kind of hierarchy.

Example 4-4. Scolding Wife

1. Monday morning I married me a wife
   A'thinking I'd live a happy life.
   Oh fiddle invention was all that I craved,
   To think how happy I were made,
      To think how happy I were made.

2. Tuesday morning I brought her home
   I had a wife and scolding tongue.
   She tuned up her pipe and scolded more
   Than ever I heared in my life before,
      Than ever I heared in my life before.

3. Wednesday morning I went to the woods
   A'thinking that I would do her some good.
   I cut me a stick, the hickory so green
   I believe it's the toughest that ever I seen,
      I believe it's the toughest that ever I seen.

4. Thursday morning I banged her well
   The truth to you young man I will tell.
   And if you're no better tomorrow
   The devil may take you away from me,
      The devil may take you away from me.

5. Friday morning before it was day
   She laid on her pillow a'scolding away
   Come one, come two, come three little devils
   And carried her off in a shower of rain,
      And carried her off in a shower of rain.

6. Saturday morning come dine at home,
    I had neither wife nor scolding tongue.
    Oh, my big bottle was my best friend,
    And my week's work was all to an end,
        And my week's work was all to an end.

Progressive chain—simple repetition tied to principle of progression; as in the last type, changes occur in relation to numbers, letters, days of the week, months of the year, and so on.

Example 4 - 5 Darlin', You Can't Have One

1. Darling, you can't love one.
    Darling, you can't love one.
    You can't love one and still have fun,
    Oh, darling you can't love one.

2. Darling, you can't love two.
    Darling, you can't love two.
    You can't love two and still be true,
    Oh, darling you can't love two.

3. Darling, you can't love three.
    Darling, you can't love three.
    You can't love three and still have me,
    Oh, darling you can't love three.

4. Darling, you can't love four.
    Darling, you can't love four.
    You can't love four and still have more,
    Oh, darling you can't love four.

Cumulative—a causal or progressive chain which has a new element added as the piece is consecutively repeated. Some of the more common songs in this form are "The Green Grass Grows All Around" and "The Twelve Days of Christmas."

Example 4-6. I'll Sing You One Ho!

1. I'll sing you one Ho
   Green grow the rushes O
   What is your one Ho?
   One is one and all alone,
   And ever more shall be so.

2. I'll sing you two Ho
   Green grow the rushes O
   What is your two Ho?
   Two, two lily-white boys,
   Clothed all in green O
   One is one and all alone,
   And ever more shall be so.

3. I'll sing you three Ho
   Green grow the rushes O
   What is your three Ho?
   Three, three rivals,
   Two, two lily-white boys,
   Clothed all in green O
   One is one and all alone,
   And ever more shall be O.

This pattern continues adding in each subsequent stanza;

4.   Four are the gospel makers.
5.   Five are the symbols at your door.
6.   Six are six broad waiters.
7.   Seven are the seven stars in the sky.
8.   Eight are the eight commanders.
9.   Nine are the nine that brightly shine.
10.   Ten are the ten commandments.

Suspended chain—progression of action here is not reliant on cause-effect relationships, but rather on the linguistic similarities between the final word of one stanza and the first word of the next. Most songs using this formulaic pattern are bawdy or obscene and use the sound substitution to emphasize obscene words and at the same time excuse their use.

> Country boy, country boy,
> Sitting in the grass,
> Along came a bumble-bee
> And stung him on the
>
> Ask me no questions,
> I'll tell you no lies, etc.

Another type, instead of providing a sound-alike word, rather withholds the imperative obscenity and substitutes the inanity of a nonsense chorus.

> There were two men in Darby town
> And they were very rich.
> One was the son of a millionaire
> The other was a son of a
>
> Hoky, poky diddly okey,
> If you think I lie, etc.

chapter

STYLE AND THE
ORGANIZATION
OF MEANING

In distinguishing between song types in terms of the narrative-lyric continuum, we were making generalizations about story-telling technique as modified by the process of oral transmission. We were establishing a methodology by which the different song types could be related. The songs placed on that spectrum share the characteristic of telling a story. But they differ in the techniques which they use, especially in the way in which they focus their energy. We have already noted how ballad is an eclectic form which uses many techniques of narration in order to center upon a dramatic happening, but that third-person narration tends to be qualitatively emphasized. Similarly, lyric tends to arise in first-person terms and dialog song to rely almost completely on interpersonal conversation to convey drama. These differences occur because the dramatic focus differs in the three song types, and not all Anglo-American songs are dramatic; that is, not all tell a story. Some present a series of vignette stories, focussing on a central character, while others discuss the characteristics of some interesting object, animal, or occupation.

In this chapter we will discuss in detail the different ways in which the meaning of songs is focused, organized. All Anglo-American songs are built around one central idea, action, situation, or character. Each song then directs our attention with singular devotion to the focusing element and rejects extraneous details. In telling a story, elements such as scene are neglected in favor of a purely dramatic focus. Similar single-mindedness can be observed in other song types as well.

Story-Songs—The Ballad

By now the ballad as a form is most familiar to us, and it thus seems most convenient to begin our discussion with it. Ballads are organized by focussing on an action. The action is generally one in which a dramatic transformation occurs, leading to someone's death or marriage or some other cataclysmic event. Because of this focus on action, most ballads direct the attention to a single dramatic episode, an encounter between characters in collision which results in dramatic change. This centering on the single episode, reliance on impersonal (often third person) narrative method, and concentration on the story action are the three most important characteristics of the ballad (Gerould: 1932, 10–11; Wilgus: 1959, 262).

We have already noted that ballad change often causes the action to be compressed. But the genre is such that it has already been concerned with the telling of its story in which our introduction to the action is quite close to the climax. The narrative is therefore short, exhibiting little interest in the exhibition of ornate story-telling techniques, especially when viewed in contrast to epic or wonder tale. The action is generally simple, usually composed of one act or series of acts which is the "cause" of the dramatic conflict, and which leads directly to the climax or "effect." Commonly, there is an incidental short scene between the dramatic "cause" and "effect" which serves as something of a "breather," heightening the dramatic tension somewhat. The scenes are chronologically arranged, but equal time is not spent on each, a technique called "leaping and lingering" (Gummere: 1902, 91). Action after the climax is very unusual, though the conventional ending does serve something of a postlude function, just as the conventional opening functions as a prelude. The limited action is also reflected in the limitation of characters; the *dramatis personae* is always small, generally limited to two characters, seldom greater than four except when a collective "character" such as the seven brothers in "Earl Brand" appears.

Because of the emphasis on the economy of action, ballads often neglect other aspects of story-telling technique: scene, motivation, theme, and so on (Leach: 1949, 106; Friedman: 1956, xiii-xiv.). Scene is given only by brief allusion in the opening stanza, if it is given at all, and then more because of the force of the conventional opening than because of the necessity to establish dramatic place. Furthermore, characters may perform the most incredibly illogical or inhuman actions and the audience will usually be provided with no rationale at all. Motivation, as well as scene and other such elements, must be implied from the dramatic situation or imagined.

Nowhere is the limitation of ballad technique more strongly felt than in the impersonal manner in which the tale is sung. Except in those ballads which descend from the minstrel tradition and use the insertion of the singer in first-person terms to testify to the veracity of the events being described, there is little intrusion on the objective tone of the narration. The way in which the story is told underlines the psychic distance between performer and the events being celebrated. No editorial comment is generally needed (though the broadside hacks often inserted one); the story speaks for itself. Attraction or disdain for the events described may be expressed after the performance by the performer or one of the audience, but it is not generally stated overtly in the song itself, which is not to say that a song is really objective in its approach. On the contrary, ballads generally insist that everyone view the ethics of the action in the same way, but they do so with the appearance of objectivity about the whole matter. Truly we hate the cruel captain of "The Golden Vanity" (286) not because of the singer's expression of attitudes, but because of the captain's unreasonable actions which speak for themselves.

Example 5-1 Golden Willow Tree

1.   There was a little ship that sailed upon the sea,
     And the name of that ship was the *Golden Willow Tree,*
     Sailing on the low and lonesome low,
     Sailing on the lonesome sea.

2.   Now she hadn't been out but a week, two or three,
     Until she sighted the British robberie,
     Sailing on the low and lonesome low,
     Flaunting the Jolly Roger on the lowland sea.

3. Up stepped the captain, wringing of his hands,
   Saying, "Alas, what shall we do?
   They will sink us in this low and lonesome low,
   They will sink us in this lonely lowland sea."

4. A boy then said, "Captain, what will you give me
   If I sink this British robberie?
   I'll sink them in this low and lonesome low,
   I'll sink them to the bottom of this lonely sea."

5. "I'll give you wealth, I'll give you fee,
   My oldest daughter and you shall married be,
   If you'll sink them in this low and lonely low,
   If you'll sink them in this lonely sea."

6. Then he picked up a tool and he jumped overboard.
   He said, "I'll be as good as my word."
   And he was swimming in the low and lonesome low,
   Swimming in the lonesome, lowland sea.

7. Then he took his little tool just made for that use,
   And he made twelve holes just to let in the juice,
   And she was sinking in the low and lonesome low,
   She was sinking in the lonesome lowland sea.

8. The sailors offed with their hat and same with their caps,
   All trying to fill up the salt water gaps,
   But they sunk in the low and lonesome low,
   They sank to the bottom of the lonesome sea.

9. Then he turned around and away swam he
   Till he came back to the *Golden Willow Tree*.
   Swimming in the low and lonely low,
   Still swimming in the lonely lowland sea.

10. "Oh, captain, are you good as your word?
    Then take this poor sailor man aboard.
    For I'm drowning in this low and lonesome low,
    I'm drowning in the lonely lowland sea."

11. "I will not give you wealth, nor give you your fee,
    Nor my oldest daughter to you shall married be.
    I'll just leave you in this low and lonesome low,
    I'll just leave you in this lonesome lowland sea."

12. "Well, if it wasn't for your daughter and your being such a man,
    I would do unto you what I did to them.
    I'd sink you in this low and lonesome low,
    I'd sink you to the bottom of this lonesome sea."

13. Then he turned on his back and away floated he,
    Saying, "Fare you well, *Golden Willow Tree*,
    I'm drowning in this low and lonesome low,
    I'm drowning in this lonely lowland sea."

This song graphically illustrates the most salient characteristics of the ballad technique: the limited number of characters, the commencement of the action near the climax, the restricted number of scenes, the light sketching of setting, the implication of motivation, and the objective tone maintained throughout.

The ballad is one type of traditional narrative, and as such, conforms in most respects to Axel Olrik's "Epic Laws of Folk Narrative" (Dundes: 1965, 129–141). The ones most applicable here are:

> The law of opening and the law of closing: folk narrative does not begin with sudden action and does not end abruptly. This is clearly evidenced in the conventional openings [like "In Scarlet Town, where I was born" or "It fell upon a high holiday, . . ."] and closing [like the ubiquitous rose and briar motif].
>
> The law of repetition: the use of repetition, often formulaic, when emphasis is called for.
>
> The law of two to a scene: two is the maximum number of people who appear at one time in a traditional narrative. If a third is involved, it is only as a viewer. Only two confront each other at once, and this is made clear in the dialog.

Beyond these, Olrik points to other characteristics of folk narratives which he does not put in terms of a law but which are equally useful in relating ballads to other kinds of folk narratives: "each attribute of a person and thing must be expressed in actions . . ."; "folk narrative is single-stranded. It does not go back in order to fill in missing parts"; "folk narrative does not know the perspective of painting; it knows only the progressive series of bas-reliefs . . . tableaux scenes in . . . [which] the actors draw near each other"; and "each narrative element works within it so as to create an event, the possibility of which the listener had seen right from the beginning and which he had never lost sight of." Ballads differ from other types of folk narratives, in other words, only in that they are brief, quick in coming to their climax, more limited in number of characters involved in total story, and are sung.

Most of these generalizations concerning ballads are derived from the scholarly analysis of the songs in the Child canon. However, except for the metrical changes described in the last chapter and important differences in convention of character and situation, the techniques employed by the later ballad-makers were derived from the older creations. And this tendency became even more marked as songs of broadside origin became current in the folk repertoire.

However, just as the broadside writers tended to stretch the bounds of folk meter, they also gravitated toward less story compression and a dilution of dramatic effect. The major reason for this was that many of their songs celebrated recent events and were therefore closely tied to the minutiae of such reportage. This detail tended to be lost as the memory of the immediate incident faded, and if the song remained in traditional currency it gravitated toward the shape of the older ballads. Even so, the effect of the street ballad is sometimes more diffuse because the story may begin well before its climax, and the climax then comes to take a place of secondary interest in favor of an effect of dramatic sweep, often made somewhat ludicrous by its severely rushed feeling and its reliance on sentimental attitudes and diction. This is perceivable in one of the most common traditional street ballads, "Jackie's Gone a-Sailing" (N7).

Example 5-2. Jackie's Gone A-Sailing

1. There was a wealthy merchant, in London he did dwell.
   He had an only daughter, this truth to you I'll tell.
   Sing lay the lillies low, sing lay the lillies low.

2. Said she, "I'm being courted by men of high degree,
   Yet none but Jack the sailor can take my heart from me."
   Sing lay the lillies low, sing lay the lillies low.

3. "Oh daughter, oh daughter, your body I'll confine,
   If none but Jack the sailor can ever suit your mind."
   Sing lay the lillies low, sing lay the lillies low.

4. "My body you may prison, my heart you can't confine,
   For none but Jackie the sailor will ever suit my mind."
   Sing lay the lillies low, sing lay the lillies low.

5. Poor Jackie's gone a-sailin' with trouble on his mind,
   Because he had to leave his darlin' girl behind.
   Sing lay the lillies low, sing lay the lillies low.

6. Poor Jackie's gone a-sailin', his face you'll see no more.
   He's landed on San Flanders, an awful sandy shore.
   Sing lay the lillies low, sing lay the lillies low.

7. She went into a tailor shop and dressed in man's array,
   And went onto a vessel to take herself away.
   Sing lay the lillies low, sing lay the lillies low.

8. "Before you step on board, sir, your name I'd like to know."
   She smiled at him and said, "Sir, my name is Jack Monroe."
   Sing lay the lillies low, sing lay the lillies low.

9. "Your waist it is too slender, your fingers long and small,
   Your cheeks too red and rosy to face the cannon's ball."
   Sing lay the lillies low, sing lay the lillies low.

10. "I know my waist is slender, my fingers long and small,
    But it would not make me tremble to see ten thousand fall."
    Sing lay the lillies low, sing lay the lillies low.

11. The awful battle over, they hunted all around,
    Among the dead and dying, her sailor boy she found.
    Sing lay the lillies low, sing lay the lillies low.

12. She gathered him all in her arms and carried him to town,
    And sent for a physician to heal his bleeding wound.
    Sing lay the lillies low, sing lay the lillies low.

13. This couple they got married, and well did they agree;
    This couple they got married, so why not you and me?
    Sing lay the lillies low, sing lay the lillies low.

This dissipation of effect is characteristic of only certain street ballads, and is not unknown in the Child songs (for instance, see "Lord Bateman," Chapter 6, Example 6–4, which is probably of broadside origin, but included by Child because of the antiquity of the theme). The broadside songs which achieved greatest currency in tradition were those which conformed more closely to the esthetic of the folk narrative, especially those which relied heavily on economy of effect through dialog.

Blues Ballads, Coronachs, Last Goodnights

A special problem in ballad study are those compositions which center upon an event like a ballad but which do not tell the story in full. Generally, such songs take for granted a knowledge on the part of the audience of the story and simply make allusions to the goings-on, with perhaps some moral commentary. This is the spirit behind the Scottish lament or coronach, the most well known example of which is "The Bonny Earl of Murray" (181). The song laments the death of the good earl, and implicates the slayer, but tells almost nothing of the events by which the killing took place. The major emphasis is upon the sense of loss attendant upon Murray's death.

Such a lament tradition is carried on in this country, most notably in songs which Tristram P. Coffin has named "narrative obituary verse." (His prime example is "Springfield Mountain.") However, these lament songs are not as allusive in their method as they are in Great Britain; they tell of the events of the death in funereal tones. On the other hand, there are compositions of the "last goodnight" type which do allude rather than describe. These are songs which are written from the point of view of a man about to die, in which he reflects on his deeds. These are often, like the song of Tom Dula ("Dooley"), a recording of a local crime, and the references to it the singer can assume will be understood by everyone because of the notoriety of the events. Consequently, Tom's allusions to Sheriff Grayson and Laura Foster are capable of being understood by the song's original audience.

There are some songs falling between this type and the ballad proper, compositions which D. K. Wilgus has called "blues ballads" (Wilgus: 1960, 52). These songs tell some of the events of a story but in a "loose, emotional narrative style, emphasizing situation and delineating character sharply, economically, often obliquely." The lack of detail of events may, in such songs, be a result of the fact that everyone in the audience knows the story, or that the song has an accompanying spoken narrative in which the events can be filled in. (This may have been the case in the gravitation toward lament in "Mary Hamilton.") The following song is the one used by Wilgus to illustrate his point.

Example 5-3. Arch and Gordon

From *Kentucky Folklore Record.* Used by permission.

1. When Archie went to Louisville,
   When Archie went to Louisville,
   When Archie went to Louisville,
   Not thinking that he would be killed.

2. When Gordon made his first shot,
   When Gordon made his first shot,
   When Gordon made his first shot,
   O'er behind the bed Arch did drop.

3. Arch says "Gordon, I didn't mean no harm."
   Arch says "Gordon, I didn't mean no harm."
   Arch says "Gordon, I didn't mean no harm."
   When Gordon shot Arch in the right arm.

4. Hush now Guv'nor, don't you cry.
   Hush now Guv'nor, don't you cry.
   Hush now Guv'nor, don't you cry.
   You know your son Arch has to die.

5. Now you see what a sporting life has done,
   Now you see what a sporting life has done,
   Now you see what a sporting life has done,
   It has killed Guv'nor Brown's only son.

These blues ballads (or "banjo songs") recount an event like a coronach, emphasizing the emotional situation (somewhat like a lyric), celebrating an event through allusion rather description.

Dialog Songs

Whereas ballads are organized around an event and discussed in terms of action, a large group of story-songs focuses on a confrontation between characters, and these we have called dialog songs because they rely so heavily on dialog to tell their story. In the ballad, movement occurs through a progression of causally related scenes; in the dialog song, movement is of a more limited sort, focussing on the back-and-forth alternation of speakers. Such songs are usually arguments or pleadings, and it is only in the unusual song like "Lord Randall" (12) or "Edward" (13) that a story is revealed in retrospect through the dialog. In these, as in many other dialog songs, the movement is conveyed through a question-answer alternation. The conventional nature of the dialog shows the tendency of compositions of this type toward formulaic expression. Besides the question-answer construction, dialog songs also use an offer-rejection pattern (as in such songs as "Paper of Pins," "Jennie Jenkins," and "The Pretty Fair Miss All in the Garden") or the trading of mutual vows. The question-answer form especially can attain a great deal of dramatic vitality when the consequences of the answer are large ones, such as in the various riddle songs such as "Captain Wedderburn's Courtship" (46) and "The Devil's Nine Questions" (1).

Example 5-4. The Devil's Nine Questions

1. If you can't answer my questions nine,
   Sing ninety-nine and ninety.
   Oh, you're not God's, you're one of mine,
   And you're not the weaver's bonny.

2. Oh, what is higher than the tree?
   Sing ninety-nine and ninety.
   And what is deeper than the sea?
   And you're not the weaver's bonny.

3. Oh, Heaven is higher than the tree,
   Sing ninety-nine and ninety.
   And Hell is deeper than the sea,
   And I am the weaver's bonny.

4. Oh, what is whiter than the milk?
   Sing ninety-nine and ninety.
   And what is softer than the silk?
   And you're not the weaver's bonny.

5. Oh, snow is whiter than the milk,
   Sing ninety-nine and ninety.
   And down is softer than the silk,
   And I am the weaver's bonny.

6. Oh, what is louder than the horn?
   Sing ninety-nine and ninety.
   And what is sharper than the thorn?
   And you're not the weaver's bonny.

7. Oh, thunder is louder than the horn,
   Sing ninety-nine and ninety.
   And hunger's sharper than the thorn,
   And I am the weaver's bonny.

8. Oh, what is heavier than the lead?
   Sing ninety-nine and ninety.
   And what is better than the bread?
   And you're not the weaver's bonny.

9. Oh, grief is heavier than the lead,
   Sing ninety-nine and ninety.
   God's blessing's better than the bread,
   And I am the weaver's bonny.

10. Now you have answered my questions nine,
    Sing ninety-nine and ninety.
    Oh, you are God's, you're none of mine,
    And you are the weaver's bonny.

Not all dialog songs begin immediately with the dialog, as here. Many have a conventional opening, such as the *chanson d'aventure* type in which a person is walking out one morning and overhears the conversation going on; sometimes he becomes one of the speakers himself, though not always (see "Across the Blue Mountains," Chapter 2.). Sometimes the scene is objectively described in an opening stanza, often with the same bucolic sentiment as in the "As I Walked Out" stanzas. (See "A Pretty Fair Miss All in the Garden," Chapter 6, Example 6–10.)

Lyric Songs

Lyric folksongs have provided the scholar with some of his greatest headaches because of their amorphous forms. In ballads and dialog songs, organization arises out of dramatic focus. Ballads cohere because they tell a story chronologically and in terms of beginning, climax, and ending. Dialog songs achieve coherence because they are unified in time and place and because they have speech alternation. These characteristics help to show the basic interest of the song: the revelation of a dramatic confrontation and its outcome. Lyrics are organized around a situation and its attendant mood, and consequently have nothing inherent in construction to cause the lyric song to cohere. Lyrics, as a result, tend to be assemblages of conventional stanzas which could go in any order without harming the feeling. In other words, where ballads and dialog songs call for a movement to dramatize, lyrics invoke only the force of mood. For this reason, it has been much harder to arrange, to classify lyrics; they are made of such random stuff that it is difficult to name them and establish relationships between them.

Yet some lyrics do have a coherence which arises not just out of dramatic predicament. Some, like the well-known "On Top of Old Smoky," have a progression of stanzas determined by causal or associational relationships. For instance, the first stanza ends with the idea of slow courtship, and the second extends that discussion; the second ends with the allusion to the thieflike qualities of the false-hearted lover and the third discusses why such a love is worse than a thief; and so on, throughout the whole song. To a lesser extent, some lyrics will have a series of stanzas related by a common theme or image, such as "Little Sparrow."

Example 5-5. Little Sparrow

1. Come all you maids and pretty fair maidens,
   Take warning how that you love young men;
   They're like the bright star in a summer's morning,
   First appear and then are gone.

2. It's once I had a own true lover,
   Indeed I really thought he was my own;
   Straight way he went and he courted another
   And left me here to weep and moan.

3. I wish I was a little sparrow,
   Or some of those birds that fly so high;
   It's after my true love I would follow,
   And when he talked I would be nigh.

4. When he was talking to some other,
   A-telling her of many those fine things;
   It's on his bosom I would flutter
   With my little tender wings.

5. But now I ain't no little sparrow,
   Nor none of those birds that fly so high;
   I'll go home full of grief and sorrow
   And sing and pass the time by.

Legendary Songs

Another group of songs often known as ballads are those which center not on events but on a legendary personage and tell a series of verse-long stories about his life. Many outlaw songs are constructed in this way, such as "Sam Bass" (E4) and "Jesse James" (E1). (The song, Chapter 6, Example 6–18, has some of this organization, but centers dramatically on Jesse's death.) A number of compositions ultimately of Negro origin, like "John Henry" and "Railroad Bill" are also of this type. And certain dance songs like "Old Joe Clark" concoct a number of stanzas about the legendary title character, like:

Old Joe Clark's a friend of mine,
Tell you the reason why.
Keeps good whiskey round his house,
Good old rock-and-rye.

Old Joe Clark had a house
Sixteen stories high.
And every story in that house
Was filled with chicken pie.

Old Joe Clark is dead and gone,
I hope he's doing well.
He fed me on so many beans
They made my belly swell.

To which the chorus contributes:

Round and round, Old Joe Clark
Round and round I say.
Round and round, Old Joe Clark
Goodbye Lucy Gray.

Other Song Types

Though the foregoing types are the dominant ones in the Anglo-American tradition, there are numerous other ways in which songs are organized. Most of them, like the legendary songs, establish a figure or subject which the song proceeds to examine. The subjects may be as various as courtship, politics, death, and the problems of living one place or another. Generally, a song will discuss a subject by embodying it in a symbol and talking about the symbolic object from many points of view. Thus courtship is discussed in terms of "Bachelor's Hall" (see Example 6–12) or the figure of an old man or a young man who has come courting. Similarly, death is portrayed in terms of an old churchyard or the heavenly city.

One interesting group of songs seems to arise just to provide a catalog of attributes or explanations of the parts of a whole or of the members of a class. For instance, songs like "The Red Herring," "The Sow Took the Measles," or "The Derby Ram" seem to exist just to describe the character and uses of the parts of the creatures announced in their titles. The ram, for instance, is dissected, and his gigantic stature described in suitably hyperbolic terms in relation to his feet (they covered an acre of land), his eyes (used for footballs because of their proper size), his wool (reached up to the sky), and so on. Similarly, there are a number of songs that are centered on the animal kingdom and its various members (like "Who Killed Cock Robin?"), a tree or bush (like "There's a Hole in the Bottom of the Sea"), or different kinds of birds.

Example 5-6. Bird Song

1. (O) Says the robin as he run
   "Wished I had a bottle of rum
   And a pretty little girl a' sittin' on my knee
   Lord, how happy I would be."

2. Says the little humming bird,
   "I would go if I wasn't so small.
   I am so small I can't get a wife
   'Mongst these flowers I'll spend my life."

3. Says the peckerwood to the crow
"What makes the white folks hate us so
Ever since ole Satan's been born
It's been our trade for to pull up corn."

4. Says the owl with his two shiny eyes
"This dark lonesome night
O the best of courting I've heard say
Court all night and sleep all day."

chapter 6

THE CONTENT
OF THE SONGS:
LOVE AND DEATH

Central to the study of a group is the discerning of the subjects which they choose to talk and sing about repeatedly. In the Anglo-American tradition there is a remarkable preponderance of songs on the themes of love and death. Perhaps because of the functional importance of these songs in the courtship proceedings in American rural communities, sex, the war of the sexes, and sentimental love provide the subject and conventions of a great majority of their songs. There is a very narrow range of dramatic situations, character-types, and relationships between characters in these pieces. Love is nearly always frustrating or frustrated; death is pictured as a common consequence of courtship. Dramatic interest most commonly arises from the separation of lovers, but seldom are they reunited as the dramatic resolution. This chapter will explore the patterns of dramatic situations of Anglo-American love songs and the conventional characters and relationships which grow from these situations.

Once More, The Child Ballads

The limited range of dramatic convention is most easily seen in those ballads in the Child collection which have persisted in North American tradition. Of the 305 ballads canonized by Child, only 115–120 have been collected in North America, in spite of the active search for these songs (Coffin: 1963; Abrahams: 1966). More important, only some 36 are commonly found in the repertoires of traditional singers on this side of the Atlantic.*

* These are: (1) "Riddles Wisely Expounded"; (2) "The Elfin Knight" (commonly called "The Cambric Shirt"); (3) "The False Knight Upon the Road"; (4) "Lady

The scholar M. J. C. Hodgart divides the Child ballads in the following manner:

1. Ballads belonging to the common stock of international folksong:
   (a) Ballads of magic
   (b) Romantic and tragic ballads

2. Ballads from the repertoire of late medieval minstrelsy

3. Ballads of yeoman minstrelsy

4. Historical ballads:
   (a) Fully historical, dealing with real national events
   (b) Semi–historical, dealing more vaguely with minor and local events

5. Comic songs

(Hodgart: 1950, 14; Wilgus: 1959, 264)

Of these, only 1(b) and 5 occur with any regularity in the New World. Lost are the ballads of border conflict, the medieval battle songs (such as "Chevy Chase") and other historical pieces, the Robin Hood songs, and many others.

A great majority of these American Child ballads fit clearly into two simple binary structural patterns, which we will call the *morality* and the *romance modes*. In both there is a simple dramatic movement from an initial conflict to its resolution without much intermediate detail or dramatic complication. In the morality pattern, action begins because of a *violation* of law, taboo, or common sense; it is ended by the imposition of an appropriate punishment. In the romance mode, action arises from a feeling of need or lack (usually a separation of the lovers) and resolves in the elimination of that lack.

Isabel and the Elf Knight"; (7) "Earl Brand"; (10) "The Twa Sisters"; (12) "Lord Randall"; (13) "Edward"; (18) "Sir Lionel" (usually called "Bangum and the Boar"); (20) "The Cruel Mother"; (26) "The Three Ravens"; (49) "The Twa Brothers"; (53) "Young Beichan" (usually "Lord Bateman"); (54) "The Cherry Tree Carol"; (68) "Young Hunting" (commonly "Love Henry"); (73) "Lord Thomas and Fair Annet" (Eleanor); (74) "Fair Margaret and Sweet William"; (75) "Lord Lovel"; (79) "The Wife of Usher's Well" (usually "The Lady Gay"); (81) "Little Musgrave and Lady Barnard" (more commonly "Little Mattie Groves"); (84) "Bonny Barbara Allen"; (85) "Lady Alice" (usually "George" or "Giles Collins"); (93) "Lamkin"; (95) "The Maid Freed from the Gallows" (also called "The Hangman" or often "The Hangman's Tree"); (105) "The Bailiff's Daughter of Islington"; (155) "Sir Hugh or the Jew's Daughter"; (167) and (250) "Henry Martyn" and "Andrew Barton" (commonly regarded as a single ballad now); (200) "The Gypsy Laddie"; (209) "Geordie"; (243) "James Harris" ("The Daemon Lover"), (most commonly called "The House Carpenter"); (274) "Our Goodman" (usually "Three" or "Five Nights Drunk"); (277) "The Wife Wrapt in Wether's Skin"; (278) "The Farmer's Curst Wife"; (286) "The Sweet Trinity" ("The Golden Vanity"); (289) "The Mermaid"; and (293) "John of Hazelgreen."

Most of the American Child ballads which conform to the morality pattern are concerned with a murder and its consequences. For instance, "The Two Sisters" (10) has an ugly sister dispatch her more attractive sibling-rival and wind up at the stake when the crime is discovered. Similarly, "The Cruel Mother" (20) is concerned with the killing of new-born twins by their mother, "Lamkin" has a nurse doing a similar deed to her charges, "Sir Hugh or the Jew's Daughter" (155) involves the death of a child lured into the murderess's garden, while in "Lord Thomas and Fair Eleanor" (73) a "new bride" kills her rival and is killed by the bridegroom, who then commits suicide. In such songs, the description of the murders constitutes the emotional core; the punishment is secondary and consequently is often omitted.

In "Mattie Groves" (81) adultery is the violation, but the description of death punishment is pursued more graphically than any other element. "The House Carpenter" (243) also involves an adulterous relationship which is punished by death, in this case a prolonged drowning scene, and "The Gypsy Laddie" (200) again involves marital infidelity. In many of these songs, permanent separation from abandoned children is regarded as a punishment, though not necessarily a final one, and in "The Lady Gay" (79), such a separation is regarded by the neglected mother as a punishment, though the mother's only clear violation is mourning too long and vociferously for her dead babes.

"Geordie" (209), "Sir Andrew Barton" (167 and 250), and "The Wife Wrapt in Wether's Skin" (277) also conform to the morality pattern, but differ in their particulars. Geordie is killed for stealing; piracy is Barton's violation; in "The Wife. . . .," a version of "The Taming of the Shrew," a newlywed wife is beaten for insubordination.

The Child ballads which fit into the romantic pattern are equally limited in their dramatic vocabulary. Most of the songs in this group begin with a separation of lovers and end in reunification of some sort. Superficially, this sounds like the typical pattern of comedy or medieval romance, but how very different the particulars of the ballad world from that of romance or comedy. These later types characteristically have males who initiate the action and who carry it through to its dramatic conclusion. Quite the opposite happens in these ballads. Here the male-heroes are usually docile, in fact, immobilized (Lomax: 1960, xxi). "Lord Bateman" (53) is firmly ensconced in jail during the initial period of his romance, and when he runs away from jail he manages to forget his lover-accomplice; Jemmy Grove (in "Barbara Allen" [84] is safely in bed with psychosomatic complaints; and "John of Hazelgreen" back home, out of the picture completely, lets his father do his courting for him. When heroes do act, it is usually to effect the separation from the loved one: Lord Lovel (75) simply rides away "strange countries for to see"; George Collins (in "Lady Alice" [85]) is, without explanation, "riding on a cold winter's night" when he is taken sick; both Lord Thomas (73) and Sweet William (74) marry someone other than their real loves. Only Earl Brand (7) and the young cabin boy in "The Golden Vanity" (286) go out to fight for their loves and both are killed for their troubles.

In only four of these romantic ballads is wooing successful. In both "Lord Bateman" and "The Bailiff's Daughter of Islington" (105) it is the young lady who actively overcomes the obstacles in the way of marriage. John of Hazelgreen lets his father do the wooing and winning for him.

Example 6-1. John of Hazelgreen

1. An old knight rode one summer's day,
   Down by the greenwood side;
   And there he spied a fair young maid,
   And all alone she cried.

2. As he drew nearer unto her,
   To learn what it could mean,
   All her lamentation was
   For John of Hazelgreen.

3. "You're welcome home, my fair young one,
   You're welcome home with me,
   And you may wed my oldest son,
   A bold young man is he."

4. "I would not wed your oldest son,
   If he were lord or king,
   For I never intend to be the bride of none,
   Save John of Hazelgreen."

5. "Oh, he is tall, his shoulders broad,
   He's the fairest of the king,
   His hair hangs down in links of gold,
   My John of Hazelgreen."

6. He took her up before him then,
   And they rode near the town,
   Bold John of Hazelgreen sprang out,
   To lift his lady down.

7. Three times he kissed her ruby lips,
   Three times he kissed her chin,
   He took her by her fair white hand,
   To lead his lady in.

8. The tears were dry, the sorrow gone,
   But her surprise was seen,
   To learn the old knight's oldest son
   Was John of Hazelgreen.

9. "If I should ever thee forsake,
   May heaven forsake me,
   And cast me in the brimstone lake
   Forever and eternity."

Only in the fourth, "The Maid Freed from the Gallows" (95) (see p. 41), does the male lover actively come in to free his maid, though in well over half the American variants there is either a reversal of sexes, and the saver is the girl, or there is no indication of the sex of either the condemned or the sweetheart. In this regard, Coffin notes that one text carries this a step further and has the son rescued by the mother "because mother love is stronger than 'sweetheart love'" (Coffin: 1963, 91).

This role-reversal is one typical development of the romantic pattern in American variants of Child ballads. Perhaps even more representative is a transformation of the pattern from life into death terms. In these renderings, there is the usual separation of lovers, but they are reunited not in the marriage bed but in the shared grave. Lord Thomas and Fair Eleanor (73) do not find happiness and fulfillment in their love until they are both dead, and even then, the "other girl" joins them in the grave. Similarly, Lord Lovel and Lady Nancy Bell, Fair Margaret and Sweet William, Barbara Allen and Jemmy Grove, and George Collins and Lady Alice find final union in the grave. The symbol of this matchmaking, the lover's knot of rose and briar, is found in connection with all of these songs.

This romance pattern shares some of the repeated actions of the morality ballad, emphasizing once more the limited dramatic vocabulary of these songs. If death is the reward of love, the whole business of love seems to be something to be condemned. In the morality ballads, our disapproval at the original dramatic conflict is immediate and obvious. In the death-romance, the original love situation seems to be one which we approve; it is only when we see the outcome of the story that we realize that such love is not so admirable.

In both the morality and romance ballads a picture of life is presented in which death is the resolution of most conflicts. Any "identifying" action of a potential hero or heroine (especially in association with love or sex) seems doomed. This is explainable in part by the pattern of relationships between figures of authority and those seeking to assert themselves. The situation, then expressed in family terms, is almost classically Freudian in its presentation of the constellation of the family; mothers oppose the love alliances of sons with other women, and fathers frustrate the romantic aspirations of daughters (Friedman: 1958, xxi). These authority roles are often assumed by characters who are simply older, but in such cases, the defeat of the young (and of the erotic motive) can be more explicit, bloody, and final.

In many of the ballads, especially those in the morality mode, an older woman initiates an emasculating series of events. "Lamkin," "Sir Hugh" and "The Cruel Mother" are all stories in which children are cruelly butchered with knives. Equally emasculating is the murderess of "Love Henry" (68).

Example 6-2. Love Henry

1. Lady Marg'ret was a-goin' to her bed one night,
   She heard the sound of a Jericho (?) horn,
   And which it made her sad and glad
   To think it was her brother, brother John,
   But who should it be but her true love Henathree
   Come in from his wild hunting.

2. Oh light, oh light Love Hen-ri-ee
   And stay all night with me.
   For you was a-playing of a Jericho fair
   The best that I can give thee.
   For you was a-playing of a Jericho fair
   The best that I can give thee.

3. I will not light nor I won't not light
   To stay all night with thee,
   For there's some pretty girls in merry Greenleaf
   That I love more better 'an thee.
   For there's some pretty girls in merry Greenleaf
   That I love more better 'an thee.

4. He went to the bed to little Marg'ret
   And give her a farewell kiss.
   And with a penknife in her right hand
   She wounded him full death.
   And with a penknife in her right hand
   She wounded him full death.

5. Woe be, woe be, Lady Marg'ret, woe be,
   Woe be, woe be, on to you,
   Oh don't you see my own heart's blood
   Come twinkling down by me?
   Oh don't you see my own heart's blood
   Come twinkling down by me?

6. She called in her old missy servant
   "Keep a secret, keep a secret on me,
   And those fine robes on my body
   It's you shall a-bein' of them.
   And those fine robes on my body
   It's you shall a-bein' of them."

7. One taken him by his long yellow hair,
   And the other by his feet,
   And throwed him into the well water
   Which was both cold and deep.
   And throwed him into the well water
   Which was both cold and deep.

8. "Lie there, lie there, Love Hen-ri-ee
   Till the flesh rots offa your bones,
   And them pretty girls in merry Greenleaf
   A-thinking of your comin' home.
   And them pretty girls in merry Greenleaf
   A-thinking of your comin' home."

9. There is a parrot on the limb,
   A portion of the willow tree,
   Says, "There never was a pretty girl in merry Greenleaf
   That he ever loved half well as thee.
   There never was a pretty girl in merry Greenleaf
   That he ever loved half well as thee."

10. "Come down, come down, my pretty parrot,
    And sit upon my knee,
    For your cage door can be lined with gold
    Can stay in the willow tree.
    For your cage door can be lined with gold
    Can stay in the willow tree."

11. "I won't come down nor I shan't come down
And sit upon your knee,
For you have murdered your own true love
And sooner you will kill me.
For you have murdered your own true love
And sooner you will kill me."

12. "If I had my iron(t) in my hand
And strung it out full death,
Oh I'd pierce a ball through your little tiny heart
'at you couldn't sing no more.
Oh I'd pierce a ball through your little tiny heart
'at you couldn't sing no more."

13. "If you had your iron(t) in your hand
And strung it out full death,
Oh I'd take a flight and I'd fly, fly away
And tune my voice to sing.
Oh I'd take a flight and I'd fly, fly away
And tune my voice for to sing."

This termagant character-type is rendered in comic terms in the heroine of "The Devil and the Farmer's Wife" (278), who is capable of outdoing any man, including the Devil.

Example 6-3. The Devil and the Farmer's Wife

1. The old Devil came to our field,
    Said, "One of the family I'm goin' to steal,"
    Hi-iy-iy-ay.
    The old Devil came to our field,
    Said, "One of the family I'm goin' to steal."
    Twice fi-dum, fi-diddle, fi-day.

2. "You can't have my oldest son,
    Too much hard work gotta be done."
    Hi-iy-iy-ay.
    "You can't have my oldest son,
    Too much hard work gotta be done."
    Twice fi-dum, fi-diddle, fi-day.

3. "You can have my scoldin' wife,
    Devil couldn't keep her for to save his life."
    Hi-iy-iy-ay.
    "You can have my scoldin' wife,
    Devil couldn't keep her for to save his life."
    Twice fi-dum, fi-diddle, fi-day.

4. The old Devil took her to Hell's Gate;
    Bet your life he made her walk straight.
    Hi-iy-iy-ay.
    The old Devil took her to Hell's Gate;
    Bet your life he made her walk straight.
    Twice fi-dum, fi-diddle, fi-day.

5. Three little devils came peekin' o'er the wall;
    Up with her foot she kicked them all.
    Hi-iy-iy-ay.
    Three little devils came peekin' o'er the wall;
    Up with her foot she kicked them all.
    Twice fi-dum, fi-diddle, fi-day.

6. Three little devils came rattlin' a chain;
    Up with her foot she kicked them again.
    Hi-iy-iy-ay.
    Three little devils came rattlin' a chain;
    Up with her foot she kicked them again.
    Twice fi-dum, fi-diddle, fi-day.

7. The old Devil put her on his back;
    Like a blame fool come packin' her back.
    Hi-iy-iy-ay.
    The old Devil put her on his back.
    Like a blame fool come packin' her back.
    Twice fi-dum, fi-diddle, fi-day.

8. When she got home they were all in bed;
    Up with a hammer she hit them on the head.
    Hi-iy-iy-ay.

When she got home they were all in bed;
Up with a hammer she hit them on the head.
Twice fi-dum, fi-diddle, fi-day.

9. The old man went whistlin' over the hill;
"If the Devil can't keep her, I don't know who will."
Hi-iy-iy-ay.
The old man went whistlin' over the hill;
"If the Devil can't keep her, I don't know who will."
Twice fi-dum, fi-diddle, fi-day.

Equally sadistic and considerably more mysterious are the authoritative father-figure characters. Such ogres are found in many Child ballads, but in few of them do we learn much about their motivations. They are generally faceless representatives of power, often functioning more offstage than on, but making their influence felt throughout any song in which they appear. For instance, Earl Brand is defeated by his love's father (and seven brothers); but he fares much better than most heroes, for he takes his adversaries with him to his grave. Less fortunate are: Geordie, put to death by the judge, over the pleas of his wife; Mattie Groves, killed by his lord in the midst of a love feast; and the little cabin boy of "The Golden Vanity" (286) drowned by his captain because he presumed to the hand of his daughter. Only the heroes of "Lord Bateman," "The Maid Freed from the Gallows," and "The Bailiff's Daughter of Islington" manage to overcome this dreaded figure, and then usually not through male challenge but through female deception.

Example 6-4. Lord Bateman

1. Lord Bateman was a noble lord
And held himself in high degree.
He could not rest nor be contented
'Til he had voyaged across the sea.

2. Now he sailed East and he sailed westward
Until he reached that Turkish shore.
There he was taken and put in prison
To live in hopes of freedom no more.

3. This Turk he had an only daughter,
The fairest maiden you ever did see.
She stole the keys to her father's prison
And said, "Lord Bateman, I'll set you free."

4. "Have you got houses, have you lands, sir,
And are you of some high degree?
What would you give to the Turkish lady
If out of prison she'd set you free?"

5. "Yes, I have houses, I have lands, love,
Half of Northumberland belongs to me.
I'd give it all to the Turkish lady
If out of prison she'd set me free."

6. Then she took him to her father's cellar
And gave him a glass of the choicest wine,
Saying, "Every moment seems an hour.
I wish Lord Bateman that you were mine."

7. "Let's make a vow, let's make a promise.
Let's make a vow, let's make it stand."
He vowed he'd marry no other woman;
She vowed she'd marry no other man.

8. Then she took him to her father's harbor,
And gave to him a ship of fame.
Saying, "Farewell to you, my own Lord Bateman,
I fear I'll never see you again."

9. For seven long years she kept her vow, sir,
For seven long years seemed twenty-three.
Then she gathered all her gay, fine clothing,
And said, "Lord Bateman I'll go see."

10. Then she sailed East and she sailed westward,
Until she reached that English shore.
And when she reached Lord Bateman's castle
She lighted down before the door.

11. "Is this Lord Bateman's gay, fine castle,
And is his lordship here within?"
"Oh yes, oh yes," cried the gay young porter,
"He's just now taken his young bride in."

12. "Bid him remember a slice of cake, sir,
Bid him remember a glass of wine,
Bid him remember the Turkish lady
Who did release him when confined."

13. Off then went that proud young porter,
     Fast up the flight of stairs went he.
     And when he come to Lord Bateman's chamber
     He then went down on bended knee.

14. "What news, what news, my proud young porter?
     What news, what news have you brought to me?"
     "Oh, there's the fairest of all young ladies
     That my two eyes, sir, ever did see."

15. "She has got rings on every finger.
     And on one finger she has three,
     With enough gay gold about her middle
     As would buy Northumberland of thee."

16. Lord Bateman rose from where he was sitting,
     His face it was as white as snow.
     Saying, "If she is the Turkish lady
     With her, my love, I bound for to go."

17. Up then spoke the young bride's mother,
     "She's none the better nor worse for thee.
     You brought her here on a horse and saddle,
     You may return in chariots three."

18. "You brought her here on a horse and saddle,
     You may return in chariots three.
     And I will marry the Turkish lady
     Who crossed the roaring seas for me."

"The Golden Vanity" (see p. 79) is perhaps the most complete statement in the ballad literature of the defeated hero, death-romance pattern. Here, it will be recalled, the action is precipitated by the confrontation with an English pirate ship (or more frequently Turkish or Spanish). The valiant cabin boy offers to sink the enemy, and the captain offers him his daughter if the boy succeeds. He swims to the other ship and bores holes in the hull, causing it to sink. As he swims back, the captain from his vantage of power capriciously rescinds his offer, and the cabin boy, who has just exhibited great valor toward the enemy, suddenly acquiesces to his captain's command and drowns.

Though the cabin boy does not return home to any comforting mother to die (the sea and "His messmates" perform her function in those versions where he is wrapped in a sheet), in many of the ballads in which the lovers are defeated, one or another of them does return. One of the commonplace stanzas found in a number of Child ballads found in North America states this explicitly:

> Mother, mother, make my bed,
> Make it long and narrow.
> ————— died for me today,
> I'll die for him (her) tomorrow.

The most extensive statement of this relationship between the child wounded in love and the comforting mother is in "Lord Randall" (12); each stanza is emotionally charged by an implicit comparison of the murderous sweetheart and the consoling mother. Each stanza begins with a question couched in concerned terms by the mother and a self-pitying answer by the son. This mother-son emotional tie is emphasized in the burdens: "Lord Randall, my son," and "My sweet little one," murmured by the mother, and Lord Randall's response, "Mother, make my bed soon,/For I'm sick at my heart and I want to lie down."

The composite picture of the character relationships and the outcome of the love-adventures is strongly colored by puritanical attitudes which are both restrictive and authoritative. In every regard older characters stifle initiative in the young, either through overt action or through smothering. Efforts at independent action on the part of the young are, more often than not, half-hearted. The young, especially the young men, in the face of the power struggle of the generations acquiesce in docility, asking for affections that are based more on pity than attraction. That most common of American Child ballads, "Barbara Allen" dramatically exhibits this masochistic pose. Jemmy, dying of love for Barbara, forces *her* to make the trek to *his* house where he receives her from his bed. His strategy is clear; she is to feel sorry for him and thus give him comfort. The ploy doesn't work; comfort comes only in the death-union.

Erotic love is explicitly rejected in these ballads. Sex leads not to love, but to sin, adultery, and death. Whenever a normal love encounter between a boy and girl is suggested, some motive is injected into the story to defeat it: a fateful event; parental advice; emasculation in the hands of an older person; or stubbornness or flightiness on the part of one of the prospective pair.

1. It was a day and a high old day
   The very best day in the year,
   When Little Matha Grove went up to church
   Some holy words for to hear,
   Some holy words for to hear.

2. O some came there in velvet green
   And others came there in pearl,
   But among them was Lord Arnold's wife
   The fairest of them all,
   The fairest of them all.

Example 6-5. Matha Grove

From Helen Creighton and Dareen H. Senior, *Traditional Songs from Nova Scotia* (Toronto: The Ryerson Press, 1950).

3. O Little Matha Grove being standing by
   On him she cast an eye,
   She says, "This very night Little Matha Grove
   In bed with me you'll lie,
   In bed with me you'll lie."

4. "If you are whom I take you to be
   I would not for my life,
   By the look of the ring on your finger
   You are Lord Arnold's wife,
   You are Lord Arnold's wife."

5. "If I am now Lord Arnold's wife
   Whom you take me for to be,
   Lord Arnold's gone to St. James's Castle
   King Henery for to see,
   King Henery for to see."

6. O the little foot page being standing by
   And hearing what was said,
   "I'll hie away to St. James's
   Lord Arnold for to tell,
   Lord Arnold for to tell."

7. He run till he came to the riverside,
   He knelt to his breast and he swum,
   He swam till he came to the other side
   And he took to his heels and he run,
   And he took to his heels and he run.

8. He run till he came to St. James's Castle,
    He knocked at the ring,
    There was no one as ready to arise
    As Lord Arnold and let him in,
    As Lord Arnold and let him in.

9. "What news? What news, my little foot page,
    What news do you bring unto me?"
    "This very night Little Matha Grove
    Is to lie with your wedded lady,
    Is to lie with your wedded lady."

10. "O if this be a lie, a lie,
    A lie you tell unto me,
    I will have a gallows to be rigged
    And hangèd you shall be,
    And hangèd you shall be."

11. "If this be a lie, a lie,
    A lie I tell unto thee,
    You'll need no gallows to be rigged
    For I'll hang all on a tree,
    For I'll hang all on a tree."

12. "But if this be the truth, the truth,
    The truth you tell unto me,
    I have one only daughter dear
    Your wedded wife she'll be,
    Your wedded wife she'll be."

13. O Lord Arnold called his merry men all
    And he placed them in a row,
    He caused not one word to be spoke
    Or yet for a horn to blow,
    Or yet for a horn to blow.

14. But there was one among them all
    Who loved Little Matha Grove full well,
    He put his horn unto his mouth
    And he blew it loud and shrill,
    And he blew it loud and shrill.

15. He put his horn unto his mouth
    As much as for to say,
    Who's ever in bed with another man's wife
    It's time to be jogging away,
    It's time to be jogging away.

16. Little Matha Grove he heard this horn
    And jumpèd out of bed,
    He says, "By the sound now of that horn
    It is Lord Arnold's horn,
    It is Lord Arnold's horn."

17. Come back, come back Little Matha Grove
    And keep me from the cold,
    It's only Lord Arnold's shepherd boy
    A-calling his sheep to the fold,
    A-calling his sheep to the fold."

18. 'Twas there they tossed and tumbled
    Till they fell fast asleep,
    They never knew no more until
    Lord Arnold stood at their feet,
    Lord Arnold stood at their feet.

19. "Get up, get up Little Matha Grove
    And put your garments on,
    I would not have it to be said
    I slew a naked man,
    I slew a naked man."

20. "If I have now then to get up
    And fight you for my life
    When you have two swords by your side
    And I have neither knife?
    And I have neither knife?"

21. "If I have two swords by my side
    They cost me deep in purse,
    I'll give to you the best of them
    And I will take the worse,
    And I will take the worse.

22. "Now I'll give you the first good stroke
    And I will take the other,
    Any fairer than that I would not do
    If it was to my own born brother,
    If it was to my own born brother."

23. O Little Matha Grove took the first good stroke
    And wounded Lord Arnold sore,
    Lord Arnold took the next good stroke,
    Little Matha could strike no more,
    Little Matha could strike no more.

24. He took his fair lady by the hand
    And placed her on his knee,
    Saying, "Which one do you love the best,
    Little Matha Grove or me?
    Little Matha Grove or me?"

25. "O fine do I like Little Matha Grove
    And fine do I like his chin,
    And better do I like his malavering tongue
    Than Lord Arnold and all his kin,
    Than Lord Arnold and all his kin."

26. He took his lady by the hand
    And laid her in the hall,
    And neither one of them spoke one word
    Till he split her head in twain,
    Till he split her head in twain.

27. Now loud loud sings the nightingale,
    Now loud loud sings the sparrow,
    Lord Arnold killed his fair lady
    And he'll be hung to-morrow,
    And he'll be hung to-morrow.

The anti-erotic element in "Our Goodman" is presented in farcical and masochistic rather than tragic and sadistic terms. The increasing evidence that he is being cuckolded, and his drunken acquiescence (except for the sarcastic asides condemning his wife's excuses) make it clear that the drunk is being emasculated by his wife and not objecting to it much.

Example 6-6. Our Goodman

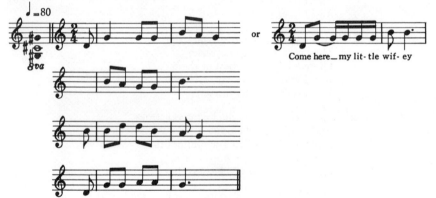

1. First night that I came home
   Was drunk as I could be.
   Found a horse in (the) stable
   Where my horse ought to be.

2. Come here my little wifey,
   Explain this thing to me.
   How come a horse in (the) stable
   Where my horse ought to be?

3. You blind fool, you crazy fool,
   Can't you never see;
   It's nothing but a milk cow,
   You drunk as you can be.

4. I've traveled this world over,
   Ten thousand miles or more.
   A saddle upon a milk cow's back
   I never saw before.

5. Second night that I came home
   Was drunk as I could be.
   I found a coat hanging on a rack
   Where my coat ought to be.

6. Come here my little wifey,
   Explain this thing to me.
   How came a coat hanging on a rack
   Where my coat ought to be.

7. You blind fool, you crazy fool,
   Can't you never see;
   It's nothing but a bed quilt,
   You drunk as you can be.

8. I've traveled this world over,
   Ten thousand miles or more.
   But pockets on a bed quilt
   I never saw before.

9. Third night that I came home,
   Was drunk as I could be.
   Found a hat a–hanging on a rack
   Where my hat ought to be.

10. Come here my little wifey,
    Explain this thing to me.
    How come a hat a–hanging on a rack
    Where my hat ought to be.

11. You blind fool, you crazy fool,
    Can't you never see;
    It's nothing but a milk churn,
    You drunk as you can be.

12. I've traveled this world over,
    Ten thousand miles or more.
    But a hat-band on a milk churn
    I never saw before.

13. Fourth night that I came home
    Was drunk as I could be.
    Found a head layin' on a pillow,
    Where my head ought to be.

14. Come here my little wifey,
    Explain this thing to me.
    How come a head layin' on a pillow
    Where my head ought to be?

15. You blind fool, you crazy fool,
    Can't you never see.
    It's nothing but a cabbage head,
    You drunk as you can be.

16. I've traveled this world over,
    Ten thousand miles or more.
    But a mustache on a cabbage head
    I never saw before.

We can tell from the behavior of the drunkard that he has willingly abdicated his husband's role in favor of that of the child. The drunkard is one of the standard clown-figures in our folklore, the character who seems to be a man but who through the limitations on his motor and mental activity imposed by alcohol becomes a child once again. This is emphasized not only by the drunkard's attitude toward an obvious challenge, but by his relationship with his wife. He asks questions of her like a foot-stamping boy, and her evasive answers indicate that indeed she regards him as little more than a child. We see by his reactions to her answers that he sees through her act, but we never see him doing anything about it. (In the ballad, "The Wife Wrapt in Wether's Skin," the husband acquits himself as a man by putting his new wife in her place, but such stories are unusual. See also the broadside "Will the Weaver," Laws Q9, and its neighbors Q5, Q6, and Q8 for other facetious tales.)

The dominant patterns observable in these North American Child ballads are continued and embroidered upon in other song types. For instance, in one large group of later songs the faceless father's successful opposition to the lovers is dwelt upon at great length, while another group emphasizes the indissoluble ties of son and mother. These will be discussed according to theme.

Father's Opposition to Lovers

There is a large group of songs in Anglo-American tradition, most of them ultimately of broadside origin, in which lovers are separated because the girl's father or some other male in the family objects to the union. The basis of the objection generally given is the inequality of status. In most cases, the objectors manage to keep the lovers apart. In the 39 songs which Laws includes under the heading "Ballads of Family Opposition to Lovers" in his *American Balladry from British Broadsides* (Laws [1957]: 179–200), only fourteen have a successful courtship. Of these, three involve a reversal of roles in which the lady takes the initiative, eight are of very limited currency, and only three are commonly found in which the male-hero seizes his love and manages to carry her away. These are "Locks and Bolts" (M13), "The New River Shore" (M26), and "The Bold Soldier" (M27), a replay of the "Earl Brand" story in which the hero manages to beat the father and brothers and survive.

Example 6-7. Rainbow Willow

1. Last night I dreamed of my true love
   All in my arms I had her;
   When I awoke there was no such there
   I was forced to lie without her.

2. Her yeller hair like links of gold
   Were dangling over my pillow;
   She is the darling of my heart,
   She is the rainbow willow.

3. I went into her uncle's house
   Inquiring for my sweet one.
   They answered me, the're no such there
   She's in another room, sir.

4. But locks and bars to flender (splinters?) fly,
   And quickly I got to her.
   I took her and I followed on
   And after us did follow.

5. Her uncle and another man
   All after us did follow.
   They swore before I returned home
   All in my blood they'd waller.

6. There was blood spilled on ever' side
   I drew my love from amongst them;
   And if you want to gain your love,
   Just fight and overcome them.

Much more common are the pieces in which the hero is somehow eliminated unheroically; generally he is not even allowed the heroism of the cabin boy of "The Golden Vanity." Sometimes he is waylaid and murdered, as in "The Bramble Briar" (M32). More commonly he is simply sent away through the maneuverings of her parents, often by being "pressed to sea" or taken away for the army, after she has been confined to her room. Such detail reflects realistic elements of British life of the eighteenth and nineteenth centuries, employing them as a rationale for the separation of the lovers. These conditions did not prevail so strongly in the more democratic American society of these times, and thus few native American ballads were penned using this method of separation; but the idea must have appealed to American singers, for many of these songs of British origin did find their way into the Anglo-American repertoire.

Example 6-8. Charming Beauty Bright

1. Once I courted a fair and beauty bright,
    I courted her by day and I courted her by night.
    I courted her for love and love I did intend.
    I'm sure she never had any right to complain.

2. When her cruel old parents came this to know,
    That I was a-courting his daughter also,
    He locked her up so high and he treated her so 'vere, (severe)
    I never, never more got the sight of my dear.

3. Then to the war I thought it I would go,
    To see what I would forget my love or no,
    Oh when I did get there the army shined so bright
    It put me in fresh remembrance of my own heart's delight.

4. Sevent long years I served as a king,
    Oh sevent long years I 'turned home again,
    With my heart full of war and my eyes full of tears,
    But I never, never more got the sight of my dear.

5. Then her cruel old parents I thought it I would go,
    To see what I could see my love or no,
    Her mother saw me coming, she wringed her hands and cried,
    "My daughter loved you dearly and for your sake she died."

6. Then I was struck like one had been slain,
    The tears from my eyes like showers of rain,
    This crying lordy mercy this pain I cannot bear,
    My true love is gone and I wish that I was there.

The force of this separation pattern can be seen clearly operating in the case of the William Reilly songs. These are three interrelated ballads of Irish broadside origin which discuss William Reilly's courtship and marriage with his "Colleen Bawn." They are found printed together in American songbooks, notably the very popular *Forget-Me-Not Songster*. The first ballad deals with the early days of the courtship, his asking for the hand of his love, the refusal by the parents, the elopement of the couple, their capture, and Willie's imprisonment (M9). The second begins with the elopement and capture and ends with his being sentenced to transportation to the colonies (M10). The third begins with the sentencing and goes on to describe his petition to the Lord Lieutenant, his release, and his rescue of the girl before she is sent to Bedlam, and it ends with their marriage. Characteristically, the first two ballads are widely collected. The third has not been observed at all in oral tradition (Laws: 1957, 185).

The theme of parental separation of lovers does indeed occur in native American song, but the parting most often arises because of the pride of the man at being scorned by the girl's parents, not because of anything the parents do. This is more common in lyric and dialog songs, where the following stanza or one of its many variations serves as its clearest statement.

> Your parents don't like me, they say I'm too poor,
> They say I'm not worthy to be seen at your door;
> I work for my living, my money's my own,
> And if they don't like me, they can leave me alone.

The major exception to the pattern of thwarted love has already been observed in the Child ballads: the woman seizing the initiative, and marriage occurring through her devices. The technique used in the broadside ballad "The Bailiff's Daughter of Islington" (inexplicably included by Child), in which the girl disguises herself as a man, is found in many other broadside ballads which attained traditional status in America. The most common disguise in these songs is to dress as a soldier and to fight alongside the exiled lover, or as in "Jack Monroe" (N7; see p. 82) to assume this disguise to be free to search for him. The conventional statement of this masking is the challenge given to the girl-dressed-as-boy:

> Your waist is too slender, your fingers are too small;
> Your cheeks too red and rosy to face the cannon ball.

The parental opposition in these songs becomes secondary dramatically, even fades away; the reversal of roles becomes the complete *raison d'être* for the song. The final direction of this movement occurs in a dialog song like "The Girl Volunteer" (O33), in which the girl simply threatens to dress like a soldier so that she can remain with her lover.

Separation of Lovers by Their Own Devices

As in certain Child ballads, the separation of lovers is either unmotivated or brought about by the perversity of one of the pair. This particularization of the separation pattern is widely observable in the Anglo-American repertoire in both comic and melodramatic guise. In serious statements of the theme, the songs often fall into the morality pattern; love is a violation which leads to further violations and punishments. A common rationale for such separation is that the man grows tired of the girl, especially if she is pregnant. There are a large number of lyric songs which are expressed from the bereft girl's point of view, describing her condition and warning others not to fall into the same trap (See "Little Sparrow," p. 88).

In one group of ballads the girl is killed either because she has become pregnant or been promised marriage, or both. This story is embodied in a number of imported British broadsides, such as the ubiquitous "The

Oxford Girl" (P35), found attached to many locales in the United States, such as Knoxville, Waco, and so on.

Example 6-9. Knoxville Girl

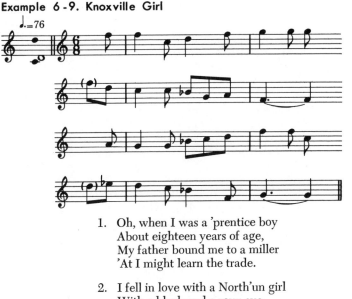

1. Oh, when I was a 'prentice boy
   About eighteen years of age,
   My father bound me to a miller
   'At I might learn the trade.

2. I fell in love with a North'un girl
   With a black and a rovy eye,
   I told her that I'd marry her
   If she would not deny.

3. My father he persuaded me
   To take her as my wife,
   The devil he persuaded me
   To take away her life.

4. I went on to her sister's house
   'Bout eight o'clock that night,
   And little did her sister think
   'At I had any spite.

5. I asked her wouldn't she take a walk
   Down through the flowers so gay,
   That we might have some pridest (private) talk
   And set the wedding day.

6. We hadn't walked so vary fur
   A-looking 'round and 'round,
   It's I drew out a stiffen-stick
   I knocked her to the ground.

7. She fell upon her bending knees,
   "Oh, mercy," did she cry,
   Says, "Eddie dear, don't murder me
   For I'm not fit to die."

8. I took her by her lily-white hand,
   I slung her 'round and 'round,
   I took her to the riverside
   I plunged her in to drown.

9. I went on to my miller's house
   'Bout ten o'clock in the night,
   And little did this miller think
   That I had been about.

10. He looked at me so very close
    Saying, "Sir, what bloodied your clothes?"
    The very reply I made to him
    By bleeding at the nose.

This story has been taken up by American song writers so often that it is, in a very real sense, *the* American Tragedy. The American songs of "Fair Florella" (F1A) and "Pearl Bryan" (F1B) (see pp. 30) are of this type; so are "Omie Wise" (F4), "Rose Connley" (F6), "The Banks of the Ohio" (F5), and most others in the large "Murder Ballads" section of G. Malcolm Laws's *Native American Balladry*.

The perfidy of men is matched in these songs by the fickleness of women, most often expressed in the "girl I left behind me" type of composition. In these, a man is forced through circumstances (usually economic) to leave home and sweetheart. His friend vows eternal fidelity, but he soon hears by letter that she has married someone else. The theme is usually treated gravely in song, but ones like "Joe Bowers" present it in a more comic light. The "other man" is richer, or just more immediately accessible, and sometimes, as in "Jack and Joe" turns out to be his best friend (see p. 67).

The dialog and lyric counterparts of the "girl I left behind me" type are the departure songs. At the port, or at the girl's front door, the lovers take their parting, needing to vow their undying love. One of the commonplace stanza groups which clusters about this dramatic situation is the "Who's gonna shoe" verse:

Who's gonna shoe your pretty little feet,
And who's gonna glove your hand?
Who's gonna kiss your red ruby lips;
Who's gonna be your man?

Poppa's gonna shoe my pretty little feet,
Momma's gonna glove my hand.
Sister will kiss my red ruby lips,
And I don't need no man.

(For an example of a lyric which uses these stanzas, see pp. 52–53). Of course, these sentimental songs end with a note of hope, not the despair and cynicism of the ballads of forsaken love.

This feeling of trust and hope is carried over to one important type of dialog song; that which tells the story of the "broken token." A man returns after a long separation and wants to test the fidelity of his love. He approaches her as a stranger and asks her to marry him, and she refuses. He then reveals himself, often by showing half of the ring they had used to swear eternal love. She then consents to go away with him. No fewer than fifteen traditional songs devoted to this story are widely found in North America, most of them in the form of an "As I walked out" song, in which the narrating observer becomes one of the principals. The emphasis in all of them is not on the pleasures of reunion, but on the value of chastity and fidelity. Common songs on this theme are "The Mantle So Green" (N38), "John Reilly" (N37), and "A Pretty Fair Miss All in a Garden" (N42).

Example 6-10. A Pretty Fair Miss All in a Garden

1. A pretty fair miss all in the garden,
   A brave young soldier came passing by.
   He stepped up and thus he 'dressed her
   Says, "Pretty fair miss, will you marry me?"

2. "It's no kind sir, a man of honor,
   A man of honor 'at you may be."
   "It's how can you 'fuse this single soldier
   Has late-lie 'turned from across the sea?"

3. "I have a true love on the ocean,
   Been gone to sea it's seven long years
   And if he stays it's seven years longer,
   No man on earth can marry me."

4. "So supposin' your true love is drowned?
   So supposin' he's in some battle slain?
   So suppose he's took some fair girl and married,
   Why you'll never see his face again."

5. "It's if he's drowned, I hope he's happy,
   And if he's in some battle slain,
   And if he's took some fair girl and married
   I'll love the girl that married him."

6. He run his hand all in his pocket,
   His fingers being slim and small,
   He pulled out the ring that she had give him
   And down before him she did fall.

7. He picked her up all in his arms,
   The kisses that he gave her was one, two, three.
   "Oh don't you remember the promise that I made you,
   No girl on earth could'a married me."

The counterpart of these dialog songs emphasizing fidelity is the courting song in which a man and a woman make a futile attempt to bridge
the gap of the sexes and arrive at a marriage settlement. The tone of
these songs is always comic, emphasizing the incompatibility of male and
female. Men are pictured as incompetent and pesky courters, while
women are presented as avaricious or flighty, or simply impossible to
please.

Example 6-11. The Drunkard's Courtship

1. Sir, I see you coming again.
   Pray tell me what it's for?
   'Cause when we parted on yonders hill
   I told you to come no more, no more,
   I told you to come no more.

2. Miss, I have a very fine horse,
   He paces against the tide.
   And he shall be at your command
   Whenever you wish to ride, to ride,
   Whenever you wish to ride.

3. Sir, I know you've a very fine horse
   Standing on yonders turn.
   His master drinks and does get drunk
   And I'm sure the horse'll learn, 'll learn,
   And I'm sure the horse'll learn.

4. Miss, I have a very fine farm,
   It's sixty acres wide.
   And that shall be at your command
   If you will be my bride, my bride,
   If you will be my bride.

5. It's sir, I know your very fine house,
   And also a very fine yard.
   Who shall stay with me at night
   When you a-playing at cards, at cards,
   When you a-playing at cards?

6. Miss, that's something I never did,
   I never thought was right.
   If you'll consent to be my bride
   I won't stay out nary a night, a night,
   I won't stay out nary a night.

7. Sir, I know just what that's for,
   It's just to take me in.
   If I consent to be your bride
   You'll drink and gamble again, again,
   You'll drink and gamble again.

8. Miss, I have a very fine mule,
   He pulls my buggy well.
   I'll drink my drugs and throw my cards,
   And you can go to hell, to hell,
   And you can go to hell.

Closely allied to these banter songs are the other courting songs which castigate one or another of the sexes by direct comment and from a unitary point of view (songs like the male "I Wish I Was Single Again" and the female "I Wish I Was a Single Girl Again"). In these songs, old men are chastised for their lack of virility, young men for keeping the girls up all night, young women for being skittery, and old women for being jealous, and wanton. Typical of this type is "Bachelor's Hall."

Example 6-12. Bachelor's Hall

1. When young men goes courtin' they'll dress up so fine.
   They'll talk to the young girls and all of them mind.
   They'll hug them, they'll kiss them, likewise they will lie;
   They'll keep the girls up till they're ready to die.

2. So early next morning they will rise;
   They'll brush off the straws and wipe out their eyes.
   And onto their horses and home they will ride,
   Like gentlemen proper, all puffed up with pride.

3. Oh, when they get there they'll stagger and reel;
   It's "Damn all the women, how bad I do feel.
   I believe it's the best to court none at all,
   And to live by myself and keep bachelor's hall.

4. "A bachelor hall I believe would be best.
   Get drunk or get sober, lie down and take rest.
   No wife to control you, no children to bawl.
   I pity the man that gets married at all."

5. When young men get married their pleasures all gone
   Adieu to the young girls and trouble comes on,
   The wife to control them, the children to bawl,
   I pity the man that gets married at all.

American Songs of Death

There is a great deal of death in the American Child ballads, but, by comparison with later songs on the theme, very little dying. Death is seen as the fitting climax to wrongdoing or to attempts at courtship. Death is less inextricably connected with separation in later lovesongs, except in the latter-day moralities such as the murder ballads. Separation is simply made permanent by physical removal and by marriage to someone else. However, death continues to exert dramatic interest in later Anglo-American songs, especially in sentimental and religious compositions.

Not only is death dramatically important in sentimental songs—in many cases it provides the occasion for the song. Sentiment involves the elaboration of the most passionate and poignant moments of life, often to such an extreme that the word "sentimental" has accrued negative connotation. Given the strong tradition of songs emphasizing separation, it is not surprising that when the sentimental exerted its influence on American song it chose to elaborate parting. Consequently, we have numerous highly sentimental songs dwelling on the pain of lovers' partings, the suspense of reunion, and most prominently, the agony of the separation of loved-ones through death.

Among the most common songs encountered among traditional singers in North America are "The Little Rosewood Casket," "The Letter Edged in Black," and "The Baggage Coach Ahead." Each of these deals very sentimentally with the shock of the death of a loved one: a sweetheart, wife, or child. However, none of these describes the death of the loved one; just the effect on others of discovering their demise. There *are*, however, many sentimental songs which do describe such death-throes at great length. The two situations used repeatedly in such songs concern the deaths of young children and of people far away from home.

The death of small children has always been a subject of interest in English-language folksongs—witness the many Child ballads in which children are sadistically dispatched by mysterious adults, such as "Little Sir Hugh," "Lamkin," "The Cruel Mother," and so on. In the totally sentimental vein, one song, "The Babes in the Woods," has been widely popular for at least three centuries, and is still often encountered in tradition.

> 1. Oh, don't you remember a long time ago,
>   Two little children, their names I don't know,
>   Were walking alone one long summer day—
>   Got lost in the woods so I heard people say.
>
> 2. Now when it was night, so sad was their plight,
>   The moon was not shining, the stars gave no light,
>   They cried and they cried so bitterly cried;
>   Then the poor little things just lay down and died.

Example 6-13. The Babes in the Woods

3. Now when it was morning a robin so red,
   Brought strawberry leaves and over them spread.
   Sang them a song the whole summer long,
   Poor babes in the wood who had never done wrong.

This song, though sentimental, is considerably more objective in point of view than more recent songs of this type. Later compositions place the audience much closer to the actual drama so that we may more fully savor the moment of death. Some will intensify the drama by casting the victim as an orphan, a blind child, or the offspring of a drunkard, but any child will do.

Example 6-14. Little Bessie

1. Hug me closer, mother, closer;
   Put your arms around me tight.
   For I'm cold and tired mother
   And I feel so strange tonight.

2. Something hurts me here, dear mother,
   Like a stone upon my breast
   And I wonder, wonder, mother,
   Why it is I cannot rest.

3. All the day while you were working
   As I lay upon my bed,
   I was trying to be patient
   And to think of what you said.

4. Just before the lamps were lighted,
   Just before the children came,
   When my room was very quiet,
   I heard someone call my name.

5. "Come up here, my little Bessie,
   Come up here and live with me,
   Where no children ever suffer
   Through a long eternity."

6. An' I wondered, wondered, mother,
   Who so sweet upon me smiled,
   An' I knew it must be Jesus
   When he whispered, "Come, my child."

7. An' I wondered, wondered, mother,
   Who had called and I must go.
   Go to sleep no more to suffer,
   Mother don't be crying so.

8. There were little children singing,
   Sweetest songs I ever heard.
   They were sweeter, mother, sweeter,
   Than the sweetest singing bird.

9. Way up yonder in the portals
   That is shining very fair,
   Little Bessie now is sheltered
   By the Savior's love and care.

Just as dramatically immediate, extended, and sentimental, are the songs of the dying stranger. There is a group of such songs which are from the lips of a soldier wounded in battle, in which he asks that messages be carried back home. Usually he is very young and leaves a doting mother and a sweetheart behind. Another recurrent figure is the dying pilgrim, the life-journeyer who has finally found an end to his travels, but is far from home.

Example 6-15. The Dying Nun

1. Let the air blow in upon me,
   Let me see the midnight sky.
   Stand back sisters from around,
   It is so hard to die.
   Raise the pillow up, oh Martha,
   Sister Martha, you are kind;
   Come and stand alone beside me,
   Ere I leave you all behind.

2. Oh, my father and my mother
   Have you not forgave the past
   When you hear some stranger telling
   How your stray lamb died at last?
   Out of all who used to love me
   Who will weep when I am dead?
   None but you dear Sister Martha,
   Keep their last watch round me bed.

3. Hark those heavenly strains come stealing
   Through the midnight dark and dim.
   And I hear some chime bells pealing
   As I float away with him.
   I am coming Douglas, Douglas,
   Where you are I'll soon be there.
   Yes I come at last, my darling,
   Death gives back your little Clare.

4. Hold my hand so cold and frozen,
   Once it was so soft and white.
   And this ring that drops down from it,
   Once it clasped my finger tight.
   Little ring they thought so worthless
   That they let me wear it here.
   It is but one plain golden circlet,
   With a braid of Douglas' hair.

5. Sister Martha, are you near me?
   You are kinder than the rest.
   Raise my head and let me lay it,
   While I live, upon your breast.
   I was thinking of some music
   That I heard long, long ago;
   Oh, how sweet the nuns are singing
   In the chapel there below.

6. Sister Martha, Sister Martha,
   Has the moon gone down so soon?
   And this cell is cold as winter,
   Though I know it's now in June.
   Sisters in their white beds lying,
   Dreaming in the pale moonlight.
   To their dreams their comes no message,
   Clara dies alone tonight.

In such songs, there is a real theological basis for the sentiments involved. Life is pictured by many folk revivalist groups as just a stopover on the way to the Heavenly City to which all Christians are bound. Individuals have the lonely responsibility of their own salvation. They picture life as lonely and as a prison for the body. Consequently, death is seen as something to be desired as an end to the struggle, and as a way of becoming reunited with loved ones. This picture of the transience of life and the desire for death is expressed in many religious folksongs in this tradition.

Example 6-16. Wayfaring Stranger

1. I'm just a poor wayfaring stranger
   While traveling through this world of woe.
   Yet there's no sickness, toil, or danger
   In that bright world to which I go.

2. I'm going home to see my father,
   He said he'd know me when I come.
   I'm just a going over Jordan;
   I'm just a going over home.

3. I'm going home to see my mother.
   She said she'd know me when I come.
   I'm just a going over Jordan,
   I'm just a going over home.

4. I'm going there to see my classmates,
   Who's gone before me one by one.
   I'm just a going over Jordan;
   I'm just a going over home.

Men Away from Women: The Occupational Ballads

An important group of native American ballads are those pieces connected with occupational groups such as lumberjacks, miners, railroadmen, and cowboys. These songs are eclectic in their sources of subject and compositional technique. Ultimately, the most vital styles are the "come-all-ye" and the sentimental ballad, those in greatest vogue during the time when these occupations were at their height—the later nineteenth and early twentieth centuries.

These songs are generally concerned with the dangers of hazardous occupations, and they usually deal with the work realistically and with a minimum of complaints. In surroundings such as were found in connection with these jobs, where men were removed from their women, heroic values tended to reassert themselves. The songs of these men concern the brave deeds of certain of their number. But these events are reported generally within a sentimental frame, as the hero is often portrayed as being small or young, and when he dies he leaves behind mother and sweetheart to mourn. As opposed to other Anglo-American types of ballad, the hero is allowed heroic action, but his reward is also death. And this death is something that he seems to court directly, because it provides him with his moment of glory.

The occupational hero dies doing his job. These occupations were difficult ones involving constant risks, and men naturally died while performing them; it was these deeds that became celebrated. In each occupation there seems to have been one recurrent situation which provided the greatest risks and consequently the greatest number of heroic deaths. In the lumberjack trade, it was the log-jam preventing the logs from getting down the river to the mill. One person could break up a jam, but it was a very hazardous duty and often led to the death of the chosen one. A number of ballads came out of just such situations, the most common being "The Jam on Gerry's Rocks."

Example 6-17. The Jam on Jerry's Rocks

Reprinted by permission of the publishers from Franz Rickaby, *Ballads and Songs of the Shanty-Boy*, Cambridge, Mass.: Harvard University Press, copyright 1926 by Harvard University Press, 1954 by Lillian Rickaby Dykstra.

1. Come all ye true born shanty-boys, whoever that ye be,
   I would have you pay attention and listen unto me,
   Concerning a young shanty-boy so tall, genteel, and brave.
   'Twas on a jam on Gerry's Rocks he met a wat'ry grave.

2. It happened on a Sunday morn as you shall quickly hear.
   Our logs were piled up mountain high, there being no one to keep them
       clear.
   Our boss he cried, "Turn out, brave boys. Your hearts are void of fear.
   We'll break that jam on Gerry's Rocks, and for Agonstown we'll steer."

3. Some of them were willing enough, but others they hung back.
   'Twas for to work on Sabbath they did not think 'twas right.
   But six of our brave Canadian boys did volunteer to go
   And break the jam on Gerry's Rocks with their foreman, young Monroe.

4. They had not rolled off many logs when the boss to them did say,
   "I'd have you be on your guard, brave boys. That jam will soon give way."
   But scarce the warning had he spoke when the jam did break and go,
   And it carried away these six brave youths and their foreman, young
       Monroe.

5. When the rest of the shanty-boys these sad tidings came to hear,
   To search for their dead comrades to the river they did steer.
   One of these a headless body found, to their sad grief and woe,
   Lay cut and mangled on the beach the head of young Monroe.

6. They took him from the water and smoothed down his raven hair.
   There was one fair form amongst them, her cries would rend the air.
   There was one fair form amongst them, a maid from Saginaw town.
   Her sighs and cries would rend the skies for her lover that was drowned.

7. They buried him quite decently, being on the seventh of May.
   Come all the rest of you shanty-boys, for your dead comrade pray.
   'Tis engraved on a little hemlock tree that at his head doth grow,
   The name, the date, and the drowning of this hero, young Monroe.

8. Miss Clara was a noble girl, likewise the raftsman's friend.
   Her mother was a widow woman lived at the river's bend.
   The wages of her own true love the boss to her did pay,
   And a liberal subscription she received from the shanty-boys next day.

9. Miss Clara did not long survive her great misery and grief.
   In less than three months afterwards death came to her relief.
   In less than three months afterwards she was called to go,
   And her last request was granted—to be laid by young Monroe.

10. Come all the rest of ye shanty-men who would like to go and see,
    On a little mound by the river's bank there stands a hemlock tree.
    The shanty-boys cut the woods all round. These lovers they lie low.
    Here lies Miss Clara Dennison and her shanty-boy, Monroe.

The songs which seem to have been most popular among the cowboys, "Little Joe, the Wrangler" (B5), "An Empty Cot in the Bunkhouse Tonight," and "When the Work's All Done this Fall" (B3), all tell the story of a cowhand killed while heading off a stampede, while "Utah Carroll" (B4) involves the further interest that the hero is killed by the rampaging cattle while saving the boss's daughter.

Example 6-18. Utah Carroll

1. You ask me why, my little friend, I am so quiet and still;
   And why a frown sits on my brow like a storm cloud on a hill.
   Rein in your pony closer, I'll tell to you a tale
   Of Utah Carroll, my partner, and his last ride on the trail.

2. In the land of Mexico in the place from whence I came,
   In silence sleeps my partner in a grave without a name.
   We rode the trail together and worked cows side by side.
   Oh, I loved him like a brother, and I wept when Utah died.

3. We were rounding up one morning, our work was nearly done,
   When off the cattle started on a wild frightened run.
   Now the boss's little daughter was holding in that side.
   She rushed in to turn the cattle, 'twas there my partner died.

4. In the saddle of the pony where the boss's daughter sat,
   Utah that very morning had placed a red blanket
   That the saddle might be easier for his little friend,
   But the blanket that he placed there brought my partner's life to an end.

5. When Leonora rushed in to turn the cattle, her pony gave a bound,
   And the blanket slipped from beneath her and went trailing on the ground.
   Now there's nothing on a cow ranch that will make the cattle fight
   As quick as some red object would just within their sight.

6. When the cattle saw the blanket there trailing on the ground
   They were maddened in a moment and they charged it with a bound.
   When we cowboys saw what had happened, everyone just held our breath,
   For if her pony failed her, none could save Leonora from death.

7. When Leonora saw the cattle, she quickly turned her face.
   And leaned from out her saddle, caught the blanket back in place.
   But in leaning lost her balance, fell before that maddened tide.
   "Lie still, Leonora, I'm coming dear," were the words old Utah cried.

8. About fifteen yards behind her Utah came riding fast.
   I little thought that moment that ride would be his last.
   The horse approached the maiden with sure feet and steady bounds
   And he leaned from out the saddle to catch her from the ground.

9. In falling from her pony, she dragged the blanket down,
   And it lay there beside her where she lay upon the ground.
   As he leaned to reach Leonora and to catch her in his arms
   I thought my partner successful and Leonora safe from harm.

10. But such weight upon the cinches, they never had felt before.
    His hind cinch burst asunder, and he fell beside Leonore.
    Utah picked up the blanket, "Lie still again," he said.
    And he ran across the prairie and waved the blanket over his head.

11. And thus he turned the cattle from Leonora his little friend,
    And as the cattle rushed upon him, he turned to meet his end.
    And quickly from his scabbard, Utah his pistol drew.
    He was bound to fight while dying, like a cowboy brave and true.

12. His pistol flashed like lightning, the reports rang loud and clear,
    As the cattle pinned down on him, he dropped the leading steer.
    But they kept right on coming, my partner had to fall.
    No more he will cinch the bronco or give the cattle call.

13. And when at last we reached him, there on the ground he lay,
With cuts and wounds and bruises, his life-blood oozing away.
Oh, I tell you what, little one, it was most awful hard,
I could not ride the distance in time to save my pard.

14. As I knelt down by him I knew his life was o'er,
But I heard him faintly murmur, "Lie still, I am coming, Leonora."
'Twas on one Sunday morning, I heard the parson say,
"I don't think your young partner will be lost on that great day."
He was just a poor young cowboy, maybe a little wild.
But God won't be too hard on a man who died to save a child.

The analogous situation in railroading songs is the attempt of the engineer to bring his late train in on time.

In all of these occupational songs there is a common element: heroism occurs in the course of doing the job properly. The forces against which the hero contends are impersonal, dehumanized. Not so that other occupational hero who dies in the carrying out of his profession—the outlaw —for his deeds are directed against human enemies and his death is often engineered by treachery.

Example 6-19. Jesse James

1. Living in Missouri was a brave bold man,
Known from Seattle, Washington to Birmingham,
From Boston, Massachusetts across the states,
From Denver, Colorado to the Golden Gate.

2. Sitting in the saddle he won his fame,
Every nook and corner knew of Jesse James.
Perhaps you read about him in your homes at night,
And if the wind blew down the chimney you would shake with fright.

3. Jesse said, "Some more coin we need."
   He oiled up his rifle, got his trusty steed.
   Galloped over to his brother Frank,
   Says, "We'll have to have some money from the Pettsville bank."

4. He rode into town about ten o'clock.
   The cashier and the banker 'ceived a terrible shock.
   While Jesse kept him covered with his forty-four,
   His pals got a half a million dollars or more.

5. Jesse was sitting in his home alone;
   His wife had left him there to straighten out the home.
   He was sitting in the kitchen when the doorbell rang.
   In stepped Ford, a member of the outlaw gang.

6. Ford said, "Tonight we will make a haul."
   Jesse's wife's picture was hanging on the wall.
   The western mail ran through the town,
   Jesse reached for his rifle, knocked the picture down.

7. Jesse said to Ford, "I will hang it back up there."
   He picked up the picture, climbed upon a chair.
   Ford aimed the forty-four at Jesse's head,
   And news rang around the world that Jesse James was dead.

8. Next week on his tombstone, these words they ran:
   "If you're going to live a bandit live a single man."
   For perhaps Jesse James wouldn't have lost his life
   Hadn't been for the picture of his darling wife.

It is not for lack of evidence that so many people have asked why American folksongs are so sad. The Anglo-American tradition is suffused with stories of futility, destruction, and death. Life is pictured in fatalistic terms. Even when stories are given in comic terms, they often picture individuals as defeated and self-defeating, as bound by internal limitations to an ineffectual life—it is these inabilities that we laugh at. Only in the songs of the occupations do we see action valued highly, and we get a sense of fulfillment, even though here, too, death is the common result—but it is a hero's death.

chapter 7

THE METRICAL
ASPECT OF FOLKSONG

Folksong is the uniting of traditional verse and music. Although both are capable of existing separately, their combination in song presents special problems. Verse and music have in common the elements of rhythm and meter which give them motion and pace, and in a larger sense, structure and organization.

Rhythm and Meter

Any series of audible impulses possesses the element of rhythm which can be expressed symbolically. A series of impulses may range from the mono-rhythmic tick, tick, tick of a watch to the equally repetitive, but more complex rhythm of train wheels or to the chaotic rhythm of a tray of glasses being dropped. In the last example, the rhythmic possibilities range from all glasses reaching the floor simultaneously, thereby producing a single impulse, to each glass striking at a different point in time, producing a separate impulse for each glass. Rhythm is a physical reality subject to the most objective representation. This representation is achieved by symbolically indicating the time lapse between consecutive impulses. Any series of sounds in which the impulses bear an expressible relationship constitutes a rhythmic unit.

The organization of rhythmic units, or small groups of impulses into larger patterns of predictable stress is called meter. Meter is artificial; it is the result of man's need to organize and impose form upon small components. This is not to say we do not *feel* meter, but it is something we create. For this reason, meter is individually and culturally subjective. The mono-rhythm of the equally spaced and identical ticks of a metronome will begin to suggest groupings and patterns of relationship and stress to the listener. Each listener may set up a different grouping, the only limitation to the possibilities being the imagination and experience of the individual.

The subjective nature of meter may be proven by a simple experiment based on suggestibility. Set a metronome in motion without divulging the nature of the mechanism to the experimental group. Suggest to them that the impulses are in stress patterns of three pulses to the group—*tick* tick tick. Stop the metronome after sufficient time to let each member of the group organize his hearing. Then suggest that you have readjusted the mechanism to produce a stress pattern of four pulses to the group— *tick* tick tick tick. The experimental group will almost invariably agree that they heard the suggested groupings although in physical fact all impulses were of equal stress and without varying relationship to one another.

The organization of rhythmic impulses into preconceived patterns of predictable occurrence is meter. Rhythm, then, is the actual relationship of consecutive impulses and exists both in and outside of art; meter is the organization of rhythmic units and exists exclusively in art. There may be rhythm without meter but meter is merely an artistic concept of rhythmic patterns based on repetition and predictability.

Meter in Traditional Verse and Song

Traditional verse, being simple and unselfconsciously con- structed, cannot fruitfully be described in the usual terms employed for the poetry of record. The conventional "school-book" analysis of poetic meter (that is, in terms of *iamb, trochee, dactyl*, etc.) is meaningful in *belles lettres* because these concepts are often known, accepted, and utilized by the creative writer. Traditional verse is coarser and less con- sciously contrived in its organization, and therefore requires broader units of measure for a useful descriptive analysis. Furthermore, it is just such broad units which enable us to see how the music and words of a song fit together, complementing each other. Gerould describes the units and the interrelationship perceptively:

> Whatever the length of line and whatever the stanza form, the stresses fall with heavier and lighter weight in strict alteration. They are, as we say, primary and secondary.... This alternation of primary and secondary stresses in the verse scheme corresponds, of necessity, to a similar alter- nation of stress in the musical setting. The matter becomes far plainer, indeed, when the melodies are examined than when the verse is read ... primary stresses almost invariably fall at the beginning of measures and thus correspond with the normal musical stresses. Secondary stresses, on the other hand, ordinarily fall within the musical measures, though by no means always.
>
> (Gerould: 1932, 129)

This kind of analysis, which emphasizes the relationship of stresses within the unit of the line is called *isochronic*. Here focus is directed toward the ways in which the line naturally divides itself, and the ways the component parts fit together; the number of unstressed syllables is disregarded for the most part. The duration between stresses and the way in which slack syllables articulate the duration are emphasized. Furthermore, the relationship of primary and secondary stresses in alternation pointed out by Gerould emphasizes the basic unit of traditional verse in English, the *dipod* (literally "two feet").

Meter in Traditional Music

The dipodic-isochronic approach to verse metrics is parallel in many respects to the metrics of traditional music. Our musical heritage, in both traditional music and art music, has conditioned us to accept meter as an integral part of music.* Just as oral tradition has established certain commonplaces in folk verse, natural selection has established certain metrical patterns as basic to folk music.

* By conditioning, we think of music as inherently metrical, but there exists in other cultures today and there existed in Western culture until the twelfth century, music without meter. That is, music whose rhythmic components defied organization into the larger framework we call meter.

Prior to the thirteenth century, the formalization in music of record was directed by the Church. Sacred music through the twelfth century (i.e. plainsong and liturgical chant) was all but invariably monorhythmic with the grouping of notes to the syllables of the liturgy accomplished in a manner foreign to metric organization. The thirteenth and fourteenth centuries saw the development and use of the "rhythmic modes." These correspond to classical verse metrics and they equated greater duration in time with accent or stress. Thus, the Iambic foot (⌣—), would assume the musical expression of a short note followed by a longer note in the ratio 1/2 or ♩ o . The further projection of the rhythmic modes into larger units resulted in the principles of mensuration, which closely parallels the modern concept of musical metrics. The underlying principle of mensuration was that durations of time might be divided in various ways. Each note value in decreasing order (whole note o , half note ♩ , quarter note ♪ , etc.) could be divided by two or by three. In this way a note of long duration might be divided into three notes, each a third the duration value of the original note. These, in turn, might be divided into three notes, each one ninth the duration value of the original note.

o

♩   ♩   ♩

♩♩♩♩♩♩♩♩♩

The basic unit of musical meter is similarly an alternation of two stresses, one strong and one weak, found within the musical bar:

The bar represents a predetermined period of time and may be divided into many combinations of lesser values.

There are four meters or metrical families which we may consider basic to the study of Anglo-American traditional song.* These are 2/4, 3/4, 6/8, and 9/8.

A division of the original value in twos was similarly possible.

o

𝆺 𝆺

𝆺 𝆺 𝆺 𝆺

Divisions into smaller values might be accomplished in combinations of divisions by two and three.

o

𝆺   𝆺

𝆺 𝆺 𝆺 𝆺 𝆺 𝆺

𝆺𝆺𝆺𝆺𝆺𝆺 𝆺𝆺𝆺𝆺𝆺𝆺

Since music of record in Medieval times was exclusively sacred and no documented history of the popular or secular music exists, the tracing of influence, one upon the other, is difficult. The direction of influence (i.e. sacred to secular, or secular to sacred) is impossible to reconstruct accurately, and indeed the stylistic differences between Church and vulgar music in earlier periods are one of conjecture.

Since a bilateral influence is found in later periods, we may assume that considerable interchange of idioms occurred between Church and popular music before the fifteenth century. It is therefore possible that the formalization of theory and practice within Church music, for example, mensuration, reflected idioms which already existed outside the Church. Church theorists may have given organization to secular musical practices which were influencing sacred music and displacing the mono–rhythmic style of early plainsong.

* The meter 4/4 is omitted from this discussion because it behaves in the same fashion as 2/4 regarding value divisions. Expression of a tune may be accomplished

In 2/4 meter the bar has a durational value of two beats or pulses, and the total value is expressed by a half note ($\rho = 2$ beats). The normal division of 2/4 meter is as follows:

In 3/4 meter, the bar has a durational value of three beats or pulses and the total value is expressed by a dotted half note ($\rho \cdot = 3$ beats). The normal division of 3/4 meter is as follows:

In 6/8 meter, the bar has a durational value of two beats or pulses and the total value is expressed by a dotted half note ($\rho \cdot = 2$ beats). The normal division of 6/8 meter is as follows:

in either 4/4 or 2/4 obtaining the same result by using differing note values. The 4/4 meter is more convenient in representing tunes of slower tempo. The pattern of accent and stress found in the four quarter notes of a 4/4 bar is the same as found in the four eighth notes of a 2/4 bar.

In 9/8 meter the bar has a durational value of three beats or pulses and the total value is expressed by a dotted half note combined with a dotted quarter note ($\mathcal{P}\cdot\ = 3$ beats). The normal division of 9/8 meter is as follows:

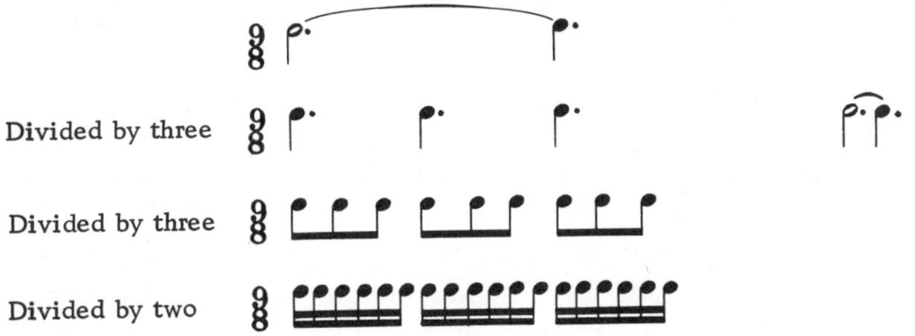

Divided by three

Divided by three

Divided by two

These different time values may occur in any combination without altering the character of the meter providing they are consistent with the preconceived pattern of division.

There may be seen in the accompanying tables and in transcriptions of traditional tunes the amount of variety achieved in merely altering the number of divisions of a note of given value. These are the patterns of relatively simple make-up which natural selection has established as the backbone of Anglo-American traditional musical metrics. These patterns and their variants have been conventionalized along with folk verse to form the most effective word-music relationships.

Metric organization dictates that the heaviest stress shall in the majority of occurrences fall on the first beat of each bar. In 2/4 and 6/8 meters the heaviest stress falls upon the first beat and a secondary stress on the second beat of each bar. The intervening notes of smaller value are unstressed.

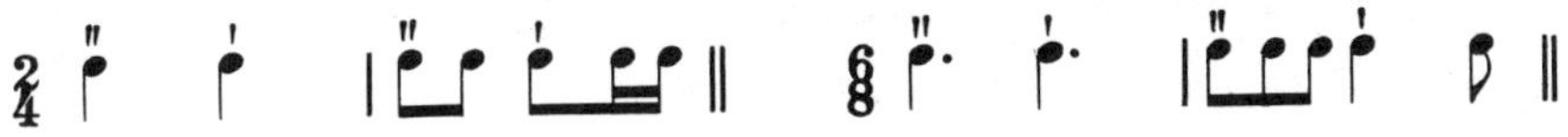

In 3/4 and 9/8 meters the heaviest stress falls upon the first beat and a secondary stress upon the third beat of each bar. The second beat and all intervening notes of smaller value are unstressed.

These are general characteristics of the four basic meters as found in Anglo-American folksong and many exceptions to this strict pattern may be found. If this were not the case our folksong would be nothing more than a tedious sing-song.

The two most common departures from the metrical patterns of sub-division and stress are alteration and syncopation. Alteration is the changing of the expected division of note values; for example the division of a quarter note in 2/4 by three instead of by two. These alterations are labeled to readily indicate their departure from expected metrical behavior.

Alteration is most often done to accommodate words whose number of syllables necessitates a change in the normal division in order that the larger pattern of beats or stresses remain unaltered. Such an alteration occurs on the word "merrily" in the line:

Young   gyp - sy   Da - vey came   mer - ri - ly   by

Young gypsy Davey came merrily by

Syncopation is the displacement of the normal points of stress. This is accomplished by placing the stress at points in the bar other than the beats upon which they are expected to fall. In the line "Git down, git down pretty Polly" the secondary stress on the second syllable of "Polly" does not fall upon the second beat of the bar where it is anticipated but is advanced by a half beat.

Git   down   git   down   pret - ty   Pol - ly____

Git down, git down pretty Polly

In the following example a heavy stress is expected upon the word "on" which here is delayed beyond the first beat of the bar.

She ta - ken her lit - tle ba - by___ on her___ knee

She taken her little baby on her knee

These displacements of the normal stress pattern create tensions within the song by the conflict between the preconceived metrical background against which the tune is set and the more erratic handling of the melody itself.

The strict adherence to the inherent stress pattern of the meter gives a sense of repose as seen in this example:

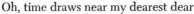

Oh time draws near my___ dear - est___ dear

Oh, time draws near my dearest dear

Syncopation and, to a lesser extent, alteration cause tension by interruption of the metrical pattern. An extreme use of syncopation and/or alteration will cause a complete breakdown of the metrical characteristics and destroy its sense of organization.

The Interdependence of Text and Tune

When Gerould spoke of verse and music as having a common method of stress organization, he pointed toward the basic way words and music are co-ordinated in folksong. The full relationship of tune and text has not been examined because of differences in terminology. But there are a number of terms in poetic analysis which have almost exact parallels in music analysis. The following is a correlation of those terms having direct relationship to the verse and the music of folksong.

TERMS OF TEXT	TERMS OF TUNE
Stanza	*Tune*
the basic unit of song verse	the complete melodic construction of song
Line	*Phrase*
a sentence or phrase; a segment of the stanza	a segment of melody; each line of verse is represented by a phrase of music. A stanza of four lines will be matched usually by a tune of four phrases.

TERMS OF TEXT	TERMS OF TUNE
Dipod	*Measure*
a group of syllables containing two stresses, one primary and one secondary with their intervening unstressed syllables	a unit of meter containing a primary and secondary stress
Foot	*Pulse*
a single stress with its adjacent unstressed syllable(s)	a single musical beat; each beat of a 2/4 and 6/8 bar; the first and third beat of a 3/4 and 9/8 bar

Since most folk verse in English consists of two dipods to the line and four lines to the stanza, most traditional tunes consist of two bars to the phrase and four phrases to the tune. The most common exception to this is the second and fourth line of "ballad meter" in which the second dipod is incomplete, because the second foot of the second dipod is missing. This is paralleled in music by a long tone, usually a full bar in length with no enunciation at the second stress point in the bar. In the verse and music the missing stress is implied by the over-all metrical background and by the pause which occurs at that point.

Metrical Rigidity

Of verse and music, the latter is the more abstract idiom. The word within verse must conform to grammar and syntax in order to communicate. The organization of words into metrical patterns (i.e. verse) must be secondary to the necessity for communication. Music, or a series of tones comprising a melody, does not communicate a concrete thought or image. The organization of musical tones into metrical patterns tends to be more formal and less flexible than verse meter. When a tune is abstracted from words (hummed, whistled, or played instrumentally), its metrical organization tends to be rendered more rigidly. Conversely, the addition of words to a tune modifies and tempers metrical organization to some degree because of the added dimension of verbal communication.

Analysis by stress pattern works as well with verse as with music. Once a stress pattern is established, the treatment of intervals between stresses may be as varied in words as in music. This is not meant to imply that folksong is inflexibly metrical once a stress pattern has been established. On the contrary, there is a wide range of metric variability in folksong from the strictest adherence to time values and stress patterns to an arrangement of stresses only slightly suggestive of a constant meter.

The range of metrical organization found within speech and song may be best shown by use of a spectrum. The poles of the spectrum have on one end "utterance," the least organized and predictable in its stress pattern, and on the other end, certain song types of inflexible musical meter. Between these poles can be found all the degrees of formalization in speech rhythm.

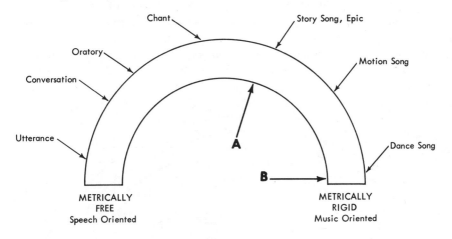

Normal speech does not utilize the full range of stress/slack patterns. As the patterns of stress/slack become more predictable, the time lapses between stresses become more regular, and thus, introduction of meter becomes more evident. Just such a thing happens when conversation becomes argument, argument becomes speech or debate, debate becomes oratory, oratory becomes preachment, preachment becomes chant, chant becomes song.

The rhythms of casual speech, being usually unpredictable, are found near the pole of greatest freedom. As speech patterns and mannerisms become more regularized and predictable—that is, more subject to organization—they are found in positions nearer the pole of fixed meter. The combination of speech and musical idioms, with its inherent degree of formality, first appears in chant.* From this point on the spectrum to the fixed pole, the musical idiom asserts increasing influence upon words and the alteration of and formalization of casual speech patterns increases.** This trend culminates in the complete subjugation of communicative speech rhythm to rigid metrical patterns.

As is clear from this spectrum, the imposition of meter does not nec-

* Chant, while strongly speech–oriented with regard to its rhythmic freedom, does formalize inflection into various pitches.
** This formalization can, of course, exist apart from song, as in the rigidly metrical nursery rhymes; but such compositions are often referred to as sing-song, emphasizing their song-like characteristics.

essarily mean that rigid metricality becomes the norm. Some creations emphasize such rigid patterns more firmly than others, justifying a distinction between the flexibly metrical and the rigidly metrical. This is a difference literary critics often imply between poetry, which is flexibly metrical, and verse, which is rigidly metrical. (The distinction breaks down, of course, with compositions like Blake's "Songs of Innocence and Experience.") All of Anglo-American folksong is relatively fixed. However, there is a variation in the degree of adherence to meter which is well worth more detailed consideration. Here is a more detailed look at that part of the spectrum (A to B) which contains Anglo-American folksong.

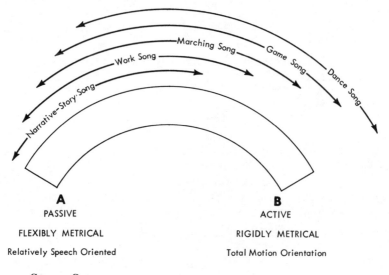

<table>
<tr><td align="center">**A**</td><td align="center">**B**</td></tr>
<tr><td align="center">PASSIVE</td><td align="center">ACTIVE</td></tr>
<tr><td align="center">FLEXIBLY METRICAL</td><td align="center">RIGIDLY METRICAL</td></tr>
<tr><td align="center">Relatively Speech Oriented</td><td align="center">Total Motion Orientation</td></tr>
</table>

Story–Song

The songs which are most speech oriented, nearest the passive pole of the spectrum, are those story–songs which are sung for an audience—which relate a story by lyric, narrative, or dialog techniques. Being fictive, they elicit an emotional more than a physical response from the listener. The oldest of the English and Scottish ballads and songs exhibit speech orientation to a greater degree than any other group or type. This may be because these songs have existed in oral tradition longer than others. It is also likely from what we know of the creation of recent songs within Anglo-American tradition, that texts are conceived to "fit" a pre-existing tune. Abstract melody (which a pre-existing tune would be) contains a high degree of metrical orientation with *no* element of speech orientation. In the early stages of the combination of a text and tune, the musical element dominates and the speech rhythm is at its most altered and formalized stage. Clearly, one thing which oral tradition and transmission does is to allow the two idioms to "live together." This co-existence over a long span of time and through many transmissions causes the idioms to modify one another at points of greatest friction. The hundreds of years in oral circulation temper the older story song and separates its style from the abstract melody or dance tune to which it may originally have been set. When the function of dance is no longer a part of a song's existence, the necessity for retaining strict meter is relaxed, allowing a shift of functional interest to the tale.

Oral tradition works not only on the combination of text and tune but on each component separately. Thus, a tune may change from a well–defined and complex melody to a mere contour outline, and its meter from a well–organized pattern to a series of rather free stress groups. This is, of course, the same process which scholars have long described in regard to text modifications as "oral change." The following example demonstrates the breakdown of what was probably at one time a rather well-defined meter. The dwelling upon certain words and the fore-shortening of other words in disregard for an abstract metrical background shows the singer's shift in emphasis from musical to verbal focus. In order to compare this version with a highly metrical realization, a projected tune is given to coincide. Despite the great metrical freedom displayed, there is still sufficient organization of stresses to indicate an influence of constant meter.

There are a number of ways in which the traditional singer tends to relax the feeling of rigid metricality or to ameliorate a strong meter. There is in the singing of many traditional performers the tendency to relax the meter at the end of the verse line (i.e. musical phrase). This is especially so at the end of the second line or the musical mid-cadence.

These departures from the prevailing meter of the tune take the form of extensions and/or compressions of the predictable values. Many traditional singers, rather than hold a note at the end of a phrase until the metrical value has been filled, will arbitrarily shorten the final note and proceed to the next phrase. This is most often found in tunes of rather slow pace.

Love   o love o care-less   love, ____   Love o love o care-less   love ____

Traditional singers will sometimes expand or stretch those values expected in a certain meter at the points of relative repose occurring at the end of the phrase. These extensions of the phrase may take the form of a short rest or silence prior to the next phrase or they may be an expansion of note values immediately prior to the phrase ending. Both of these interrupt the constant flow on the metrical background and the latter may even be of such a nature to give the feeling of a new, if temporary, meter.

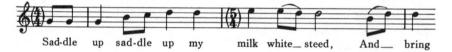

Sad-dle   up sad-dle up   my   milk white__ steed,   And__ bring

Some traditional singing styles, especially those of the Southern Appalachian Mountains, are so rich in ornamentation and so free from rigid stress patterns that meter is greatly modified. Although a tune may be sung consistently in a certain meter the presence of ornamentation will "camouflage" its rigidity. This style obscures any persistent meter, as does alteration and syncopation, but does not produce a feeling of tension. This characteristic is responsible for the feeling of wonderful fluidity of many Southern Appalachian folksongs which upon analysis are found to be rather tightly organized metrically (see music on page 145).

These modifications, rather than being an irreversible process of decay and degeneration, are the outcome of a shifting emphasis, a changing function, and an evolving esthetic fashion. This can only be considered as a vitally creative process. Since these songs were and are intended to express a dramatic situation in an effective manner, any change which makes them more effective must be considered creative and not degenerative. Within the older story–songs are to be found the modifications which compromise musical abstraction in favor of natural and colloquial speech. Within this body of song is also found the greatest flexibility of meter due to its long disassociation with abstract music and/or dance function.

There are story–songs of certain types which tend to maintain adherence to metrical rigidity. These are story–songs which are: (1) humorous, (2) sung to a dance tune which has continued in dance tradition, (3) parodies of a song which remains in circulation, and (4) of recent currency and under the influence of recent commercial instrumental conventions.

Humorous songs are generally rather rigidly metrical. This is perhaps because most humorous songs are sung to fast tunes which allow less latitude for alteration and metrical flexibility. Fast tunes tend to rely upon a one syllable to one note ratio. The kinds of departures from natural speech rhythms which occur in this type of setting heighten comic effect and are therefore more likely to be retained. Here are two examples of the native American song, "Springfield Mountain." One retains a somber mood and its style is strongly narrative with a high degree of speech orientation and metrical flexibility. The other, although from the same story source, takes a more humorous bent. Its style is much more rigid metrically, its tempo quicker, and its tune lighter in mood.

Example 7-1. Springfield Mountain

1. On Springfield Mountain where we all do dwell,
   This likely youth was known full well,
   Old Tennessee rode for his own dear son,
   This likely youth was twenty one.

2. A Friday morning he did go
   Down in his meadow for to mow,
   He mowed all 'round in his meadow field,
   This pizen serpent came at his heel.

3. He laid his scythe down on the ground,
   A-looking at this deadly wound,
   And to go home it was his intent,
   Crying out all as he went.

4. His voice were heard both fur and near,
   But none of his friends they did not 'pear,
   They thought it was some workman's call,
   But poor man alone at last did fall.

5. Oh the night a' been gone and the day coming on,
   This old man went to see his son,
   It was his own dear son he found,
   Dead as a rock lying on the ground.

6. This old man thought he were taking his rest,
   His hands was placeted across his breast,
   His hands were placeted across his breast,
   His mouth and eyes were closed fast.

Example 7-2. Springfield Mountain

From *The Bulletin of the Folksong Society of the Northeast.* Used by permission of The American Folklore Society.

1. Come all ye gee-wee-wents
     And a story I will tee-wee-well,
   About a young ma-wa-wan
     Whom I knew quite wee-wee-well.
   Come a roo-di-roo-di-roo!

2. He mowed the hay-way-way
     All round the fie-wee-wield,-
   Come a rattle, come a snaa-y-kay,
     And bit him in the hee-wee-weel.

3. He set right dow-wow-wown
     Upon the grow-wow-wound,
   Closed both his eye-wye-wyes,
     And looked around-wow-wound.

4. "Oh, go, good da-wa-wad,
     And to spread the new-wew-wews,
   For here comes Sa-wa-wal
     Without her shoe-woo-woos!"

5. Oh, all ye gee-wee-wents,
     Come a warning come a ta-wa-wake,
   Don't get a bee-y-t
     From a rattle, come a sna-wa-wake!

In songs which are set to pre-existing dance tunes, metrical rigidity is inherent in the tune. The song tends to remain rigid so long as the dance tune continues to be identified with the dance when apart from the song.

Certain ballads have long been acknowledged to bear strong association with dance; for example, most common Anglo-American versions of "The Two Sisters" and the many songs set to the jig tune "The Irish Washerwoman." These generalizations are true also of story songs which are set to older tunes or are parodies of existing songs. So long as the original tune remains in popular currency, an identity is maintained between the original and the newer setting. Any metrical rigidity found in the former will be duplicated and maintained and, in many cases, reinforced in the latter.

The Influence of Instruments

Although instruments have been used in regions where Anglo-American folksong has flourished for the same length of time, there is evidence of a separation between the song and instrumental traditions. The fiddle was the earliest and remains the dominant instrument in many rural areas. However, there are few reports of traditional singers accompanying themselves on this instrument. Other instruments associated with traditional music in America made their appearance in roughly the following order: dulcimer, banjo, guitar, mandolin, string bass, and more recently, instruments of electrical amplification.

The methods by which the early string instruments were played tended to establish a rigid metrical style or "beat." Naturally, the tunes accompanied by these instruments tended to conform to that musical style. The playing and singing of traditional music by two or more performers necessitated an agreement between them upon a single formalized or metrical version of the tune. This was necessary to enable the performers to complement and coordinate with one another.

The increasing popularity of instruments, the establishment of the string-band tradition, and the exposure via radio and phonograph of these idioms did much to popularize a "country music" style which is overwhelmingly metrical. This movement is probably no more than sixty to eighty years old, but was greatly accelerated by the invention and widespread use of mass media of communication. Examination of the earliest recordings of country music from the 1920's indicates that ensemble tradition was by no means the dominant one. Of equal importance were the solo singers playing their own instrumental accompaniment. Record companies almost totally ignored the unaccompanied singing tradition that was the dominant style in most rural areas. Since ensemble performance, with its metrical beat and often complex and contrapuntal arrangements, excited the most commercial interest, its wide exposure altered the development of rural singing styles. The major manifestation of the new country music, so far as this study is concerned, was that many old songs received a radically different esthetic treatment which was rapidly disseminated via radio and phonograph. The new treatments were invariably rigid in meter and the setting of words was dominated by a preoccupation with the musical factors.

Motion Songs

The progression from free to strict musical style travels across the metrical spectrum toward songs with the functional purpose of coordinating or directing physical movement. Whereas the passive story-song elicits primarily an emotional response, the metrically rigid action songs tend to excite a physical one. We talk of hearing a tune and having to tap our feet or clap our hands—this is the response intended in the heavy metered tunes with a strong and relentless "beat." A great many such tunes have their origin in some form of physical activity. Songs are sung in association with many types of motion: children's games, play-parties, dances, and instrumental pieces. These tunes tend toward quick pulsations (rapid tempo), with consequently few subdivisions of stress. They are all but invariably bound to a constant meter and its most direct rhythmic patterns and subdivisions. The placement of words within so formalized a metric-rhythmic style must necessarily adhere to musical considerations rather than those of natural speech.

I been work-in all my life   aint got no-thin but a   bar-low knife

Often auxiliary syllables such as "a" or "o" are inserted for rhythmic unity without any consideration for their intrusion upon the normal sense of the words.

(Oh)There's a   coon from Ten-nes-see   Just (a) wic-ked as (a) he could be

But the addition of melody and musical organization to our common, everyday tools of communication, our words, gives them a new dimension. Psychologically we do not hear song as words being treated musically. Our response to the words of a song is entirely different from our response to conversation, drama, oratory, and recitation. For this reason we tolerate, or perhaps do not even become aware of, distortions of words in music which would be ludicrous and esthetically intolerable if heard apart from the tune. As a simple experiment take the old dance tune "Old Joe Clark":

I went down to   old Joes house   old Joe was - n't   home

Now eliminate the melodic element. Set a metronome at 200 and speak each syllable in exact rhythmic unison with a corresponding metronomic "tick" (/).

/   /   /   /   /   /   / /   /   /   /   /   /
I   went down to   old   Joe's house-   Old   Joe   was   n't   home

This dramatizes how our word-rhythms may be distorted away from natural speech patterns without our objection within the confines of a song. The word-rhythm of song is a distinct and psychologically different entity from non-musical communication. This is because folksongs are a fusion of words *and* music and the fusion is irrevocable.

chapter

THE NATURE
OF FOLK TUNES

In examining the musical aspects of folksong there are factors which must be considered with regard to their texts. There are also factors which must be considered solely from a musical point of view and divorced from the form and literal meaning of folk verse. For example, chapter seven describes certain parallels which exist between text and tune; a stanza is sung to a tune and as the stanza is divided into lines so the tune is divided into phrases. Since the four line stanza is the dominant convention in Anglo-American folk verse the conventional folk tune is of four phrases.

What Is a Folk Tune?

A folk tune is a unit of musical expression or more simply a melody which has entered into the cycle of oral transmission common to all folklore. A folk tune may be associated directly with other genres of folklore as in folksong where the tune is bound to a corresponding folk verse, or it may exist somewhat more independently but still be associated with some form of folk activity as in dance. The important factor in the definition of a folk tune is its place in oral tradition, rather than its origin or age, and the effect of oral transmission upon it.

In the musical study of folk tunes the problems are many and varied. Informants who may even be illiterate sometimes have considerable language skills and powers of self-expression. They may, in discussions with the collector, yield valuable information about the lore they impart. Such questions as what a word or phrase means to the singer or what appeal a song text holds for the singer may be pursued with meaningful results.

151

To some extent, technical factors such as rhyming patterns or verbal corruptions may be discussed with the traditional performer. However, the discussion of musical factors with the folk singer or traditional musician is virtually pointless. Only a discussion of the most general and nontechnical aspects of music is possible such as a tune being "pretty," "lively," or "played in a far-off tuning." * This is due to the traditional performer's lack of a specialized technical vocabulary. In musical matters we cannot learn from the performer directly what is meaningful to his esthetic point of view. We must base our appraisal of traditional music idioms on continued observation of stylistic phenomena. Those characteristics which occur and reoccur in traditional tunes must be accepted as meaningful and gratifying to the traditional performer's esthetic sense. It is upon these characteristics that the technical study of folk tunes must be based. "Folksong has developed orally, without consciousness of the aesthetic principles according to which it is moulded; but the principles are there" (Gerould: 1926, 13).

Melody

Since the term melody is so much a part of the definition of folk tune, perhaps a definition of *melody* is in order. Melody is a succession of tones of different pitch. There are several factors about a succession of tones which give it individuality; the order of their succession, the repetition of tones, the relationships between adjacent tones, the total number of different tones, etc. While a succession of tones can exist without regard to rhythm, the correlation of a given succession of pitches (melody) and a set variety of durations (rhythm) conforms to the generally accepted concept of melody. This combination of tones and rhythm gives the melody its musical identity and makes recognition and retention possible.

It can be demonstrated experimentally that the proper series of tones is not alone sufficient for recognition of a melody. The sequence of tones found in the most familiar melody, for example, "Happy Birthday" (g-g-a-g-c-b-g-g-a-g-d-c-etc.), can be played slowly and without a variance in the duration of each tone, to a group. The result will be that many of that group will fail to recognize the melody from its tone sequence alone. The reaction of performing the same tones again with the equivalent rhythm is one of surprise at not having recognized so "obvious" an example.

* Because of the common singing schools, it is not unusual to find informants who know their notes; but this has little to do with their traditional repertoire except in regard to folk spirituals in shape-note. Occasionally, because of this background, a singer will remark, "Here's a song that can be chorded" or some similar comment.

Common Characteristics in Folk Tunes

Folk tunes, or melodies which have entered into and been modified by Anglo-American oral tradition, tend to possess these common characteristics:

1. Conventions of structure and form directly relating to Anglo-American folk verse.

2. Diatonicism and incomplete diatonicism; i.e. the use of the seven stepwise degrees found in western scales as the maximum number of different tones found within the tune, or the limitation of the tune to fewer than the seven diatonic degrees. Chromaticism is rare.

3. Singability or vocal orientation of the tunes in regard to their over-all range and the easily produceable relationships between successive tones within the tunes; the strength of the singing tradition has exerted a strong shaping influence on the instrumental idioms so that no basic differences exist and the two idioms share a single musical style.

4. The tunes are monophonic in concept, i.e. conceived as pure melody divorced from or without regard to polyphonic or harmonic considerations. Later ensemble traditions have produced songs which are undoubtedly polyphonic in orientation but the great body of existing Anglo-American folk tunes was conceived and performed as melody alone.

As well as these general stylistic similarities, Anglo-American folk tunes show patterns of consistency when analyzed technically in regard to the following ingredients: *Scale, Melodic progression, Contour,* and *Form.*

Scale

The scale, or group of different specific pitches, found within a folk tune may be considered the raw material from which it is fashioned. The scale is both a basic unit for study of the single tune from which it is abstracted and a basis for comparison with other folk tunes. (A methodology for analyzing and classifying the scales found in Anglo-American folk tunes is found in Appendix III.)

There exists within the musical study of folksong many approaches varying widely in method, accuracy, and applicability. This frequently confusing state of affairs may not be attributed entirely to the inaccurate use of musicological concepts by other than musicians. The attempts of some musicians to apply the doctrines established in formal music history and theory to the peculiarities of folksong have also led to confusion in techniques and terminology. The documentation of music history is entirely that of formal music, i.e. secular "art" music or religious music. To apply the theories and methods meaningful to this body of documentation to traditional music and song is therefore attempting to apply the "rules" of formal music to the traditional music idiom. This is at best impractical and most frequently impossible.

The most persistent efforts to place folksong study within the framework of formal music theory are found in the attempts at describing and classifying the scales found in folksong. This is most obvious in the widespread use of modal theory and terminology in the study of British and Anglo-American folksong.

The church modes, with their inherent theoretical systems and codifications, dominated recorded European music from 400 A.D. to 1500 A.D. The influence of modal concepts was felt in formal music throughout the 16th century. Then followed the decline of modal music and the growing importance of the factors which evolved into the system of tonal keys and harmonically oriented music. The history of church mode theory, from the establishment of the four Ambrosian and four Gregorian modes in the fourth and fifth centuries until the sixteenth century, is one of endless differences and contradictions among theorists.*

* Before the sixteenth century, the theory of ecclesiastical music recognized but four basic modes. These were based upon the finals d, e, f, and g. Each mode had two forms, authentic and plagal, each having a different overall range in relation to the final. A comparison of the terminology of Glareanus and that common to modal theory before 1547 is:

Mode	Ecclesiastical Name	Glareanus' Name	Final	Range
I	Protus Authenticus	Dorian	d	d-d^1
II	Protus Plagius	Hypodorian	d	A-a
III	Deuterus Authenticus	Phrygian	e	e-e^1
IV	Deuterus Plagius	Hypophrygian	e	B-b
V	Tritus Authenticus	Lydian	f	f-f^1
VI	Tritus Plagius	Hypolydian	f	c-c^1
VII	Tetrardus Authenticus	Mixolydian	g	g-g^1
VIII	Tetrardus Plagius	Hypomixolydian	g	d-d^1

To these eight modes Glareanus added, in his theoretical system, the four modes:

IX		Aeolian	a	a-a^1
X		Hypoaeolian	a	e-e^1
XI		Ionian	c	c^1-c^2
XII		Hypoionian	c	g-g^1

The possible mode based upon the final b was rejected, being comprised of two imperfect tetrachords. In theory this mode bears the name Locrian.

Although adopting the general classifications of Glareanus to describe the scales of folksong, some scholars (Sharp, Bronson, Schinhan) retain the terms authentic and plagal to indicate the range of melodies.

That modal systems were of supreme importance in shaping the formal music of Western Europe before 1600 is undeniable. It is equally undeniable that this period saw the formation of the folkmusic idioms in Western Europe which were the precedents of Anglo-American folkmusic. The application of modal theory and terminology to folksong would seem to indicate that formal music exerted a strong and formulative influence on traditional music. This position is highly speculative. It is probably more accurate to speculate that the decline of formal modal music was due to an invasion of popular music or to the spirit of folksong and the growth of harmonized music.

The decline of modal music and the subsequent evolution of scales with different internal relationships and patterns of harmonic behavior established the esthetic concept of tonic or tonal center. This concept has been the shaping factor in our understanding of music for the past three hundred years. Because of this constant conditioning to a tonal center, we now hear music in terms of a tonic or key note. The concept of a tonal center, with the melodic and harmonic ramifications, is relatively new to formal music. It may be questioned that singers and musicians who have been free of formal music influence for the past three hundred years (i.e. Anglo-American traditional performers) indeed "hear" or feel the necessity of a tonal center. Vincent D'Indy stated the problem of hearing in this manner: "The idea of tonality is very subtle because of its subjective character: it changes following the difference of musical education and the degree of perfection of our understanding."

Modal theory stressed the importance of the final in shaping the character of the scale. Monody, the predominant idiom of the Middle Ages, did not require the establishment of strong tonal centers. The growth of polyphony, the changing nature of scales, and the sense of harmonic progression dictated the necessity for a tonal center. The application of these differing concepts, i.e., modality and tonality, to the study of folksong and traditional music seems historically and esthetically incongruous.

Other terminologies of Western art music theory are not applicable to Anglo-American folksong because of differences in the formal and traditional music idioms. In specifying the number of tones in a given scale, use of the Greek designations Di-, Tri-, Tetra-, etc. is frequently misleading when applied to traditional music.* These designations require the use of the qualifying suffixes -chordal and -tonic, which imply scales of consecutive diatonic degrees and scales containing intervals larger than the whole step respectively. Certain of these terms have acquired con-

---

* The scale G A C D E or any of its four possible inversions shall be termed "pentatonic." All other scales consisting of but five different tones shall be described as five-tone scales.

notations in musicology which are contradictory to the practices found in traditional music.

The above tune is comprised of a six-tone scale with the distribution:

This scale would be expressed theoretically G A B – D E F# and described as Hexatonic. This specifies a scale of six tones but implies the presence within the scale of an interval greater than a whole step, in this case the "gap" between B and D which is inferred by the term "hexatonic." However, as the tones are used in the last example, they are consecutive. The distribution or range of the six tones precludes the B to D interval. A tune containing all seven tones is theoretically Heptachordal, implying a scale of consecutive diatonic degrees. However, in the following example the seven tones are used but are distributed so as to produce a "gap" within the tune.

The seven tones of this example are not consecutive in distribution:

The description of this scale as Heptachordal is, therefore, misleading. The term Heptatonic is theoretically anomalous, implying a "gap" within a scale of seven diatonic degrees.

The use of the term "heptachordal" in this instance assumes that different octaves of the same pitch or scale tone should be treated as theoretically the same. This assumption may well be in conflict with the traditional performer's use or "idea" of the octave. We have observed while collecting in the Southern Appalachians that traditional singers never compensate for the difficulties caused by the extreme ranges of a tune by the use of an octave displacement, but continue at the original pitch level despite obvious difficulty caused by range. When the range of a tune is entirely beyond the singer's capabilities, he will stop and comment that he has "set the tune too high" or "too low." It is common for the singer to then begin again at the identical pitch level and meet with the same difficulty. Several attempts may be made before a different and more practical pitch level is found. The absence of octave transposition among Anglo-American traditional singers seems to indicate that they have a different esthetic feeling for the octave than those preconditioned to Western art music. While different octaves of tones are found and sung in traditional tunes, their placement and melodic integrity are maintained so one is not substituted for the other.

It would seem, then, that the scale of a traditional tune must be considered and expressed not only in terms of the different tones present, but also with regard to the overall range of the tune and the distribution of scale members within that range. This must include what we think of as *octave repetitions of the same pitch*.

The study of folksong and particularly Anglo-American folksong must abandon the use of theories, concepts, and terminology (such as modes, tonal centers, and musicological jargon) which in the forced application to traditional idioms results in technical, semantic, and esthetic anomalies.

In keeping with the philosophy of basing our study on recurring phenomena of folk tunes rather than using arbitrary formulae pre-set to express music of a contrasting idiom, we must accept the final tone of the tune as the most important functional tone of the scale. This tone, by the very fact that it is the final of the tune, represents to the performer the point in the scale of ultimate repose. That most editors do not accept the final as the point of ultimate repose is evidenced by the considerable number of traditional tunes described as "circular" or as "ending on" some tone not tonic. Cecil Sharp writes in the introduction to the 1917 edition of *English Folksongs from the Southern Appalachians:* "In some tunes . . . the tonic is frequently and patently *not* the final of the tune. Airs of this kind are called 'circular,' because the final phrase is fashioned so that it may lead into the initial phrase without pause or break of continuity and thus complete the melodic circle. Strictly speaking, the singer on the final repetition of a circular tune should vary the last phrase so as to conclude upon the tonic, but this singers very rarely do—No. 29A is the only tune in this collection in which this is done." It is obvious that Sharp's esthetic sense was not gratified by the general practice of the traditional singer's treatment of "circular" tunes. The shaping of a melody to provide smooth transition from stanza to stanza should not be judged as the reason for ending on a tone "patently not" the tonal center. The singers (with one exception) were satisfied with their tune ending and this is of significance.

The final tone of the folk tune will all but invariably be found to have further functional importance within the tune, usually by way of durational emphasis (or time value spent upon that tone) or numerical repetition (separate occurrences of that tone).

The vast majority of Anglo-American folk tunes have scales of five, six, or seven different pitches along with their octave forms. We must not consider octaves as the same pitch except in the most abstract description of tune scales because, as previously mentioned, the Anglo-American traditional singer preserves the integrity of the octave as a distinct melodic entity.

The five-tone scales almost always conform to the accepted definitions of the term *pentatonic;* that is, a scale having five tones within the octave arranged in intervals of one or one-and-one-half steps between adjacent tones of the scale; further, there are no two consecutive intervals of one-and-one-half steps within the octave. There are five such pentatonic scales:

g a b d e	G A B D E
a b d e g	G A C D F
b d e g a	G Bb C Eb F
d e g a b	G A C D E
e g a b d	G Bb C D F

The term *pentatonic* is meaningful to the Anglo-American traditional music idiom and will be used to describe scales which conform to one of the patterns given above. Any scale of but five tones which does not conform to these pentatonic scales may be considered simply a "five-tone" scale. *Any* scale not conforming to one of the pentatonic scales is best described for purposes of Anglo-American folk tune study as seven-tone scale, six-tone scale, etc.

Occasionally a folk tune will have, in addition to the seven degrees of the full diatonic scale, two chromatic degrees of a single scale tone, for example G A B C D E F F#. When two chromatic degrees of a tone occur within the scale of a folk tune, that tone is said to be inflected. Thus the scale quoted above is a seven-tone scale with an inflected tone (F–F#). Such inflection may be the result of inaccuracy in performance or may indicate a dual nature of that particular tune's scale. However, chromaticism or inflection is uncommon within Anglo-American folksong to such a degree that it cannot be considered idiomatic.*

Melodic Progression

The order in which the tones of a tune follow one another may be called *melodic progression*. Tunes having the same scale may have contrasting melodic progressions. While the sequence of tones within a scale is important to the tune's identity, melodic progression is not alone sufficient to establish the characteristics of a tune. As we discussed in an experimental example, there must be added to the simple progression of tones the elements of rhythm and meter. This establishes the durational and metrical importance and function of each tone within the tune. The use of a given set of tones (scale) in a specific order (melodic progression) with different durations (rhythm) and stresses (meter) establishes a tune's complete individuality.

Before discussing the results of melodic progression plus rhythm and meter, it is worthwhile to mention some aspects of melodic progression which may be considered without regard to rhythm and meter. There is the quality of Anglo-American folksong mentioned earlier—*singability*. This accounts for the great preponderancy of small, easily singable intervals in the melodic progressions of folk tunes. The small intervals of seconds (adjacent tones of a diatonic scale) and thirds (alternate tones of a diatonic scale) are in the great majority both in ascending and descending melodic progressions. The incidence of the third is especially frequent in Anglo-American folk tunes because it is inherent as adjacent tones of pentatonic and six-tone scales. The slightly larger intervals of fourths, fifths, and sixths are found with less frequency. Occasionally the octave is encountered as a melodic interval. Other more difficult intervals for the voice are quite rare.

* A high occurrence of chromaticism is idiomatic of American Negro musical idioms and has therefore exerted considerable influence upon Anglo-American folk tunes in many regions of the United States.

Contour

The next aspect of folk tunes to be considered is *contour*. While scale indicates the building blocks of which the tune is constructed and melodic progression dictates the order of their use, *contour* expresses the functional use of tones within melody. Contour indicates the relationships between the tones of the scale as they exist within a single specific tune. These internal relationships establish a pattern of tension and repose which is the essence of a tune's identity. The relationships occurring between tones may be considered in the following ways: those between tones within a single phrase, those between tones of different phrases, and finally the relationships which exist between the phrases of a tune. In this way each phrase has an expressible contour and the combinations of phrases which is the total tune has its larger and more complex contour.

Any number of songs may share identical scales without "sounding alike." On the other hand, songs with the same or similar patterns of contour will cause a response of recognition or familiarity in the listener. This recognition of similarity will occur although the variance between the scales and melodic progression of the different tunes is considerable. Contour then is the most important factor in establishing the ingredient of individuality which is necessary to memory and retention.

Just as tune finals serve as the basis for description and classification of scales, phrase finals are used as the major factor in the comparison of tune contours. In examining a wide range of traditional tunes and tune variants, it would seem that phrase finals are the most constant of the many variables in Anglo-American folk tunes. Other melodic characteristics of a tune may be altered, but so long as the phrase endings, with their patterns of tension and repose, remain unchanged, the basic flavor of the tune is retained. It may well be that this outline of phrase endings is the "germ" or melodic idea upon which the traditional performer reconstructs the tune. This would allow and account for variation within the tune without altering the pattern of the phrase endings.

The opening of the phrase seems to be the next most important characteristic. This does not necessarily mean the initial tone of each phrase. Traditional singers often "throw in" one or more notes as a pickup to the phrase proper. This note(s), frequently on the Vth degree or an anticipation of the first note of the phrase, is often sung to such words as "Oh," "Says," "Well," or "Then." These will appear and disappear from stanza to stanza and are not constant with the same informant from one performance to the next. We shall then consider the phrase opening as the first "stressed" tone of the phrase, that is, the first tone of metrical importance in the phrase.

In each phrase, the highest and lowest tones occurring between the relative constants of phrase openings and phrase finals indicate melodic shape within the phrase. Melodic progression is then of importance in forming the contour within a phrase.

We have spoken of contour as establishing a pattern of tension and repose. To be more specific, we may compare the melodic pattern or contour with the structure of folk verse. There is in Anglo-American folk verse a fixed rhyming scheme, usually occurring at the ends of lines two and four of the conventional four line stanza. This corresponds to the musical cadences or pauses which conventionally occur at the ends of the second and fourth phrases. "The mid-cadence and final cadence of a folk tune are a kind of musical rhyme ... when reinforced, as they usually are, by the cadential pause or held note, they almost automatically prompt a corresponding verbal rhyme" (Bronson: 1959, x). As the verbal rhyme brings a sense of repose and finality to the stanza, so are the melodic cadences arranged to produce tension at the mid-cadence and repose at the final cadence. This is done musically by placing a tone other than the final at the mid-cadence, the final tone representing to the traditional singer the tone of greatest repose within the scale. The most frequently found relationship between the tones of mid-cadence and final cadence is that of the perfect fifth (three and one half steps or seven semitones within the interval), the mid-cadence tone being a perfect fifth above the final of the tune. The inverted form may likewise be found in which the mid-cadence tone is a perfect fourth (two and one half steps or five semitones within the interval) below the final of the tune. While the fifth relationship and its inversion, or fourth relationship, are the most common found between mid-cadence and final cadence, the occurrence of any scale tone other than the final tone itself at mid-cadence, will provide the traditional tune with its most important pattern:

TENSION ————→ REPOSE

There exist similar, if somewhat less striking, relationships between the finals of all phrases of the tune. These relationships between phrase finals are the determining factors in this more detailed expression of a conventional tune pattern:

> *first phrase*
> Initial impression ...

>> *second phrase with mid-cadence*
>> progressing to TENSION;

>>> *third phrase*
>>> transition to

>>>> *fourth phrase with final cadence*
>>>> an approach to ultimate REPOSE.

The total of these relationships (that is, the relationship of phrase open-ing to its phrase final and the relationships between different phrases with special regard to their finals) is the essence of the traditional tune. As long as they remain unchanged or even similar, details of scale or melodic progression may vary, because of oral tradition, but the basic tune will endure and remain recognizable. The two tunes below the ballad "The House Carpenter" are from within a one mile radius in Albemarle County, Virginia. While they have different scales and melodic progressions, there is an unmistakable identity through a preservation of the internal relationships which we have called contour.

Bronson has said, "The singer 'knows the tune' and thinks he is singing it all the time" (Bronson: 1959, xxvii). It may be more specific to say that in knowing the tune the traditional singer has a preconception or memory "echo" of the tune's overall behavior, and that any addition, omission, or change of detail which does not clash with his preconcep-tion may occur either consciously or subconsciously.

Variety of Contour

There exists, even with a limited number of tones, an infinite variety of possible relationships between those tones. This is due to the variables of melodic progression and emphasis which result in a tune's contour. A melody in its movement from initial melodic interval to final resolution may take any of virtually innumerable possible paths and patterns.

Within the single phrase there are certain patterns or contours which occur and recur with unusual frequency, even among widely divergent songs. These "staple" phrase contours are musical conventions which are analogous to the textual *conventional phrase*. ("Go saddle up my milk–white steed," "He took out a wee pen knife," etc.) The following are initial phrases from divergent songs which have noticeably similar contours:

This contour pattern apparently has the same strength of identity and appeal to the traditional performer as *conventional phrase* in folk verse.

Occasionally such similarity of contour is maintained throughout the entire tune, phrase by phrase. This phenomenon corresponds somewhat to the *commonplace* in folk verse where whole identical stanzas are found in different song (cf. Chapter 2).

Those tunes which share consistent similarities of contour when found among variants of a single story verse or with widely divergent texts are called a *tune family*. The "tune family is a group of melodies showing basic interrelation by means of constant melodic correspondence, and presumably owing their mutual likeness to descent from a single air that has assumed multiple forms through processes of variation, imitation, and assimilation" (Bayard: 1950, 33).

Conceivably then, the basic musical material for not only one song or ballad with its variant forms, but for many different song groups could come from a solitary melody. This could occur only after extreme currency in oral tradition with its inevitable variations, compressions, or less frequent expansions, adaptations, conscious and unconscious deletions, additions and changes of such detail as scale, range, rhythm, and meter. Through such a process only the most stable elements of the original tune remain to cast the light of musical relationship upon its many offspring.

chapter

THE MUSICAL
FORM OF
FOLKSONG

In discussing the relationships which exist between the contours of different phrases within the total tune we lead naturally to the consideration of *form*. It has been offered as a maxim that *repetition is the essence of form*. The recurrence of details or sections within a tune, then, give it an internal unity which we call *form*. Just as the elements of scale and melodic progression were considered interdependent, so must form and contour be considered as different expressions of the same object: the traditional tune. We shall use the term *form* to designate the repetitive relationships which occur within a tune.

The musical phrase shall be the basic unit for formal analysis. The purpose of formal analysis is to illustrate graphically any repetitive relationships which occur between the phrases of a tune. This may most conveniently be done by use of capital letters to represent each phrase (cf. Appendix II). Thus the possibilities of form present with conventional four phrase tunes are:

A	A	A	A	A	A	A	A	A	A	A	A	A	A	A
A	A	A	A	B	B	B	B	A	B	B	B	B	B	B
A	A	B	B	A	A	B	B	B	B	C	C	C	A	C
A	B	B	A	A	B	A	B	C	C	A	B	C	C	D

These range from four repetitions of the same musical phrase (which is rare in Anglo-American folksong, being usually found only in children's game chants) to a tune of four contrasting musical phrases (which is quite common in Anglo-American folksong).

While musical form may be studied apart from any regard to the corresponding verse, certain formal elements of the verse are reflected in

165

the musical form of the tune. For example, there are folksongs in which identical or similar lines of text are set to equally similar musical phrases.

> Want to get your eye knocked out?
> Want to get your fill?
> Want to get your eye knocked out?
> Go down on Sugar Hill.

Here the first and third lines of text are alike and are set to two equally related musical phrases:

Frequently in folksongs having refrains, the narrative and refrain lines receive contrasting musical treatment.

In this example the narrative lines are sung to identical musical phrases while the burden is set in a contrasting manner.

	Musical Form
She took out a long yellow hair (*narrative*)	A
Little o lily in the loney (*burden*)	B
And she bound their feet so bare (*narrative*)	A
Down by the greenwood sidey (*burden*)	C

In a more extreme example the narrative lines are treated in a manner radically different from the refrains or non-narrative elements of the text. Here the narrative is chanted or virtually recited monotone while the refrain and nonsense lines are treated in a more conventional melodic fashion.

Example 9-1. The Wife in Wether's Skin – Dandoo!

	Musical Form
1. There was an old man who lived in the West,	A (chant)
Dandoo,	b (sung)
There was an old man who lived in the West,	A (chant)
To my clash a' my klingo,	c (sung)
There was an old man who lived in the West,	A (chant)
He married him a wife which he thought the best,	A' (chant)
Lingarum, lingorum, smikaroarum, kerrymingorum,	d (sung)
To my clash a' my klingo.	e (sung)

2. Now this good man came from his plow,
      Dandoo,
   Now this good man came from his plow,
      To my clash a' my klingo,
   Now this good man came from his plow,
   "Oh wife, is breakfast ready now?"
      Lingarum, lingorum, smikaroarum, kerrymingorum,
      To my clash a' my klingo.

3. "There's a piece of bread upon the shelf."
      Dandoo,
   "There's a piece of bread upon the shelf."
      To my clash a' my klingo,
   "There's a piece of bread upon the shelf.
   If you want any more, you can get it yourself."
      Lingarum, lingorum, smikaroarum, kerrymingorum,
      To my clash a' my klingo.

4. Now this good man went out to his sheep pen.
      Dandoo,
   Now this good man went out to his sheep pen.
      To my clash a' my klingo.
   Now this good man went out to his sheep pen,
   He grabbed him up an old sheep skin.
      Lingarum, lingorum, smikaroarum, kerrymingorum,
      To my clash a' my klingo.

5. He threw that skin 'round his wife's back,
      Dandoo,
   He threw that skin 'round his wife's back,
      To my clash a' my klingo,
   He threw that skin 'round his wife's back,
   And with a big stick he went whickety-whack.
      Lingarum, lingorum, smikaroarum, kerrymingorum,
      To my clash a' my klingo.

6. "I'll tell my neighbors, I'll tell my kin."
      Dandoo,
   "I'll tell my neighbors, I'll tell my kin."
      To my clash a' my klingo.
   "I'll tell my neighbors, I'll tell my kin.
   That you beat me up with a big hickory limb."
      Lingarum, lingorum, smikaroarum, kerrymingorum,
      To my clash a' my klingo.

7. "Go tell your neighbors, go tell you kin."
      Dandoo,
   "Go tell your neighbors, go tell you kin."
      To my clash a' my klingo.
   "Go tell your neighbors, go tell you kin.
   I was only tanning my old sheep skin."
      Lingarum, lingorum, smikaroarum, kerrymingorum,
      To my clash a' my klingo.

8. Ever since that time she has been a good wife,
    Dandoo,
Ever since that time she has been a good wife,
    To my clash a' my klingo,
Ever since that time she has been a good wife,
And I hope she'll be all the rest of her life.
    Lingarum, lingorum, smikaroarum, kerrymingorum,
    To my clash a' my klingo.

There are songs in which the internal relationships of the lines of text are not reflected in the tune. Rather a tune may have internal musical relationships quite independent from those of its text. For example, the song "Careless Love" * has a formal verse pattern of three line repetitions and one contrasting line to the stanza. This pattern of text is sung to a tune with a different formal organization.

This produces an interesting interworking between the individual and distinct forms of text and tune.

	Verse Form	Musical Form
Reckon what my Ma will say,	A	A
Reckon what my Ma will say,	A	B
Reckon what my Ma will say,	A	C
When she hears her girl has gone astray.	B	A

It is through such variable combinations of text and tune segments that great structural variety is possible within the relatively restricted and simple conventions of folk verse and folk tune.**

* This song has a strong Negro influence and may be of Negro origin. This is true of many songs with similar patterns of textual repetition. The ballad "Pretty Polly" has this characteristic, to a lesser degree than "Careless Love," and probably represents a midground between Negro and Anglo-American verse styles.

** The fifteen possible forms given for a four phrase tune when combined with the same fifteen possible forms for a four line stanza produce 225 possible text tune structures possible within the four line/phrase folksong convention.

Since the elements of contour and form are so bound together, with certain phrase contours recurring within a tune and therefore establishing a formal pattern, we must consider the effects of oral transmission on the total tune and on each of those components which determine contour and form. As we have seen there are phrases of a tune which occur and recur. There are also complete tunes which maintain a strong contour identity and consequently a rather stable musical form when found with widely divergent texts. By studying the changes found within these tune families we may approach the problem of the effect of memory and oral transmission on the music of folksong.

Musical Stability in Oral Tradition

In discussing the factors within melody which maintain varying degrees of stability in oral currency, we must first mention the difficulties in making unassailable conclusions and the corresponding high degree of speculation and generalizing necessary. In order to make a totally scientific and objective study of the musical memory of traditional performers and the exact nature of musical change, we would need all versions of all songs performed in a large area carefully collected and accurately transcribed. Then a study of similarities would yield the elements of melody which are most retained and memorable. However, collecting and publishing practices have put a premium on the differences found within traditional tunes. For example, a collector might record fifty versions of "Barbara Allen" in a given area. Of these, forty-nine might be so similar as to contain only slight variations. On the other hand, one tune might be totally different. In the publication of this collection we would be presented with two examples, one typical of the forty-nine examples collected and the other being the single exception to the norm. Inevitably, without proper definition of the circumstances or statistical clarification of examples, the collection gives the erroneous inference that the two tunes appear in equal occurrence. Such collecting and publishing procedures thus exaggerate the amount of variety found among traditional tunes within an area and thereby make an accurate study of the workings of oral tradition upon a melody all but impossible.

We may deduce from the preponderancy of melodies of great similarity with few recorded deviants that some tunes have a strong total stability. The tunes associated with "Lord Lovel" demonstrate this consistently minimal degree of variation.

Other songs show a strong central tradition or a predominant tune association but with separate, distinct, and vital deviations from the strong central tune. The main tune type for the ballad "The Two Sisters"

is given in Chapter 2, but there are several relatively minor departures from this tune tradition.

Other songs such as "Barbara Allen" and "The Cherry Tree Carol" show a wide divergence of tunes associated with their stories although one tune might be heavily predominant within a given region.

Within many variants of melodies all from the same tune family, whether associated with similar texts or not, there seems to be an order of stability. This pattern of change indicates not only something about the traditional performer's musical memory but also confirms the functional importance of certain elements of folksong. We have discussed that the three most important characteristics of the phrase are, in order of importance, final, phrase opening, and intermediary range. Based on these three factors we may offer the following as an order of decreasing stability of phrases within a tune family:

Initial Phrase

This seems to be the most stable phrase of a tune's history in oral currency. This is the initial musical impression of both singer and audience and serves as a stimulus to recall of subsequent phrases. In this way it equates to the performer's grasp to recall the opening words of a text, which in turn spur further recollection.

Last Phrase

This phrase is relatively set because of its functional importance in approaching ultimate repose. Certain tunes have formulae endings as well as formulae openings.

Phrase Preceding Mid-cadence

This phrase is of relative stability in its approach to the importantly functional tone at the mid-cadence.

Transitional Phrase(s)

This phrase, the third phrase of the conventional tune, is the least stable in being of neither initial impression nor strong function. It is within such phrases that melodic variation is most likely to occur.

This represents the order in which variation may most likely be expected to occur with regard to complete phrases. Since certain elements of each phrase are more stable than others we must expect exceptions to this tendency. For example, the phrase final is a more stable element than the phrase opening and we may therefore expect the final of the second phrase to be more stable than the opening of the first phrase. In considering such small segments of the total tune we might say that next to the final (which is the base of analysis and therefore theoretically without change) the next most invariable element is the tone of the mid-cadence, next the opening of the first phrase, the final of the first phrase, and so on.

There seems to be a correlation between the changes in a text and changes in a tune due to oral transmission. Certainly such happenings as forgetting and faulty hearing will affect tune in the same way as it does text by causing a severe change within the single performer. Thus a tune or text will change significantly from his hearing to his passing on of the song. Tunes will change as much in detail as texts for these reasons but the flavor or basic idea of the tune will persist simply because it is repeated with every stanza and therefore its contour becomes more imbedded in the listener's memory. So, just as a text might change in regard to detail, so may a tune change in scale or melodic progression. But, if the important events or situations of a story remain sufficiently intact to make it recognizable, the main characteristics of a tune endure.

We find throughout Anglo-American folksong: first, several tunes used with the same song–story, and second, the same tune family found with totally unrelated song–stories.

Same Song, Different Tunes

Occasionally with the same story family we find tunes so dissimilar as to cast doubt that they could have come from a common origin despite the changes of long and extensive oral currency. Such differences have been attributed to tunes of different national or regional origin associated with the same or similar stories. For example, these versions of "The Three Ravens" from England and "The Twa Corbies" from Scotland show similar story lines but are set to different tunes.

Example 9-2. The Three Ravens

1. There were three rauens sat on a tree,
     Downe a downe, hay down, hay down,
   There were three rauens sat on a tree,
     With a downe,
   There were three rauens sat on a tree,
   They were as blacke as they might be.
     With a downe derrie, derrie, derrie, downe, downe.

2. The one of them said to his mate,
     Downe a downe, hay down, hay down,
   The one of them said to his mate,
     With a downe,
   The one of them said to his mate,
   "Where shall we our breakfast take?"
     With a downe derrie, derrie, derrie, downe, downe.

3. "Downe in yonder greene field,"
     Downe a downe, hay down, hay down,
   "Downe in yonder greene field,"
     With a downe,
   "Downe in yonder greene field,
   There lies a knight slain under his shield."
     With a downe derrie, derrie, derrie, downe, downe.

4. "His hounds they lie downe at his feete,"
   Downe a downe, hay down, hay down,
   "His hounds they lie downe at his feete,"
   With a downe,
   "His hounds they lie downe at his feete,
   So well they can their master keepe."
   With a downe derrie, derrie, derrie, downe, downe.

5. "His haukes they flie so eagerly,"
   Downe a downe, hay down, hay down,
   "His haukes they flie so eagerly,"
   With a downe,
   "His haukes they flie so eagerly,
   There's no fowle dare him come nie."
   With a downe derrie, derrie, derrie, downe, downe.

6. Downe there comes a fallow doe,
   Downe a downe, hay down, hay down,
   Downe there comes a fallow doe,
   With a downe,
   Downe there comes a fallow doe,
   As great with young as she might goe.
   With a downe derrie, derrie, derrie, downe, downe.

7. She lift up his bloudy hed,
   Downe a downe, hay down, hay down,
   She lift up his bloudy hed,
   With a downe,
   She lift up his bloudy hed,
   And kist his wounds that were so red.
   With a downe derrie, derrie, derrie, downe, downe.

8. She got him up upon her backe,
   Downe a downe, hay down, hay down,
   She got him up upon her backe,
   With a downe,
   She got him up upon her backe,
   And carried him to the earthen lake.
   With a downe derrie, derrie, derrie, downe, downe.

9. She buried him before the prime,
   Downe a downe, hay down, hay down,
   She buried him before the prime,
   With a downe,
   She buried him before the prime,
   She was dead herselfe e're euen-song time.
   With a downe derrie, derrie, derrie, downe, downe.

10. God send euery gentleman
    Downe a downe, hay down, hay down,
    God send euery gentleman,
    With a downe,
    God send euery gentleman,
    Such haukes, such hounds, and such a leman.
    With a downe derrie, derrie, derrie, downe, downe.

Example 9-3. The Twa Corbies

1. As I cam' by yon auld house end
    I saw twa corbies sittin thereon,
    The tane unto t'other did say,
    "O whare sall we gae dine the day?"

2. "Where but by yon new fa'en birk,
    There, there lies a new slain knight;
    Nae mortal kens that he lies there
    But his hawks and hounds, and his layde fair.

3. "We'll sit upon his bonny breast bane,
    And we'll pick out his bonny gray een;
    We'll set our claws intil' his yellow hair
    And big our bow'r—its a' blawn bare.

4. My mother clekit me o' an egg,
    And brought me up i' the feathers gray,
    And bade me flee where'er I wad,
    For winter wad be my dying day.

5. Now winter it is come and past,
    And a' the birds are biggin' their nests,
    But I'll flee high aboon them a'
    And sing a sang for summer's sake.

In this version from recent Anglo-American tradition there is an extreme change in both degree and feeling within the text. Only the barest of similarities exists to establish its lineage from the earlier British examples cited. The tune, however, is so different from either earlier example that it would not be associated with either except for the association with its text.

Example 9-4. The Three Crows

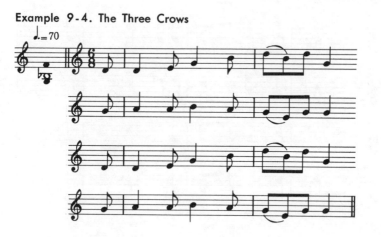

1. There was three crows on yonder's tree,
   As just as black as crows could be,
   One of them said unto his mate,
   "What shall we do for grub to eat?"

2. "There's an old dead horse in yonder's lane,
   Whose body has been lately slain,
   Let's fly up on his old breast bone,
   And peck his eyes out one by one."

3. Old satan thought to injure me,
   By cutting down his apple tree,
   But he could not injure me at all,
   For I had apples all the fall.

Just as the final stanza seems a complete intrusion upon the earlier story tradition the tune is without relationship to either of the British tunes. During the obvious changes brought about by oral transmission, exemplified by the text, the tune has become so modified that it is no longer recognizably related; or just as the final stanza intruded upon an existing tradition so a different tune may have at some point in the ballad's life become associated with the "Three Ravens"/"Twa Corbies"/"Three Crows" tradition. A less extreme example are the two tunes found with the "Springfield Mountain" examples of Chapter Seven. Here the two tunes might well have evolved from a common source but the differences between them are equatable to the varied detail and emotional content of the two texts.

Same Tune, Different Songs

The same tune or tune contour may be found with widely differing song texts and stories. This may occur because of one of the following: a singer using one tune to set more than one song/story within his repertoire; the conscious use of a pre–existing tune to set newly composed words; the unconscious reliance on a traditional contour pattern in the creation of a new song; the free exchange or borrowing of tunes which "fit" different tunes. The learning of songs from printed or written sheets has certainly been the greatest force in causing a variety of tunes to become associated with individual songs.

It is not uncommon for a traditional performer to have a "favorite tune" to which he is inclined to sing more than one song.

Careless Love

O, once I wore my apron low,
He followed me thru frost and snow.
But now I wear it to my chin
He passes by but he don't call in.

Butcher Boy

O Jersey City where I onc't dwelled
A pretty little boy that I knew well
He courted me my heart away
And then with me he would not stay.

This common tune is often coupled with such a well-known song as "Careless Love," or even more usually, with "The Butcher Boy." This seems to be an instance of an individual singer using the same tune for more than one song since the melody is not commonly associated with the tradition of both songs. Occasionally tunes unmistakably from the same tune family are associated with more than one specific song tradition. Such tune sharing is found between the song traditions of "The Wagoner's Lad" (Old Smokey) and "Little Mohee," "Villikens and his

Dinah" and "Sweet Betsy from Pike," or "Wayfaring Stranger" and "Fair and Tender Ladies."

The conscious use of an old and perhaps familiar tune as a vehicle for a new story/verse has always been the stock in trade of the broadside ballad-maker. Similar use of known tunes by traditional bards or even commercially inspired writers has been responsible for the dualities of tune traditions such as "Wagoner's Lad" and "Little Mohee."

A similar multiple use of a tune occurs when a song is "reworked" by a traditional performer. Such reworking is almost always restricted to the words, thus resulting in the continuance of a tune tradition with a new text association. Such alteration or reworking of a song can vary greatly in results from outright parody to a complete reshaping of the meaning and emotional context of a song. Here the traditional song "There's More Pretty Girls than One" has been totally reworked to present a radically different mood and meaning while utilizing the same tune.

> Little girl you turned me down
> You left me all alone.
> I'm a' leaving you with a lonesome song
> To sing when I am gone.
>
> There's more pretty girls than one,
> There's more pretty girls than one,
> Wherever I ramble 'round
> There's more pretty girls than one.
>
> Mama told me last night,
> She give me good advice,
> She told me to stop my rambling 'round
> And marry me a wife.
>
> There's more pretty girls than one,
>   etc.

This song sung to the tune:

is here totally reworked and sung to the same tune:

'Tis the lowly Lamb of God
That is my heart's delight.
I love him more than all this world
He saved me from death's night.

There's no savior but one,
There's no savior but one,
Jesus Christ the son of God,
He is the only one.

When I'm degraded by the world
It's just a crown of thorns.
I think God's smile is well worthwhile
I have no worldly charm.

There's no savior but one,
                etc.

At times a "new" song appears in tradition which seems to bear no direct relationship in story or music to earlier songs. However the strength and vitality of the prevalent style will so shape it that it becomes stylistically indistinguishable. This will happen without the creator's conscious intent by the use of conventional phrases or accepted language patterns and by the use of scales and contours within the traditional idiom. Such a song is "Across the Blue Mountain" (see pp. 14–16). While a product of original and rather recent balladry, it relies upon and is largely composed of conventional phrases and epithets; "One morning, one morning, one morning in May," "me and my love to part," etc. So, too, is the tune undeniably bound to the local folksong idioms and style. Probably without the conscious knowledge of either the creator of the ballad or of the many singers who have passed it along, it possesses a pattern of contour which is almost identical with the strong tune tradition associated with that song which shares riddles with "Captain Wedderburn's Courtship" sung throughout the Southern Appalachians called "The Riddle Song."

Blue Mountain   **Riddle Song**

There is within Anglo-American folksong the undeniable and equally unexplainable phenomenon of tune borrowing, that is the apparently free exchange of a given tune from one body of songs to another body of songs. It is often impossible to state positively in what direction a tune travels unless it is traditionally associated with a specific song and this association is verifiable at an earlier time than the existence of later songs to which the tune is sung. One assumes that tunes are passed from "older" to "younger" songs but this is not so consistently provable as to set up a rule. Here are two versions of the same tune found in tradition with "Fair Margaret and Sweet William," a ballad of considerable age, and "The Drunkard's Courtship." Since this tune is not a part of the most common tradition of "Fair Margaret and Sweet William," it may be an example of an "old" song borrowing its tune from a "young" song.

Here the tunes are identical except for the modifications, in the form of repeated phrases, made necessary by the extension of one line in "The Drunkard's Courtship" (see p. 118). Thus the two songs share the same tune with slight rearranging of phrases which results in the following forms:

"Fair Margaret and Sweet William"	"The Drunkard's Courtship"
A	A
A'	A'
B	A
C	B
	C

Tune borrowing may, in some cases, be the result of a singer's forgetting one tune and simply substituting another tune which "fits." Such tune borrowing or substituting is probably most frequent among songs which have no single strong tune tradition: that is, a story-song which a person from a folk community might hear sung to different tunes at different times thereby causing an element of flexibility to enter the memory process. It is upon such story-songs as this that a different and previously unassociated tune might most easily intrude. Here are three examples of "The Gypsy Laddie" collected within a small area of central Virginia. It is obvious from the differences in texts and tunes that no strong single tradition existed for this ballad in that area.

Example 9-5. Gypsy Davey

1. Young Gypsy Davey came merrily by
    Whistling loud and gaily,
    He whistled and sang till the green wood rang.
    Charmed the heart of a lady.

2. Merrily down the castle stair
    Came this fair young lady.
    In her hand so fine was a glass of wine,
    To drink a health to Davey.

3. Her Ingram Lord came home that night,
    Inquiring for his lady,
    The waiting maid cried, as she replied,
    "She's gone with the Gypsy Davey."

4. "Oh, saddle with speed my milk-white steed,
    Quickly make him ready,
    I will ride this night, till the broad daylight,
    Till I overtake my lady."

5. He rode that night, he rode next day,
    Till he come to the banks of the river.
    On the other side his wife he spied,
    Beside her gypsy lover.

6. "Turn back, turn back my own fair one,
   Turn back to your home and baby,
   How can you roam from your fair home,
   To follow a gypsy laddie?"

7. "I won't turn back, I shan't turn back,
   For neither lord nor baby.
   I would give your home and the rest you own,
   For one sweet kiss from Davey."

8. "Last night on a bed of down you lay,
   Your baby lay by you.
   Tonight you will lay on the cold, cold clay,
   With the gypsy lad beside you."

9. "I won't turn back, I shan't turn back,
   For all your words of honey.
   I wouldn't give a kiss from the Gypsy's lips,
   For all your land and money."

10. "Take off, take off your costly glove,
    That's made of Spanish leather.
    Your hand I will grasp in a farewell clasp,
    'Twill be farewell, forever."

Example 9-6. Gypsy Laddie O

1. It was late in the night when the Captain came home,
   Inquiring for his honey, O.
   The reply that was made unto you, my love,
   She's gone with the gypsies and the laddie, O.

2. "Saddle up, saddle up my milk-white grey,
   Saddle up, saddle up in a hurry, O.
   I will ride all night till the broad daylight,
   Till I overtake my honey, O."

3. He rode to the east and he rode to the west,
   And he rode till he came to Baltimore.
   And there he met with his prettly little Miss,
   A' going with the gypsies and the laddie, O.

4. "Here come and go along with me,
   You'll never be lacking for money, O.
   I'll lock you up in a chamber so high,
   That the gypsies nor the laddie won't come a'nigh."

5. "I won't go back nor I shan't go back,
   No I won't go back, my husband, O.
   For I wouldn't give a kiss from a gypsy boy's lips,
   For all your house and money, O."

6. "It's how can you leave your house and money,
   Or how can you leave your husband, O.
   Oh how can you leave your tender little baby,
   And go with the gypsies and the laddie, O?"

7. "I can leave my house and money,
   Or I can leave my husband, O.
   Or I can leave my tender little baby,
   And go with the gypsies and the laddie, O."

8. "Oh once you get used to a good feather bed,
   And now you get used to another one,
   And now you get used to an old tornbed,
   With the gypsies and the laddie all around you."

Example 9-7 Gypsy Laddie

1. Yes sir, the gypsies in the North
   They're bound unto Sweet Bosley-O
   They'll sing to you such a beautiful song
   It'll charm the heart of a lady-O.

2. 'Twas late in the night when the captain came home
    A-quiring for his honey-O
    The servant miss replied to him,
    "She's gone with the gypsy's laddie-O."

3. "Saddle up, saddle up my milk-white steed,
    Saddle up, saddle up in a hurry-O.
    I'll ride all night till the broad daylight
    Till I overtake my honey-O.

4. He rode to the east and he rode to the west
    And he rode on to Sweet Bosley-O
    And there he spied his own true love
    A-going with the gypsy's laddie-O.

5. "Come back, come back my own true love,
    Come back, come back, my honey-O.
    I'll lock you up in the chamber so high
    The gypsies can't come a-nigh you."

6. "I won't come back nor I shan't come back
    I won't come back my husband-O.
    I'd rather have a kiss from the gypsy's lips
    Than all of your land and your money-O."

7. "Oh how can you leave your house and land,
    Oh how can you leave your husband-O,
    Oh, how can you leave your sweet little babes
    To go with the gypsy's laddie-O?"

8. "Oh, I can leave my house and land,
    And I can leave my husband-O,
    Yes I can leave my sweet little babes
    To go with the gypsy's laddie-O."

9. She hadn't been a-travelling but a very short while
    Before she spend all of her money-O.
    She spent the gold rings off of her fingers,
    The breast pins off of her bosom-O.

10. It was once she was used to a good feather bed
    And also a parlor-O.
    But now she's come to a bed of hay,
    The gypsies lay all around her.

The last version above shows a case of unmistakable tune borrowing in its extremely similar melody with a tradition of the ballad "Edward" as sung in the Southern Appalachian Mountains.

Such borrowing of tunes from one song tradition to another is observable even in instances where one song, as is the case with "Edward" above, is not found in the same area.

AFTERWORD

We have attempted to sketch out some of the larger stylistic features of the Anglo-American folksong style in this work. Our idea has been to introduce the student and the folksong enthusiast to some of the facets of an oral art. It is our hope that this book will not only serve as a textbook but will also stimulate further examination of this tradition in its cultural context. Because of this, it seems more important than usual to point out what we have not done in this book, why, and what areas of investigation seem most important for the immediate future.

Two of the most obvious omissions here have been songs of license: bawdy and obscene materials and children's songs. The former has not been explored because we know so little about the subject. Collectors have tended to shy away from such material even if it was offered to them, but our field experience has shown us that, for most traditional singers, obscene materials are the smallest part of the repertoire. What we have collected and what we have been able to see of the collections of others have convinced us that there are few songs which glorify love while describing its enactment in North American tradition. Most obscene songs, like "The Five Nights Drunk," seem anti-erotic and castratory; this is especially true of such bawdy classics as "The Sea Crab," which facetiously describes what happens when a man brings a crab home and puts it in the chamberpot.

Even more obvious in its omission is children's material, especially lullabies, nonsense songs, children's parodies, and singing games. All of the problems in the study of oral transmission regarding verbal mutations and distortions of meaning are magnified in the folklore made up by, or taken over by, children. Those changes brought about by misunderstanding and substitution discussed earlier are more abrupt, severe, and bizarre in the hands of children with their undeveloped language skills.

A large part of the traditional repertoire of children consists of motion-oriented songs, such as singing games, and the more recent jump-rope and handclapping games. This material is part of the larger problem of song-dance which has only been lightly touched upon in the later chapters.

The major forms of adult song-dance entertainments are hoedowns and play-party games. The latter are, like children's games, designed to be sung by the participants while dancing; the directions are sometimes given in the song, sometimes simply known to all the dancers. The play-party is a purely vocal idiom in most communities—done without instrumental accompaniment. The rhythmic emphasis required for the play-party is frequently enhanced by hand-clapping, foot-stomping, etc. (The fullest treatment of the play-party is Ben A. Botkin, *The American Play-Party.*)

The hoedown, on the other hand, is primarily an instrumental idiom, utilizing from one instrument (fiddle or banjo, generally) to a group of instruments, often called a "string band." Whatever singing is done is incidental to the dancing and is usually injected by an instrumentalist for humorous purposes. Consequently, the sequence of stanzas of such songs is not fixed. The songs which emerge from this activity are made up of stanzas related thematically, the theme generally suggested by the title of the tune—like "Old Joe Clark," "Cumberland Gap," "Cripple Creek," "Ida Red," etc. These stanzas are sung in random order usually, separated by instrumental renditions of the tune. In this manner the lengths of the songs are set not by any story but rather by the length of the dance. The singer is free to sing as many or as few stanzas as he cares to. This kind of song seems to have encouraged improvised stanzas on local situations and characters. This is one of the few traditions of improvised song in the Anglo-American culture.

Because a musician of reliable skills was a necessary prerequisite to the square dance, this idiom prompted the growth of a semi-professional and even a wholly professional folk-musician class. Good instrumentalists, some paid, some not, would be called upon by a much larger community than his immediate neighbors—such groups as "Wizard Oil Shows"—but the music they played remained traditional for the most part, and their audience was primarily rural. This movement encouraged ensemble playing and the organization of bands, which eventually evolved into a traditional style of ensemble playing. This essentially popular form was given tremendous impetus by the new media of radio and phonograph recordings. This style, with addition of singing, has remained the backbone of the American commercial country music sound. For this reason, many of the conclusions which we have made concerning the make-up of Anglo-American songs is still applicable to composed country music.

The same may be said about the country music performer. He developed his skills out of a similar traditional background, utilizing a traditional style of song presentation and expanding upon the traditional role of the local songmaker or "musicianer." Though D. K. Wilgus has written of one of these songmakers, Rev. Andrew Jenkins ("The Rationalistic Approach" in *A Good Tale And A Bonnie Tune*) and the *Journal of American Folklore* has recently devoted an issue to American Country Music (Vol. 78, No. 309), a great deal more work needs to be done in describing traditional performance styles and tracing their development into contemporary country music.

Furthermore, little work has been done on the role of the creative performer or the local songmaker in the tradition-oriented community (as opposed to the great number of studies of Negro performers). Unique in this regard is Edward Ives' *Larry Gorman*, a study of a satirical songwriter from lumberjack country, Maine and the Canadian Maritime Provinces. There have been a number of studies of individual performers written as accompanying notes for recordings, a number of which are included in the Discography.

Equally neglected has been a description of the tradition-oriented community itself and an analysis of its use of folklore in its day-to-day existence. Such studies as those by Jean Thomas and Jean Ritchie, though engaging and entertaining, tend to be both sentimentalized and overly self-conscious. Because of the lack of such studies, we have not been able to make generalizations concerning the social role of the musician or the social uses of the songs. We do not yet know whether it is significant that there have a great many more women informants than men encountered by collectors. This may have had a profound influence upon the total repertoire, as well as upon the themes which have become conventionalized and the attitudes which have become embodied. That such differences may be important has been hinted at in the discussion about the heroic values introduced into the occupational songs.

Another dimension of the problem of the relation between attitude and theme is encountered in the religious song traditions, which we have also not dealt with extensively. Religious revival movements have made a significant impact on the cultural life of rural America. Various denominations and myriad splinter-sects have given rise to a wide spectrum of music and attitudes toward music. This ranges from the prohibition of all music to the creation of whole corpora of songs which were written for special ceremonial purposes, and which have relied upon oral transmission and what might be termed "folk composition." The relationships between one large group of religious songs found in shape-note hymnals and secular tunes has been investigated at length by George Pullen Jackson; these studies emphasize the symbiotic relation, especially in the area of tunes, between secular and spiritual traditions. The spiritual singing was probably the first direct use of polyphonic (harmonized) singing as a traditional idiom in white rural communities. Certain styles of harmonized hymn-singing were probably the progenitors of secular professional country music and singing family idioms of the late 19th and early 20th centuries. In some religious sects rather exotic song and performance techniques developed, such as the hymn lining-out tradition which provides a bridge between the Anglo-American and the Afro-American traditions (especially in regard to the relation between call and response). These reflect some of the positive and creative aspects of the interplay between secular and religious song traditions. On the negative side are those fundamentalist attitudes which have viewed the singing of secular songs or the playing of instruments with dancing as sinful. In some regions this has been so extreme that it has brought a complete halt to the secular folksong tradition.

Finally, in regard to totally musical considerations, we have not been able to discuss a number of potentially fruitful topics. As we pointed out, there has been a tremendous amount of influence upon Anglo-American song style from the Negro musical idioms. There also may have been important influences from other ethnic groups, such as the Pennsylvania German, who almost certainly introduced the plucked dulcimer into Anglo-American communities. Further, we do not know exactly how most of the other instruments were introduced into this tradition, nor what effect their techniques of playing had on the singing style which arose when folksongs came to be accompanied by the instruments.

It is clear, then, that there are a great many untapped areas of investigation for the student to think about when he begins collecting. In an attempt to facilitate the further study of Anglo-American folksong, we are including a number of appendices and bibliographical aids which are intended to suggest further ways of pursuing the study of Anglo-American folksongs.

CHAPTER
REFERENCES

Chapter One

The nature of the relationship between oral and written litera-
tures has received a great deal of critical attention in the last few years.
The seminal works in this field have dealt primarily with the longer
poetic forms, epic and romance, in which one can see a transition occurring from basically oral renderings to those which are self-consciously
literary. The most ambitious of these works is *The Growth of Literature*
by H. M. and N. K. Chadwick. The work which has created the greatest
critical impact is Albert B. Lord's *The Singer of Tales*. Taking ideas and
materials from the work of Milman Parry, Lord's work is concerned with
the formulaic nature of epic composition, especially in regard to Jugo-
slavian and Homeric epics. Similar compositional techniques have been
observed in a number of other traditional song forms (see, for instance,
the excellent study of the lyrics of a Dravidian group, Murray B. Emeneau, "Oral Poets of South India—The Todas"). Numerous studies, utilizing the Parry-Lord thesis, have been made in relation to the compositional elements of belleletristic works; each new one surveys most of the
past scholarship in proper academic fashion. Perhaps the most recent is
Larry D. Benson, "The Literary Character of Anglo-Saxon Formulaic
Poetry." An extremely important work on the distinction between written
and oral epic is C. S. Lewis, *A Preface to Paradise Lost*. Another
important work, tangential to the subject of the art of folksong, is Axel
Olrik's "Epic Laws of Folk Narrative," in Alan Dundes' *The Study of
Folklore*.

The works of greatest pertinence to the present discussion come from
ballad scholarship. Throughout Gordon Hall Gerould's *The Ballad of*

Tradition one finds insight into the art of balladry, but of special interest is Chapter One, "The Nature of Balladry." MacEdward Leach has also done much to anatomize the art of the ballad; for his ideas, see his introduction to *The Ballad Book*, and his definition of the ballad in *The Standard Dictionary of Folklore, Mythology, and Legend*. His most extensive statement of the art of folksong is found in his article, "The Singer or the Song," in *Singers and Storytellers*. Albert B. Friedman's brief remarks at the beginning of his introduction to *The Viking Book of Folk Ballads of the English-Speaking World* are also valuable. Tristram P. Coffin's work in the esthetics of folksong has been consistently pioneering, though he occasionally insists on using the criteria of sophisticated poetry for a judgment of folksong. See especially his " 'Mary Hamilton' and the Anglo-American Ballad as Art Form."

Behind the distinction between folk, popular, and sophisticated culture lies a huge corpus of scholarship, folkloristic and anthropological. One of the major problems of folklore studies has been the definition of the term "folk," as well as the effective description of the differences between a pre-literate (primitive or aboriginal) group, and a non-literate (generally peasant) community. Since both have predominantly oral expression for their literature, both have been referred to as "folk" communities. Folklorists usually reserve this word for peasant or rural groups who live alongside a dominant city culture, and anthropologists have often concurred in this use of the word. However, it follows that a group which has folklore should be called "folk" and one prominent anthropologist, Robert Redfield, has used the term to refer to a complex of culture traits most fully represented by aboriginal peoples. The term has, in fact, become so muddled that anthropologists tend today to shun its use as a categorical word completely. George M. Foster's article, "What Is Folk Culture?" is a splendid review of Redfield's ideas and contains some thoughtful suggestions of his own.

Chapter Two

For a brief and objective reading of recent scholarship concerning variation (to 1958), see D. K. Wilgus' *Anglo-American Folksong Scholarship Since 1898*. The introduction to Tristram P. Coffin's *The British Traditional Ballad in North America* brings together many ideas presented in the past and argues some new ones. Stanley Edgar Hyman's "The Child Ballad in America," makes critical conclusions on the basis of Coffin's data. Douglas J. McMillan's recent article, "A Survey of Theories Concerning the Oral Transmission of the Traditional Ballad," divides the scholars into three camps in regard to attitude toward oral transmission: those who see the process as totally degenerative, those who regard it as regenerative, and those who see it as both. Coffin's most extensive statement of the concept of "emotional core" is contained in the article " 'Mary Hamilton' and the Anglo-American Ballad as Art Form," reprinted in his book cited above. Another important discussion by him is "The Problem of Ballad-Story Variation and Eugene Hahn's 'The Drowsy Sleeper'." The chapter in Gordon Hall Gerould's *The Ballad of Tradition* on ballad variation is, as always in that work, intelligent and informative. An important early treatise on the subject is John Robert Moore, "The Influence of Transmission on the English Ballads." With regard to the effect of intelligence and print on oral traditions, the note by Fannie Hardy Eckstorm and Phillips Barry, "What Is Tradition?" in the *Bulletin of the Folksong Society of the Northeast* is short but informative in outlining the problems in the complex study of song traditions. Also important in respect to the effect of printed texts on tradition is W. Edson Richmond's "Some Effects of Scribal and Typographical Error on Oral Tradition." Studies of changes in individual songs are listed and commented upon in Wilgus, pp. 284–317. Those of interest in regard to songs mentioned in this chapter, not found in Wilgus, are George D. Foss, "More on a Unique and Anomalous Version of 'The Two Sisters'," the introduction to G. Malcolm Laws' *American Balladry from British Broadsides;* and Reed Smith, *South Carolina Ballads.* Wilgus has given a portrait of a ballad composer for commercial records the Rev. Andrew Jenkins, in "The Rationalistic Approach," *A Good Tale and a Bonnie Tune.* Keneth S. Goldstein has documented "The Unfortunate Rake" tradition, Folkways Record 2305, through many stages of recomposition. His notes to the album are justifiably celebrated. Also notable is the record of multiple versions of "Barbara Allen" edited for the Library of Congress by Charles Seeger, as well as the article by Ed Cray contained in *Folklore International.*

Chapters Three and Four

This discussion has not taken into account the vast scholarship on the emergence of the ballad and allied forms in terms of meter and stanzaic arrangement. This antiquarian problem was one of the many explored in the controversy between the communalist and individualist theories of ballad composition. For a recapitulation of these wars, see Wilgus, *Anglo-American Folksong Scholarship Since 1898*, Chapters One and Two. These controversies led to a few objective treatments of the problem of analyzing the meters of folksongs, usually in regard to the ones in the Child canon. The most important of these are: J. W. Hendren,

A Study of Ballad Rhythm; and George E. Stewart, Jr., "The Meter of the Popular Ballad." Both develop on the dipodic arrangement. An extension of this idea, but in more than English language folksong and in terms of units of meaning as well as metrical units is Américo Parédes, "Some Aspects of Folk Poetry." Bertrand H. Bronson has studied the different songs in the "Captain Kidd" family, in "Samuel Hall's Family Tree." The importance of formula and repetition is testified to by virtually every commentator on folk composition. Especially interesting in this regard are Axel Olrik, "The Epic Laws of Oral Narrative," and C. M. Bowra, *Primitive Song,* Chapter Three.

Chapter Six

The discussion here in regard to the Child ballads in America is primarily based upon materials in Tristram P. Coffin, *The British Traditional Ballad in North America.* For a further documentation and discussion, see Roger D. Abrahams, "Patterns of Structure and Role Relationship in the Child Ballads in the United States." Of additional interest are the brief remarks in the introduction to Albert B. Friedman, *The Viking Book of Folk Ballads of the English-Speaking World,* and the introduction to Alan Lomax's *Folksongs of North America* and his article "Folksong Style." The information on American broadsides and native American songs comes primarily from G. Malcolm Laws' two works, *American Balladry from British Broadsides* and *Native American Balladry.* For regional collections and occupational songs, see the listings in Appendix IV.

Chapter Seven

Wilgus, 268–270, mentions the important studies of ballad meter to 1959. These include those of George R. Stewart, Jr., recently reprinted conveniently in *The Critics and The Ballad,* and J. W. Hendred's *A Study of Ballad Rhythm.* Gerould's section on the subject still seems a well-balanced introduction, pp. 124–130. Bronson's article "The Interdependence of Text and Tune" makes significant observations concerning the various elements of poetic and musical meter. A development of these ideas in this chapter shows a correlation between the formal construction of tune and verse. Of interest might be a comparison of the varied styles used by musical editors and transcribers in various standard collections. Of particular note are the transcriptions of Cecil Sharp, Ernest Mead, and A. K. Davis in *More Traditional Ballads of Virginia,* and Jan Schinhan in Vols. IV and V of *The Frank C. Brown Collection.*

The discussion by Béla Bartók, in Alfred Lord's *Serbo-Croatian Folksongs* is especially meaningful in its treatment of *parlando* and full metrical styles, and his principles may be liberally applied to many Anglo-American narrative song styles. Because of the variance in transcription style and accuracy, it is important for the student to consult and listen closely to the many available oral sources on phonograph. For some of these see the Discography. Of particular help in this regard are those recordings that also have transcriptions available (such as those in Bronson, *The Traditional Tunes of the Child Ballads*, taken from various recordings, especially those issued by the Archive of Folksong in the Library of Congress).

Chapters Eight and Nine

In the formation of meaningful conclusions about the nature or "stuff" of folk tunes it is of primary importance to have available a corpus of material of such size that a survey of it will evolve generalities and detect exceptions and peculiarities. Such a study has been tremendously aided by the yet incomplete *The Traditional Tunes of the Child Ballads* of Bertrand H. Bronson. Here in one convenient source the student may examine all significant variants from printed and oral sources of American Child Ballads and their British forerunners and counterparts. Other collections which provide more than one example of songs and thereby facilitate tune comparison are *English Folksongs Sung in the Southern Appalachians* by Cecil Sharp, *The Frank C. Brown Collection of North Carolina Folklore, More Traditional Ballads of Virginia* by A. K. Davis, and a number of other regional collections referred to in the Bibliography.

Of further interest to the student is a survey of various esthetic, technical, and analytical approaches to the musical faults of Anglo-American folksong specifically and traditional song in general. For these, examine Samuel Bayard, "Prolegomena to a Study of the Principal Melodic Families of Folk Song," reprinted in *The Critics and the Ballad;* Jan Schinhan introduction to *Music of the Ballads* and *Music of the Songs, Frank C. Brown Collection of North Carolina Folklore;* Cecil Sharp, *English Folksong: Some Conclusions;* and with Maud Karpeles the introduction to *English Folksongs Sung in the Southern Appalachians, Vol. I.;* Bruno Nettle's introduction in Helen H. Flanders' *Ancient Ballads Traditionally Sung in New England.*

Dealing with idioms outside the scope of this text but of prime interest in demonstrating the formulation of new or modified techniques specifically designed to define and express traditional idioms is Béla Bartók in Alfred Lord's collection, *Serbo-Croatian Folk Songs.*

REFERENCES

Abrahams, Roger D.
  1966   "Patterns of Structure and Role Relationship in the Child Ballads in the United States," *Journal of American Folklore,* 79, pp. 448–462.

Bartók, Béla
  1951   *Serbo-Croatian Folksongs.* New York: Columbia University Press.

Bayard, Samuel
  1950   "Prolegomena to a Study of the Principal Melodic Families of Folk Song," *Journal of American Folklore,* 63, pp. 1–44.

Benson, Larry D.
  1966   "The Literary Character of Anglo-Saxon Formulaic Poetry." *Publications of the Modern Language Association,* LXXXI, pp. 334–341.

Bowra, C. M.
  1962   *Primitive Song.* Cleveland: The World Publishing Company.

Bronson, Bertrand
  1942   "Samuel Hall's Family Tree," *California Folklore Quarterly,* I, pp. 47–64.

———
  1944   "The Interdependence of Text and Tune," *California Folklore Quarterly,* III, pp. 185–207.

———
  1958–   *The Traditional Tunes to the Child Ballads.* Princeton: Princeton University Press.

Brown
  1952–   *The Frank C. Brown Collection of North Carolina Folklore.* Vols.
  1965   IV & V, Durham, N.C.: Duke University.

Chadwick, H. M. and N. K.
1932–   *The Growth of Literature.* Cambridge, Mass.: Harvard University
1940   Press.

Coffin, Tristram P.
1950   "The Problem of Ballad-Story Variation and Eugene Hahn's 'The
          Drowsy Sleeper,'" *Southern Folklore Quarterly,* Vol. 14, pp. 87–96.

———
1957   "Mary Hamilton and the Anglo-American Ballad as Art Form,"
          Journal of American Folklore, Vol. 70, pp. 87–96.

———
1963   *The British Traditional Ballad in North America.* Philadelphia:
          American Folklore Society.

———
1964   "On a Peak in Massachusetts: the Literary and Aesthetic Ap-
          proach," *A Good Tale and A Bonnie Tune,* pp. 201–209. Dallas:
          Southern Methodist University.

Davis, A. K.
1964   *More Traditional Ballads of Virginia* (musical ed., Ernest Mead).
          Chapel Hill: University of North Carolina.

Eckstorm, Fannie Hardy, and Phillips Barry
1930   "What Is Tradition?" *Bulletin of the Folk-Song Society of the
          Northeast,* No. 1, pp. 2–3.

Emeneau, Murray B.
1958   "Oral Poets of South India—The Todas," *Journal of American Folk-
          lore,* 71, pp. 312–324.

Flanders, Helen H.
1960–   *Ancient Ballads Traditionally Sung in New England.* Philadelphia:
1965   University of Pennsylvania.

Foss, George D.
1965   "More on a Unique and Anomalous Version of 'The Two Sisters,'"
          Southern Folklore Quarterly, Vol. 28, pp. 119–133.

Foster, George M.
1953   "What Is Folk Culture?" *American Anthropologist,* Vol. 55, pp.
          159–173.

Friedman, Albert B.
1956   *The Viking Book of Folk Ballads of the English-Speaking World.*
          pp. ix–x. New York: The Viking Press, Inc.

Gerould, Gordon Hall
1932   *The Ballad of Tradition.* Oxford: Oxford University Press, Inc.

Goldstein, Kenneth S.
          "The Unfortunate Rake," Folkways Record 2305.

Hendren, J. W.
1936   *A Study of Ballad Rhythm with Special Reference to Ballad Music.*
          Princeton: Princeton University Press.

Hyman, Stanley Edgar
1957   "The Child Ballad in America," *Journal of American Folklore,* Vol. 70, pp. 235–239.

Krehbiel, Henry E.
1914   *Afro-American Folk Songs.* New York: G. Schirmer, Inc.

Laws, G. Malcolm
1957   *American Balladry from British Broadsides.* Philadelphia: American Folklore Society.

_____
1964   *Native American Balladry.* Philadelphia: American Folklore Society.

Leach, MacEdward
1949   *The Standard Dictionary of Folklore, Mythology, and Legend,* ed. Maria Leach. New York: Funk & Wagnalls Co., Vol. 1, p. 106.

_____
1955   *The Ballad Book.* New York: Harper & Row, Publishers.

Leach, MacEdward and T. P. Coffin
1961   *The Critics and The Ballad.* Carbondale, Ill.: Southern Illinois University.

_____
1961   "The Singer or the Song," *Singers and Storytellers.* Dallas: Southern Methodist University, pp. 30–45.

Lewis, C. S.
1942   *A Preface to Paradise Lost.* London: Oxford University Press.

Lomax, Alan
1959   "Folksong Style," *American Anthropologist,* Vol. 61, 927–954.

_____
1960   *Folksongs of North America.* Garden City, N.Y.: Doubleday & Co., Inc.

Lord, Albert B.
1960   *The Singer of Tales.* Cambridge, Mass.: Harvard University Press.

McMillan, Douglas J.
1964   "A Survey of Theories Concerning the Oral Transmission of the Traditional Ballad," *Southern Folklore Quarterly,* Vol. 28, pp. 299–309.

Moore, John Robert
1916   "The Influence of Transmission on the English Ballads," *Modern Language Review,* Vol. 11, pp. 386 ff.

Olrik, Axel
1965   "Epic Laws of Folk Narrative," *The Study of Folklore,* ed. Alan Dundes, pp. 28–141. Englewood Cliffs, N.J.: Prentice-Hall, Inc.

Paredes, Américo
1964   "Some Aspects of Folk Poetry," *Texas Studies in Literature and Language,* VI, 213–225.

Richmond, W. Edson

    1951   "Some Effects of Scribal and Typographical Error on Oral Tradition," *Southern Folklore Quarterly*, Vol. 15, pp. 159–169.

Seeger, Charles

    "Versions and Variants of 'Barbara Allen,'" Library of Congress Recording AAFSL54.

Sharp, Cecil

    English Folksongs: Some Conclusions. London: Oxford University Press, 1907.

Sharp, Cecil, and Maud Karpeles

    1932   *English Folksongs Sung in the Southern Appalachians*, Vol. 1. London: Oxford University Press.

Smith, Reed

    1928   *South Carolina Ballads*. Cambridge, Mass.: Harvard University Press.

Stewart, George E., Jr.

    1925   "The Meter of the Popular Ballad," *Publications of Modern Language Association*, 60, 933 *ff*.

Wilgus, D. K.

    1959   *Anglo-American Folksong Scholarship Since 1898*. New Brunswick, N.J.: Rutgers University.

    ————

    1964   "The Rationalistic Approach," *A Good Tale and A Bonnie Tune*. pp. 227–237. Dallas: Southern Methodist University.

    ————

    1967   *Folklore International*. (ed.) Hatboro, Pa.: Folklore Associates.

SOURCES OF SONGS

Examples

1–1	Earl Brand	Robert Shiflett, Brown's Cove, Va., 1961.
1–2	Nottalin Town	Beckham Ritchie, Carrie, Ky., 1962.
2–1	Across the Blue Mountain	Florence Shiflett, Wyatt's Mountain, Va., 1962.
2–2	Across the Blue Mountain	David Morris, Wyatt's Mountain, Va., 1962.
2–3	Across the Blue Mountain	Effie Morris, Shiflett Hollow, Va., 1962.
2–4	Across the Blue Mountain	Marybird McAllister, Brown's Cove, Va., 1962.
2–5	The Two Sisters	Mildred Creighton, Carrie, Ky., 1962.
2–6	The Two Sisters (Wind and Rain)	Dan Tate, Fancy Gap, Va., 1962.
2–7	The House Carpenter	Robert Shiflett, Brown's Cove, Va., 1961.
2–8	Lost Jimmy Whalen	Helen Creighton, *Maritime Folksongs*, p. 115.
2–9	Fair Florella/Pearl Bryan	Virgil Sturgill, Ashland, Ky., 1958.
3–1	The Unquiet Grave	Mrs. Rosie White, Sandy Cove, Newfoundland, 1929. Greenleaf and Mansfield, *Ballads and Sea Songs of Newfoundland*, p. 23.

Examples

3–2	Hangman	Robert Shiflett, Brown's Cove, Va., 1962.
3–3	Chevy Chase	Barry, Eckstorm, and Smyth, *British Ballads from Maine*, p. 238.
3–4	Three Lovers	Viola Cole, Fancy Gap, Va., 1962.
3–5	Mary Hamilton	Charles Kilpatrick Sharpe, *The Ballad Book*, p. 18.
3–6	Mary Hamilton	Myrtle Harman, Bland, Va. Davis, *Traditional Ballads of Virginia*, p. 26.
3–7	Time Draws Near	Dan Tate, Fancy Gap, Va., 1962.
3–8	Captain Wedderburn's Courtship	Annie V. Marsten, West Goldsboro, Maine, 1929. Barry, Eckstorm, and Smyth, *British Ballads from Maine*, p. 95.
3–9	Perri, Merri, Dixie, Domini	Regor Smaharba
3–10	Queen Jane	Bascome Lamar Lunsford, Asheville, N.C., 1937. Dorothy Scarborough, *Song Catcher in Southern Mts.*, p. 254.
3–11	Old Bangum	Regor Smaharba
4–1	Jack and Joe	Obey Johnson, Crosnore, N.C., 1962.
4–2	Who Killed Cock Robin?	Florence Shiflett, Wyatt's Mountain, Va., 1962.
4–3	Foolish Boy	Marybird McAllister, Brown's Cove, Va., 1961.
4–4	Scolding Wife	Marybird McAllister, Brown's Cove, Va., 1958.
4–5	Darlin' You Can't Have One	Duke Hughes, Limona, Fla., 1948.
4–6	I'll Sing You One Ho!	Mildred Creighton, Carrie, Ky., 1962.
5–1	Golden Willow Tree	Almeda Riddle, Arkansas, 1965.
5–2	Jackie's Gone A-Sailin'	Virgil Sturgill, Ashland, Ky., 1958.
5–3	Arch & Gordon	Mrs. Will Cline, Delaware, 1956. *Kentucky Folklore Record*, April-June, 1960, No. 2.

Examples

5–4	Devil's Nine Questions	Mildred Creighton, Carrie, Ky., 1962.
5–5	Little Sparrow (Fair And Tender Ladies)	Florence Shiflett, Wyatt's Mountain, Va., 1962.
5–6	Bird Song	Marybird McAllister, Brown's Cove, Va., 1957.
6–1	John of Hazelgreen	Robert Shiflett, Brown's Cove, Va., 1961.
6–2	Young Hunting	Marybird McAllister, Brown's Cove, Va., 1958.
6–3	Devil and the Farmer's Wife	Pina Sturdivant, Paducah, Tex., 1965.
6–4	Lord Bateman	Virgil Sturgill, Ashland, Ky., 1958.
6–5	Matty Groves	Creighton & Senior, *Traditional Songs from Nova Scotia*, p. 43.
6–6	Our Goodman	Robert Shiflett, Brown's Cove, Va., 1962.
6–7	Locks and Bolts (Rainbow Willow)	Viola Cole, Fancy Gap, Va., 1962.
6–8	Charming Beauty Bright	Marybird McAllister, Brown's Cove, Va., 1961.
6–9	Knoxville Girl	Marybird McAllister, Brown's Cove, Va., 1958.
6–10	Pretty Fair Miss in the Garden	Marybird McAllister, Brown's Cove, Va., 1958.
6–11	Courtin' Case	Marybird McAllister, Brown's Cove, Va., 1958.
6–12	Bachelor's Hall	Marybird McAllister, Brown's Cove, Va., 1958.
6–13	Babes in the Wood	Almeda Riddle, Pine Top, Ark., 1965.
6–14	Little Bessie	Viola Cole, Fancy Gap, Va., 1962.
6–15	Dying Nun	Almeda Riddle, Pine Top, Ark., 1965.
6–16	Wayfaring Stranger	Marshall, Ritchie, Carrie, Ky., 1965.
6–17	Jam on Gerry's Rocks	Franz Rickaby, *Ballads and Songs of the Shanty-Boy*, p. 11.
6–18	Utah Carrol	Almeda Riddle, Pine Top, Ark., 1965.

Examples

6–19	Jesse James	Robert Shiflett, Brown's Cove, Va., 1962.
7–1	Springfield Mountain	Marybird McAllister, Brown's Cove, Va., 1958.
7–2	Springfield Mountain	*BFSSNE* No. 5, Barry, 1933.
9–1	Wife in Wethers Skin (Dandoo!)	Ernest Byrd, Culhowee, N.C., 1962.
9–2	Three Ravens	Ravenscroft, *Melismata*, No. 20.
9–3	Twa Corbies	Campbell, *Albyn's Anthology II*, pp. 26–27.
9–4	Three Crows	Marybird McAllister, Brown's Cove, Va., 1961.
9–5	Gypsy Davey	Robert Shiflett, Brown's Cove, Va., 1961.
9–6	Gypsy Laddie O	Florence Shiflett, Wyatt's Mountain, Va., 1962.
9–7	Gypsy Laddie	Marybird McAllister, Brown's Cove, Va., 1961.

APPENDIX I:
COLLECTING
PROCEDURES

The collection of folksong, folklore, and related data when done in an imaginative and knowledgeable way can greatly increase the value and interest of the material. Such an approach will make the difference between a casual gathering of quaint antiquities and a collection which is meaningful evidence of the vitality and wonder of folklore. Certain procedures may serve the student and hobbyist collector of folklore as well as they do the professional folklorist. The following suggestions will provide a guide which is easy to follow and is adaptable to most types of collecting necessary in the English speaking American folklore complex.

In addition to specimens of songs, riddles, superstitions, tales, jokes, etc., the collector should pursue and record the following information:

The local title, if any, of the material

The name of the informant

The date

The place
> This should be done with the utmost thoroughness, especially in rural areas. The noting of the state, county, town, and if necessary, directions for finding the informant will provide the opportunity to continue any valuable collecting you may begin.

How did the informant learn the lore you have collected?
> From whom did he learn the material? This may entail recording the names of the informant's family tree or his neighbors and will frequently provide valuable leads for the collector in the same vicinity. When did

203

he learn the material? Try to establish the age of the lore within that vicinity. This information is of as great a value as the date of the collecting and will often indicate the history of oral tradition within a given area. Have written sources, radio, phonograph, television, etc. had a part in his learning, re-learning, or modifying the material, and to what extent?

In addition to these basic pieces of information there should, under favorable condition, be added the following data (which generally can *not* be gathered through direct questioning):

How does the informant feel about the piece?

Does he consider the piece to be beautiful or to have esthetic value? What is there about the piece that causes its retention? Is its entertainment value based on beauty, humor, horror, excitement, etc.? This information, if recorded correctly, will give valuable insights into why the material is performed, remembered, and appreciated by the informant. It will also provide insights into the nature of the group for whom he performs it.

What are the social and cultural background of the informant?

In order to relate the material to its environment, as much data concerning physical, financial, religious, social, and cultural characteristics as possible should be added. It is often of great meaning to know the national origins, prevailing livelihoods, or other patterns of homogeniety of the area.

Are there individual or local explanations for the material?

This is an important factor in the informant's relationship to the material. Such information is vital when dealing with pieces of original composition of those dealing heavily with localized events, places, or persons, but it is also important for older songs because they often have accompanying legends of great importance in understanding the song and its reasons for retention.

Does the informant have an understanding of or explanations for all words, phrases, and references in the piece?

A discussion with an informant over his concept of various phrases and other specifics within a piece will often provide startling insights into oral process. Explanations by an informant of what the collector recognizes as oral corruptions frequently illustrate the importance of misunderstanding and transfer of meaning in folklore.

Are any peculiarities of delivery obvious?

Is there any variance in the informant's normal speech pattern, inflection, dialect, pronunciation, etc. evident in the piece? Are such affectations traditional for that piece only? Are there any physical movements or gestures which accompany the piece? Are these indirectly related, perhaps a result of the performance tension, or directly related, as in the case of demonstrative gestures, to the piece?

Does the informant or his audience exhibit an affinity for a specific piece, type, or form of folklore or is there a pattern to his performance?

> Many informants will offer only one or a limited number of types such as religious songs, dance songs, ballads, humorous songs, etc. Some informants will sing songs in a certain order. The collector should try to establish the reasons for this.

The collector's real problem is not finding material, but collecting it correctly and meaningfully. As this book has tried to indicate, folklore of great esthetic, cultural, and historical interest may be found in all strata and areas of our society. The collector who confines his efforts to illiterate octogenarians living in log cabins high atop mountains or to the pursuit of some single esoteric specimen of a rarely collected piece has chosen the path of greatest resistance and frustration. The "Don Juan" search for the perfect and unimpeachable informant and the "Holy Grail" quest for the previously unrecorded version rarely adds to the study of folklore or to the enjoyment of collecting. A fruitful collection of folklore can frequently be initiated within one's own family and friends. The collector must not only look for and note those things which most interest him and reflect his methods of study but should also try to anticipate the needs of other investigators of culture.

The aforementioned suggestions should be considered as a way of thinking about folklore rather than as a strict "check list" of questions to be asked. The relationship between the informant and the successful collector is that of friendly human exchange. The good collector learns to meet people and learn from them on a reciprocal basis. He does not interrogate, lecture, or pry to the embarrassment of his informant. He must realize that in most collecting circumstances, his is the role of the outsider. In order to overcome this, he must be genuinely friendly, interested, and anxious to enter into an exchange of human ideas and backgrounds which will enrich both collector and informant.

The actual methods and techniques of collecting vary with collectors, their interests, and their financial status. By far the most advantageous method of folksong collecting is done by electric machines, especially magnetic tape. The advantages of electronic collecting over the time-consuming and often inaccurate noting by hand are too obvious to require discussion. The collector should remember that his paraphernalia (microphones, recording machines, tapes, etc.) are tools rather than an end in themselves. The collector who is taken with his role of sound engineer and who tries to recreate a recording studio in his informant's home, usually only succeeds in making his informant uncomfortable. This negates the very advantage of carefully and thoughtfully used recording devices, the accurate and complete record of what the informant has to offer.

APPENDIX II:
TRANSCRIBING
FOLKSONG

The following are procedures which should be included in a complete expression of folksong in musical symbols. These suggestions may be fully carried out under ideal circumstances only. For example, songs collected by electronic recording may be listened to many times in the process of securing an accurate and complete transcription. Working under this most ideal arrangement permits spot checking, slowing of listening speed for analytical clarity and constant comparisons with pitch and tempo devices. If the collector must transcribe directly from his informant in the field, then many of the desirable but subtle procedures listed below will have to be overlooked.*

Each text and tune should be preceded by the name of the informant and the place of collection.

The full text, including the title assigned the piece by the informant, should be given in the usual poetic format. Words, phrases, or references requiring clarification should be numbered and such clarification given in separate footnotes.

Prior to the tune, the metronome marking of the performance should be given. The quarter note should be used as the unit of measure as consistently as possible. The quarter note is convenient from approximately 70 to 135 pulses per minute. If the pulse should be faster, say 140 per minute, the values may be halved and the quarter note restored at 70 pulses per minute ($\flat_{=140}$ $\quad \downarrow_{=70}$). If the pulse should be slower, say 60 per minute, the values may be doubled and the quarter note restored

* For a comparison of transcription styles see Bartók *Serbo-Croatian Folksongs* for an example of ultra-meticulous and detailed transcriptions from electronic recordings and Sharp *EFSSA* for excellent examples of transcriptions made directly from informants in the field.

at 120 pulses per minute ($\textrm{♩}=60$ $\textrm{♩}=120$). If different recordings of the same piece by the same informant vary in tempo, the extremes should be indicated ($\textrm{♩}=74\text{-}90$). If the tempo changes within a single performance, this may be indicated ($\textrm{♩}=80+-$) and the exact nature of the changes noted in the transcription itself.

On the staff preceding the tune should be given the actual pitch of the performance. The final tone of the tune represented as a whole note and the upper and lower extremes of range given in small black notes. If pitch level varies in different performances of the same piece by the same informant, the extremes should be given.

Variants of pitch level within a single performance should be mentioned and indicated in the transcription itself.

All tunes should be transposed so as to place their final at g^1. The selection of g^1 is not entirely arbitrary since it places most tunes within the scope of the treble clef, thereby avoiding excessive leger lines. The use of g^1 also precludes the use of extreme key signatures. Transcribing tunes at a common pitch level (or at least with a common level for the final) greatly facilitates comparative study of variant versions, scales or modes, and ranges. Since traditional singers often vary pitch levels, we should not be bound to transcribe at the pitch level of a particular performance. The indication of actual pitch of the performance given prior to the complete transcription should suffice even the most serious student.

Key signatures should be used to indicate only consistent characteristics of the tune. Assigning key signatures to tunes in which one tone involved in the signature is missing or of consistently altering tones involved in the signature with accidentals or naturals should be avoided. Key signatures used in transcriptions of folksongs need not follow the rules of formal music theory. A signature may be designed to indicate any consistent tonal alterations in the tune.

Meter signatures should be used to indicate only consistent metrical characteristics. In tunes which are very free metrically or are erratic throughout, no meter need be indicated, and barring and grouping should be accomplished solely by the stress pattern of the text-tune. In tunes which adhere throughout to a metrical pattern, the meter should be indicated in conventional fashion. The transcriber should limit himself as much as possible to the basic meters discussed in Chapter 8 (2/4, or 4/4 if tempo requires, 3/4, 6/8 and 9/8). Such meters as 3/2, 6/4 and 9/4 should be altered in values to be represented as 3/4, 6/8 and 9/8. In a tune which is fairly consistent throughout, but with slight variations, the basic meter can be given in parentheses (3/4). This would relieve the transcriber of the theoretical obligation to limit any one bar to a specific value or to fill out any one bar to its indicated value. This will further eliminate the need for exotic and distracting meter signatures at points throughout the transcription.

In the initial stanza of the transcription, each line of text should be represented by one staff of music with the corresponding phrase of the tune. This will, in most cases, place equal phrase lengths beneath one another and make phrase relationships with the tune more readily apparent. This format will further emphasize tune-text relationship.

Each bar should be numbered.

The transcription should be as accurate a representation of the performance as possible, including ornamental tones, rhythmic oddities, musical anomalies, or aberrations and stylistic peculiarities of the singer. The completeness of such a transcription will vary directly with the musical training, developed ear, and experience of the transcriber. However, basic techniques and specialized notation should be consistent among transcribers. Musical signs and indications which are only approximations (fermatas, ritards, accelerandos, etc.) should not be used but their exact values indicated by precise notation and specific indication. Ornamental tones should be represented as grace notes only if precise representation of their rhythmic value is impossible. Ornamental tones of equal volume with the more structurally important tones should be notated with their proper rhythmic values. In the Anglo-American folksong tradition ornamental tones are often noticeably at a lower volume level. These are not grace notes of indeterminate length, but rather must be represented accurately. This may be done by the use of small head notes which indicate a lower level of volume or lack of clarity rather than rhythmic uncertainties. For example:

represents rhythmically

The use of separate flags for eighth notes, sixteenth notes, etc., traditional in vocal music, should be replaced by the barring across groups of rhythmically related notes. The occurrence of two or more tones to a single syllable can be indicated by the slur. Certain specialized notations are useful to augment standard musical symbols in transcribing Anglo-American folksong. These are:

↑   higher than the pitch given (up to 1/4 tone)

↓   lower than the pitch given (up to 1/4 tone)

↟ ↡   a quarter tone higher or lower than the pitch given

~~~~~~~~~~ signifies a glissando of all microtones between

 the pitches indicated or a blurring of the notes indicated into one another

Following a complete transcription of the first stanza, there should be full transcriptions of each succeeding stanza sufficiently different to require complete representation, and transcriptions of any stanza fragments containing variation from the initial stanza. These fragments should be carefully labeled as to stanza and bar number and given with the corresponding fragments of text.

Any information relating to the rendition of the song should be included with the transcription. This might include:

Asides and interjections given by the singer which relate to the song.

Description of accompaniment including name of instrument used, style of playing, use of instrumental interludes, tunings, etc.

Mention of any stylistic peculiarities of the singer which escape transcription.

Mention of any physical gestures which relate to the song.

The dates of the recording or transcription should be given. If several recordings of the same informant were made this should be indicated and the dates given.

The name of the collector and transcriber should be indicated.

APPENDIX III:
ANALYZING AND
CLASSIFYING FOLKSONG

After a full transcription of the folksong is completed, a comparison of the stanza variants is possible. Those characteristics which occur with greatest frequency throughout the stanzas should be projected into a single representation of the tune. This projection of only the most consistent elements of the tune will result in an abstract version of the most fundamental melodic elements. This "skeletal" tune will eliminate grace notes, nonessential tones, performance anomalies, and any rhythms dependent on relationship with the words. This skeletal version or abstraction of the tune will be used for analysis and classification. The establishment of procedures for describing and classifying Anglo-American traditional tunes should be restricted to the use of methods and terminologies which are meaningful to the characteristics of our folkmusic. In this methodology, the use of existing procedures and vocabularies from formal musicology will be used only if they do not conflict with or contradict the traditional music idiom. Wherever necessary, methods will be suggested which are designed specifically to express characteristics of the folkmusic idiom as they are found in practice.

Two factors of traditional tunes shall serve as the basis for description and classification. These are scale and contour. The scale shall be considered on two points: the number of different tones found in the tune, and the distributional relationship of the tones to one another. Contour shall mean the use to which these tones are put in forming a complete musical unit.

All descriptions and classifications shall be based upon the final tone of the traditional tune. We must accept that the final tone represents, to the traditional performer, a satisfactory point of rest. If this were not the case, the traditional singer, unencumbered by "rules" of style, would change it.

For this reason the final shall be used as the basis for scale analysis and accepted as a tone of great functional importance, i.e., the point of ultimate repose of the tune.

To facilitate comparison and provide a single table for the use of numerical equivalents, all tunes shall be transposed so that their finals fall on g^1. All descriptions of the scale shall be based upon the final tone, invariably g^1. The octave below g^1 shall be expressed by the number 1 and each ascending diatonic tone numbered consecutively.

Chromatic form of the diatonic degrees may be expressed by the use of the symbols ♭ (flat) and ♯ (sharp) before the numeral indicating the altered degree. Thus the scale:

may be expressed: V-VI-♯VII-1-2-♭3-4-5. In this manner it is possible to indicate the exact scale form typographically when the use of musical notations is impractical.

The description of the scale is contingent on two factors: the number of different tones (i.e. different diatonic degrees) in the tune and the overall range of the tune.

The number of tones found within a tune shall be expressed as follows. Accepting that a variance of pitch is necessary to produce a tune, a tune having only two different pitches would be described as having a two-tone scale. The maximum number of diatonic degrees possible being seven, a tune containing the full diatonic spectrum would be described as having a seven-tone scale. The remaining possibilities are expressed as three-tone scale, four-tone scale, five-tone scale, and six-tone scale. Only diatonic degrees are counted. If two chromatic forms of the same diatonic degree occur in the tune they are considered the same tone for purposes of expressing the number of tones in the scale. This characteristic shall be termed "inflection" and added to the scale description. A scale containing all diatonic degrees and having, for example, F-natural and F-sharp would be described: seven-tone scale, inflected seven.

The number of tones within a scale plus the range of the tune combine to produce distributional characteristics of importance in the traditional music idiom.

Range may be expressed by the numerical equivalents of the lowest and highest tones found within the tune. A tune with an overall range of d^1 to f^2 may be expressed: V-7.

Having described the number of tones in a scale and its range, a representation should be given. This expression of the scale should demonstrate the distribution of tones as they occur in the tune and not be a theoretically constructed scale of the tones found in the tune. For example, in expressing the scale, octave positions of tones should be given separately as they occur (VII-1-2-3-4-5-6-7-8).

It is not possible to state with certainty that traditional singers do not hear octaves as the same tone. However, the absence of octave displacement in traditional practice, especially when considered against the widespread use of that technique among trained singers and non-traditionally oriented amateurs, would seem to indicate a different esthetic feeling for the octave.

The description of the scale is completed with the statement of number of tones, range of the tune, and a representation of distributional characteristics. Once complete transcription and projection of the tune is finished, there may be added to the scale description an indication of the relative duration of each tone within the tune. This is accomplished after the method of Jan P. Schinhan, by indicating the number of rhythmic values found on each pitch of the scale. Such an analysis would be:

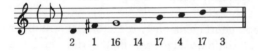

The small note at the beginning of the scale indicates the unit of rhythmic value for the computation. The number sixteen under the tone G indicates that tone is present in the tune for the equivalent of sixteen eighth-notes ( ) or eight full beats.

The above procedures present a complete picture of the nature of the distributional characteristics of a single scale. However, beyond the process of describing a single specimen is the problem of classifying it within a system to facilitate comparison with other examples. The functions of description and classification are different and should not be confused. The aim of description is the complete expression of a tune's individuality and singularity. Classification is intended to show readily the areas of similarity and common characteristics which occur between tunes. Related tunes may differ in the particulars of description but should bear similar or identical classification.

Classification is based upon the inner relationships of the tones in the scale without regard to the characteristics expressed in description. These relationships between the tones must be considered in terms of a basic unit. This "basic unit" shall be the pentatonic scale. This is not to imply that the Anglo-American traditional performer hears his tunes, consciously or unconsciously, against a background of a pentatonic scale. Nor does this imply that the pentatonic scale is a natural form or evolutionary step in the passage of music from a primitive to cultivated mode of expression. The pentatonic scale is selected because it represents, as it were, a least common denominator in the Anglo-American traditional idiom. Pentatonic scales constitute the tonal material for a great percentage of Anglo-American traditional tunes. This is true of ballads of extreme antiquity as well as material of relatively recent origin. Traditional tunes of fewer than five tones are quite rare and tunes of six or seven tones may be considered in terms of their relationship to one or more pentatonic scales. The internal characteristics of pentatonic scales may then be considered a practical unit of comparison within the Anglo-American traditional tune corpus.

The five possible forms of the pentatonic scale are derived by simple inversion. They are arranged to place those having the same characteristics adjacent and numbered I through V. Each form is transposed so as to be based on g^1.

Untransposed inversions		Transposed form								Without diatonic degrees
gabde	I	G	A	B	–	D	E	–	g	4 and 7
degab	II	G	A	–	C	D	E	–	g	3 and 7
abdeg	III	G	A	–	C	D	–	F	g	3 and 6
egabd	IV	G	–	B♭	C	D	–	F	g	2 and 6
bdega	V	G	–	B♭	C	–	E♭	F	g	2 and 5

The intervals of a minor third found within a pentatonic scale may be "filled" with tones that are a semi-tone from one adjacent degree and a whole tone from the other adjacent degree. This addition does not alter the inner relationships of the tones in the pentatonic scale. In Pentatonic scale I, the interval between B and D may be "filled" either with C or C♯ producing two six-tone scales without the seventh degree. Similarly, the interval between E and g may be "filled" with either F or F♯ producing two six-tone scales without the fourth degree. Both the fourth and seventh degrees may be added in four possible permutations. Thus, without altering the tonal relationships of Pentatonic scale I, we may form two six-tone scales lacking the 4th degree, two six-tone scales lacking the seventh degree and four different seven-tone scales. The total of nine scales, within the scope of Pentatonic scale I, are termed Scale Group I. The same procedure is followed with the remaining pentatonic scales, producing Scale Groups II, III, IV, and V. See Table I.

TABLE I

Common Groups

SCALE GROUP I

Pentatonic	G A B – D E – g	
Six-tone scales	G A B C D E – g	12
	G A B – D E F♯ g	
	G A B C♯ D E – g	
	G A B – D E F g	
Seven-tone scales	G A B C D E F♯ g	12
	G A B C D E F g	123
	G A B C♯ D E F♯ g	
	G A B C♯ D E F g	

SCALE GROUP II

Pentatonic	G A – C D E – g	
Six-tone scales	G A B C D E – g	12
	G A – C D E F g	23
	G A B♭ C D E – g	
	G A – C D E F♯ g	
Seven-tone scales	G A B C D E F♯ g	12
	G A B C D E F g	123
	G A B♭ C D E F g	234
	G A B♭ C D E F♯ g	

SCALE GROUP III

Pentatonic	G A – C D – F g	
Six-tone scales	G A – C D E F g	23
	G A B♭ C D – F g	34
	G A B C D – F g	
	G A – C D E♭ F g	
Seven-tone scales	G A B C D E F g	123
	G A B♭ C D E F g	234
	G A B♭ C D E♭ F g	345
	G A B C D E♭ F g	

SCALE GROUP IV

Pentatonic	G – B♭ C D – F g	
Six-tone scales	G A B♭ C D – F g	34
	G – B♭ C D E♭ F g	45
	G A♭ B♭ C D – F g	
	G – B♭ C D E F g	
Seven-tone scales	G A B♭ C D E F g	234
	G A B♭ C D E♭ F g	345
	G A♭ B♭ C D E♭ F g	45
	G A♭ B♭ C D E F g	

SCALE GROUP V

Pentatonic	G – B♭ C – E♭ F g	
Six-tone scales	G – B♭ C D E♭ F g	45
	G A♭ B♭ C – E♭ F g	
	G – B♭ C D♭ E♭ F g	
	G A B♭ C – E♭ F g	
Seven-tone scales	G A B♭ C D E♭ F g	345
	G A♭ B♭ C D E♭ F g	45
	G A♭ B♭ C D♭ E♭ F g	
	G A B♭ C D♭ E♭ F g	

It may be seen in Table I that some six-tone scales contain the consistent tones of more than one pentatonic scale. For example, the scale G A B C D E — g has the tones found in both Pentatonic I and Pentatonic II and, therefore, belongs to Scale Groups I and II. It is also possible that a seven-tone scale may have the tones of two or three pentatonic scales and, therefore, belongs to two or three Scale Groups. For example, the scale G A B C D E F is found in Scale Groups I, II, and III.

It is of interest at this point to consider the tri-tone in the context of Anglo-American traditional music. In Anglo-American traditional tunes, the absence of the tri-tone seems to be the basic characteristic in the predominant use of five-tone (pentatonic) and six-tone scales. The pentatonic scales are free of the tri-tone. While some six-tone scales seen in the table contain the tri-tone, the great majority of six-tone scales found in practice are also without the tri-tone. Within the table, some seven-tone scales are evident which contain two tri-tones; these, however, are highly theoretical and are not idiomatic. It is possible for a scale (especially of seven diatonic degrees) to contain two tri-tones due to inflection.

The occurrence of a tri-tone within a five-tone or six-tone scale should be considered an exception and expressed within the scale description.

We may divide the total possible scales of the five Scale Groups according to type as shown in Table II.

Scales occasionally occur in traditional music which do not belong to any of the five Scale Groups. Most notable of these are the scales containing fewer than five tones. These two-tone, three-tone and four-tone scales are classified according to the extent to which they agree with the pentatonic forms. If a two-tone, three-tone or four-tone scale agrees in *all* its tones with one or more of the pentatonic scales, it is said to bear primary relationship to that (those) group(s).

This tune is comprised of but three tones, G, A, and B. Since all three tones are found within Pentatonic I, this tune is classified as bearing a primary relationship to Scale Group I. This is expressed: PR Scale Group I.

Any three-tone, four-tone, or five-tone scale may agree in all but one of its tones to pentatonic forms. Such a scale is then said to bear a secondary relationship to those Scale Groups.

The four-tone scale of the example agrees in all its tones but one (F♯) with Pentatonic scales I and II.

TABLE II

Total scales by type		*Found in Scale Groups*	*Degrees of Tri-tone*	
Pentatonic				
	G A B – D E – g	1		
	G A – C D E – g	2		
	G A – C D – F g	3		
	G – B♭ C D – F g	4		
	G – B♭ C – E♭ F g	5		
Six-tone scales without tri-tone				
	G A B – D E F♯ g	1		
	G A B – D E F g	12		
	G A – C D E F g	23		
	G A B♭ C D – F g	34		
	G – B♭ C D E♭ F g	45		
	G A♭ B♭ C – E♭ F g	5		
with tri-tone				
	G A B C♯ D E – g	1	1–4	
	G A B – D E F g	1	3–7	
	G A – C D E F♯ g	2	4–7	
	G A B♭ C D E – g	2	3–6	
	G A B C D – F g	3	3–7	
	G A – C D E♭ F g	3	2–6	
	G – B♭ C D E F g	4	3–6	
	G A♭ B♭ C D – F g	4	2–5	
	G A B♭ C – E♭ F g	5	2–6	
	G – B♭ C D♭ E♭ F g	5	1–5	
Seven-tone scales with one tri-tone				
	G A B C♯ D E F♯ g	1	1–4	
	G A B C D E F♯ g	12	4–7	
	G A B C D E F g	123	3–7	
	G A B♭ C D E F g	234	3–6	
	G A B♭ C D E♭ F g	345	2–6	
	G A♭ B♭ C D E♭ F g	45	2–5	
	G A♭ B♭ C D♭ E♭ F g	5	1–5	
with two tri-tones				
	G A B C♯ D E F g	1	1–4	3–7
	G A B♭ C D E F♯ g	2	3–6	4–7
	G A B C D E♭ F g	3	2–6	3–7
	G A♭ B♭ C D E F g	4	2–5	3–6
	G A B♭ C D♭ E♭ F g	5	1–5	2–6

FOUR-TONE SCALE OF EXAMPLE 6

Pentatonic I				Pentatonic II
		F♯		—
E	agreement	E	agreement	E
D	agreement	D	agreement	D
—		—		C
B		—		—
A		—		—
G	agreement	G	agreement	G

The scale of Example is classified as bearing secondary relationship to Scale Groups I and II: SR SCALE GROUPS I, II.

Any four-tone, five-tone, or six-tone scale which agrees in all but two of its tones with pentatonic forms is said to bear tertiary relationship to the corresponding Scale Group(s).

Just as some scales may belong to more than one Scale Group, certain of these "exceptional" scales may bear varying degrees of relationship to more than one Scale Group. Thus the scale of the example on p. 000 (G A B) while bearing primary relationship to Scale Group I, also bears secondary relationship to Scale Groups II and III. This is because it agrees in all its tones but one (B) with Pentatonic Scales II and III. Let us examine a hypothetical scale (G B C D E) of five tones to ascertain its degree of relationship to the Pentatonic scales:

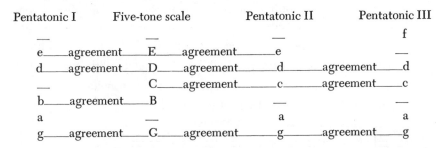

Pentatonic I		Five-tone scale		Pentatonic II		Pentatonic III
—		—		—		f
e	agreement	E	agreement	e		—
d	agreement	D	agreement	d	agreement	d
—		C	agreement	c	agreement	c
b	agreement	B		—		—
a		—		a		a
g	agreement	G	agreement	g	agreement	g

Our five-tone scale agrees in all its tones but one (C) with Pentatonic I and, therefore, bears a secondary relationship to Scale Group I. It agrees in all its tones but one (B) with Pentatonic II and, therefore, bears a secondary relationship to Scale Group II. It agrees in all its tones but two (B and E) to Pentatonic III and, therefore, bears a tertiary relationship to Scale Group III. The complete classification of the scale G B C D E would then be expressed:

SR Scale Groups I, II

TR Scale Group III

If a direct contradiction occurs between the scale of a specimen and a pentatonic scale no relationship exists. For example, our hypothetical five-tone scale agrees with Pentatonic IV in three of its tones (G, C, and D). These are the same tones of agreement which establish a tertiary relationship to Scale Group III. However, the contradiction between B in the five-tone scale and B♭ in Pentatonic IV negates any relationship between them.

Full classification by this method will result in the graphic expression of similarities of scales which have comparable structural characteristics. The classifications are sufficiently broad to include any characteristic of a scale which might indicate musical relationships to other specimens.

Classification of tune contour centers upon two factors: the basic characteristics of each musical phrase and the relationship of the phrases to one another, and the characteristics of a musical phrase which shall be considered most important to classification are phrase finals, phrase openings, and the extremes of range within the single phrase.

There is no difference in the structural formulae in songs and instrumental pieces within the Anglo-American folkmusic idiom. Instrumental or dance tunes often have incidental word settings. Statements made about the structure of folksong shall, therefore, hold true for instrumentally-oriented or non-vocal music as well.

In Anglo-American folksong, the musical structure is directly parallel or closely related to the form and structure of the text. A phrase or line of text usually has a directly corresponding musical phrase.

The final of the concluding phrase is invariably g^1. The phrase final which is at the mid-cadence or main caesura (usually the end of the second phrase) shall be designated with the symbol ☐ . Phrase finals prior to the main caesura shall be designated with the symbol ⌐ . Those occurring after the main caesura (not including the ultimate final) shall be designated with the symbol ∟ .

The contour of the above example may be expressed by musical nota-tion or typographically:

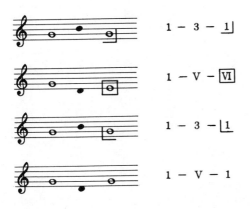

In indicating phrase finals and openings by musical notation, the first stressed tone and final are given as whole notes. The lowest and highest tone occurring between the initial stressed tone and the phrase final are indicated by small black notes. If either whole note represents an ex-treme of range for that phrase, additional indication is unnecessary. All notes occurring before the first stressed tone are indicated by small black notes. Typographically, these may be enclosed in parentheses and the initial stressed tone indicated by the accent symbol ('). In the following example the occurrence of several tones (pickup notes) preceding the first stressed tone is expressed in musical notation and typographically:

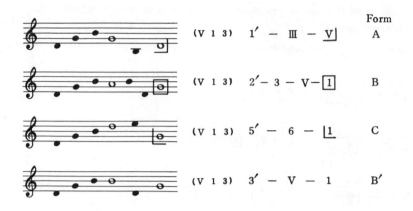

The relationship which exists between the component phrases of a tune shall be termed form. The relationship between single phrases shall be expressed by use of the capital letters A, B, C, etc. Identical phrases within the tune shall bear the same designation. A phrase bearing close similarity may be expressed by the same letter designation with the addition of the symbol ('). The relationship between the second and fourth phrases of this example is, therefore, expressed: A B C B'. No system of classification can specify to what extent two items must agree to be considered related. This is, in the last analysis, in the hands of the editor and researcher. In the matter of phrase relationships the procedures of contour classification should serve as a guide and aid. The factors affecting phrase relationship are expressed in contour classification. These should be considered in order of their importance, i.e. phrase finals, phrase openings, and melodic characteristics within the phrase.

The following examples are single stanzas from Anglo-American folksong. These are completely described and classified in Table III. The data is so arranged as to provide a suggestion for cataloguing procedure. Table IV presents a complete transcription and analysis, and additional data of a single song in accordance with the principles outlined here.

It is hoped that these procedures will provide an approach to the study and classification of folkmusic which is at once accurate and objective. This methodology is intended especially to express the idioms of Anglo-American traditional music and song. While the intent has been to combine procedures meaningful to this one idiom it is hoped that further study and application will prove its usefulness in the study of Mexican-American and American Negro idioms.

TABLE III

THE GYPSY LADDIE   Archive #
Local Title "Lord Ingram's Wife
            and the Gypsy Davey"
                                              Scale Groups
6-tone scale   III; IV
Range 1-9   Form:
1-2-b3-4-5-3-8-9   Contour:

                          (1) b3' -1-5-   1   A
                          (5) 7' -5-9-   5   B
                          (8) 9'-   1   C
                          (1) b3' -1-5-   1   A'

Meter basically 2/4 each phrase=two bars
Sung unacc. Rubato and very narrative style

Robert 'Bob' Shiflett   Brown's Cove, Va.
Collector George Foss   5/16/1961

---

cf. THE LASS OF LOCH ROYAL   Archive #
Local Title "Time Draws Near"

                                              Scale Groups
7-tone scale   I, II, III
Range V-7   Form:
                              Contour:

                          (1) V' -3-   1   A
                          (5) 5' -7-3-   4   B
                          (34) 5' -6-   V   C
                          (V) 1' -3-   1   A'

Meter 4/4 each phrase=two bars
Sung with banjo acc.

Daniel W. 'Dan' Tate   Fancy Gap, Va.
Collector George Foss   6/1/1962

Table IV Pretty Fair Miss

He step-ed__ up and__this__ he 'dresd her says pret-y fair miss will you mar-ry__ me

Its how can you fuse a sin-gle sol-dier that's late-ly__ turn - - ed from a cross the__ sea

An if hes gone_____ sev-en years__ long-er no man on__ earth_____ can mar-ry__ me

So spos hes__ took some__ fur' girl an' mar-ried An' you'll nev-er see_____ his face a - gain

And if hes__ took some fur' girl an' mar-ried I'll love the__ girl that mar-ried__ him

He pull'd out the ring that__ she__ had__ give him And down be - fore_____ him she did__ fall

O dont you re-mem - ber the promise that I made you no girl on earth_____ could a mar-ried__ me

V| I| I| Phrase finals
2   2   2   2   Bar lengths
A   B   C   B'   Form

We wish to acknowledge the free incorporation of certain procedures from other researchers into this methodology. Specifically, the transposition of specimens based upon the final and the numerical equivalents for scale designations from the methods of the late Béla Bartók, cf. *Serbo-Croatian Folk Songs.* The method of specifying the relationship of tone occurrence within a tune is from Jan Schinhan, although slightly modified, cf. *North Carolina Folklore,* Volumes IV and V.

SELECTED BIBLIOGRAPHY
OF REGIONAL
COLLECTIONS

Barbeau, Marius, Arthur Lismer, and Arthur Bourinot, *Come A-Singing!* Ottawa: E. Cloutier Printers, 1947.

Barry, Phillips, *The Maine Woods Songster*. Cambridge, Mass.: The Powell Printing Co., 1939.

———, Fannie H. Eckstorm, and Mary W. Smyth, *British Ballads from Maine*. New Haven: Yale University Press, 1929.

Beck, Earl Clifton, *Lore of the Lumber Camps*. Ann Arbor: The University of Michigan Press, 1948.

———, *Songs of the Michigan Lumberjacks*. Ann Arbor: The University of Michigan Press, 1941.

———, *They Knew Paul Bunyan*. Ann Arbor: The University of Michigan Press, 1956.

Beck, Horace P., *The Folklore of Maine*. Philadelphia: J. B. Lippincott Co., 1957.

Belden, Henry Marvin, *Ballads and Songs Collected by the Missouri Folk-Lore Society* (University of Missouri Studies, XV). Columbia, Mo.: University of Missouri, 1940, 1955.

Bone, David W., *Capstan Bars*. New York: Porpoise Press, 1932.

Botkin, B. A., *The American Play-Party Song* (University Studies of the University of Nebraska, XXXVIII). Lincoln, Neb.: University of Nebraska, 1937.

Brewster, Paul G., *Ballads and Songs of Indiana* (Indiana University Publications, Folklore Series No. 1). Bloomington, Ind.: University of Indiana, 1940.

Buchanan, Annabel Morris, *Folk Hymns of America*. New York: J. Fischer and Bro., 1938.

Bulletin of the Folk-Song Society of the Northeast, Nos. 1–12. Cambridge, Mass.: 1930–1937.

Burt, Olive Wooley, *American Murder Ballads and Their Stories*. New York: Oxford University Press, 1958.

Cambiare, Celestin Pierre, *East Tennessee and Western Virginia Mountain Ballads*. London: The Mitre Press, 1934.

Campbell, Olive Dame, and Cecil J. Sharp, *English Folk Songs from the Southern Appalachians*. New York and London: Oxford University Press, 1917.

Cazden, Norman, *The Abelard Folk Song Book*. New York: Abelard-Schuman Limited, 1958.

Chappell, Louis W., *Folksongs of the Roanoke and the Albemarle*. Morgantown, W. Va.: The Ballad Press, 1939.

Colcord, Joanna C., *Songs of American Sailormen*. New York: W. W. Norton & Company, Inc., 1938.

Colorado Folksong Bulletin. Boulder, 1962–

Combs, Josiah H., *Folk-Songs du Midi États-Unis*. Paris: Les Presses Universitaire de France, 1925.

———, *Folk-Songs from the Kentucky Highlands*. New York, G. Schirmer, Inc., 1939.

Cox, John Harrington, *Folk-Songs of the South*. Cambridge, Mass.: Harvard University, 1925.

———, *Folk-Songs Mainly from West Virginia* (American Folk-Song Publication No. 5, National Service Bureau Publication No. 81-S). New York, 1939.

———, *Traditional Ballads Mainly from West Virginia* (American Folk-Song Publication No. 3, National Service Bureau Publication No. 75-S). New York, 1939.

Creighton, Helen, *Maritime Folk Songs*. East Lansing: Michigan State University, and Toronto: Ryerson Press, 1962.

———, *Songs and Ballads from Nova Scotia*. Toronto and Vancouver, J. M. Dent and Sons, 1933.

———, and Doreen H. Senior, *Traditional Songs from Nova Scotia*. Toronto: Ryerson Press, 1950.

Davis, Arthur Kyle, Jr., *Folksongs of Virginia: A Descriptive Index and Syllabus*. Durham, N.C.: Duke University, 1949.

———, *Traditional Ballads of Virginia*. Cambridge, Mass.: Harvard University Press, 1929.

Dean, Michael C., *Flying Cloud and One Hundred and Fifty Other Old Time Songs and Ballads of Outdoor Men, Sailors, Lumber Jacks, Soldiers, Men of the Great Lakes, Railroadmen, Miners, etc*. Virginia, Minn.: The Quickprint, 1922.

Doerflinger, William Main, *Shantymen and Shantyboys*. New York: The Macmillan Company, 1951.

Eckstorm, Fannie Hardy, and Mary Winslow Smyth, *Minstrelsy of Maine*. Boston: Houghton, Mifflin Company, 1927.

Eddy, Mary O., *Ballads and Songs from Ohio*. New York: J. J. Augustin, 1939.

Finger, Charles J., *Frontier Ballads*. Garden City, N.Y.: Doubleday & Company, Inc., 1927.

Flanders, Helen Hartness, *A Garland of Green Mountain Song*. Boston: John Worley Co., 1934.

———, *Ancient Ballads Traditionally Sung in New England*, four vols. Philadelphia: University of Pennsylvania, 1960–1965.

Flanders, Helen Hartness, Elizabeth Flanders Ballard, George Brown, and Phillips Barry, *The New Green Mountain Songster*. New Haven: Yale University, 1939.

——, and George Brown, *Vermont Folk-Songs and Ballads*. Brattleboro, Vt.: Stephen Daye Press, 1931.

——, and Helen Norfleet, *Country Songs of Vermont*. New York: G. Schirmer, Inc., 1937.

——, and Marguerite Olney, *Ballads Migrant in New England*. New York: Farrar, Straus and Cudahy, Inc., 1953.

Ford, Ira W., *Traditional Music of America*. New York: E. P. Dutton & Co., Inc., 1940.

Fowke, Edith, Alan Mills, and Helmut Blume, *Canada's Story in Song*. Toronto: W. J. Gage, Ltd., 1960.

Frank C. Brown Collection of North Carolina Folklore, The, ed. Newman Ivey White, Paul F. Baum, *et al.*, six vols. Durham, N.C.: Duke University, 1952–1965.

Fuson, Henry H., *Ballads of the Kentucky Highlands*. London: The Mitre Press, 1931.

Gardner, Emelyn Elizabeth, *Folklore from the Schoharie Hills, New York*. Ann Arbor: The University of Michigan Press, 1937.

——, and Geraldine Jencks Chickering, *Ballads and Songs of Southern Michigan*. Ann Arbor: The University of Michigan Press, 1939.

Gray, Roland Palmer, *Songs and Ballads of the Maine Lumberjacks*. Cambridge, Mass.: Harvard University Press, 1924.

Greenleaf, Elizabeth B., and Grace Y. Mansfield, *Ballads and Sea Songs of Newfoundland*. Cambridge, Mass.: Harvard University, 1933.

Greenway, John, *American Folksongs of Protest*. Philadelphia: University of Pennsylvania, 1953.

Harlow, Frederick P., *Chanteying Aboard American Ships*. Barre, Mass.: Barre Publishing Co., 1962.

Henry, Mellinger E., *Folk-Songs from the Southern Highlands*. New York: J. J. Augustin, 1928.

——, *Songs Sung in the Southern Appalachians*. London: The Mitre Press, 1934.

Hubbard, Lester A., *Ballads and Songs from Utah*. Salt Lake City, Utah: The University of Utah, 1961.

Hudson, Arthur Palmer, *Folksongs of Mississippi and Their Background*. Chapel Hill: The University of North Carolina, 1936.

——, *Folktunes from Mississippi* (National Service Bureau Publication No. 25). New York, 1937.

Hugill, Stan, *Shanties from the Seven Seas*. New York and London: E. P. Dutton & Co., Inc., 1961.

Jackson, George Pullen, *Another Sheaf of White Spirituals*. Gainesville, Fla.: University of Florida, 1952.

——, *Down-East Spirituals and Others*, New York: J. J. Augustin, 1943.

——, *Spiritual Folk-Songs of Early America*. New York: J. J. Augustin, 1937.

JAF: Journal of American Folklore. The American Folklore Society, 1888–   ,
Austin, Texas: The University of Texas.

Karpeles, Maud, *Folk Songs from Newfoundland.* London: Oxford University
Press, 1934.

Korson, George, *Coal Dust on the Fiddle.* Philadelphia: University of Pennsylvania, 1943.

———, *Minstrels of the Mine Patch.* Philadelphia: University of Pennsylvania,
1938.

———, *et al., Pennsylvania Songs and Legends.* Philadelphia: University of
Pennsylvania, 1949.

Larkin, Margaret, *Singing Cowboy.* New York: Alfred A. Knopf, Inc., 1931.

Leach, MacEdward, *Folk Ballads and Songs of the Lower Labrador Coast.*
Ottawa: National Museum of Canada, 1965.

Linscott, Eloise Hubbard, *Folk Songs of Old New England.* New York: The
Macmillan Company, 1939.

Lomax, Alan, *The Folk Songs of North America.* Garden City, N.Y.: Doubleday
& Company, Inc., 1960.

Lomax, John A., *Cowboy Songs and Other Frontier Ballads.* New York: The
Macmillan Company, 1910; with additions, 1916.

———, *Songs of the Cattle Trail and Cow Camp.* New York: The Macmillan
Company, 1919.

———, and Alan Lomax, *American Ballads and Folk Songs.* New York: The
Macmillan Company, 1934.

———, *Cowboy Songs.* New York: The Macmillan Company, 1938.

———, *Folk Song: U. S. A.* New York: Duell, Sloan and Pearce, 1947.

———, *Our Singing Country.* New York: The Macmillan Company, 1941.

Lunsford, Bascom Lamar, and Lamar Stringfield, *Thirty and One Folk Songs
(from the Southern Mountains).* New York: C. Fischer, Inc., 1939.

McDowell, Lucien L., *Songs of the Old Camp Ground.* Ann Arbor: Edwards
Bros., 1937.

———, and Flora Lassiter, *Memory Melodies.* Smithville, Tenn.: Edwards
Bros., 1947.

McGill, Josephine, *Folk Songs of the Kentucky Mountains.* New York, London,
and Toronto: Boosey and Co., 1917.

MacKenzie, W. Roy, *Ballads and Sea Songs from Nova Scotia.* Cambridge,
Mass.: Harvard University, 1928.

Matteson, Maurice, and Mellinger E. Henry, *Beech Mountain Folk Songs and
Ballads.* New York: G. Schirmer, Inc., 1936.

Moore, Ethel, and Chauncey O. Moore, *Ballads and Folk Songs of the South-
west.* Norman, Okla.: University of Oklahoma, 1964.

Morris, Alton C., *Folksongs of Florida.* Gainesville, Fla.: The University of
Florida, 1950.

Neely, Charles, *Tales and Songs of Southern Illinois.* Menasha, Wis.: George
Banta Publishing Co., 1938.

Newell, William Wells, *Games and Songs of American Children.* New York:
Harper & Row, Publishers, 1883.

NEF: Northeast Folklore. Orono, Maine: University of Maine, 1958.

Owens, William A., Texas Folk Songs (Publications of the Texas Folklore Society, XXIII). Dallas: Southern Methodist University, 1950.

Peacock, Kenneth, Songs of the Newfoundland Outports. Ottawa: National Museum of Canada, 1965.

Pound, Louise, American Ballads and Songs. New York: Charles Scribner's Sons, 1922.

Randolph, Vance, and Floyd C. Shoemaker, Ozark Folksongs, four vols. Columbia, Mo.: The State Historical Society of Missouri, 1946–1950.

Richardson, Ethel Park, American Mountain Songs. New York: Greenberg, 1927, 1955.

Rickaby, Franz, Ballads and Songs of the Shanty-Boy. Cambridge, Mass.: Harvard University, 1926.

Ritchie, Jean, A Garland of Mountain Song. New York: Oxford University Press, 1953.

———, The Swapping Song Book. New York: Oxford University Press, 1952.

Sandburg, Carl, The American Songbag. New York: Harcourt, Brace & World, Inc., 1927.

Scarborough, Dorothy, A Song Catcher in the Southern Mountains. New York: Columbia University, 1937.

Sharp, Cecil J., English Folk-Songs from the Southern Appalachians, ed., Maud Karpeles, two vols. London: Oxford University Press, 1932.

Shay, Frank, American Sea Songs and Chanteys. New York: W. W. Norton & Company, Inc., 1948.

Shoemaker, Henry W., Mountain Minstrelsy of Pennsylvania. Philadelphia: Newman F. McGirr, 1931.

Smith, Reed, South Carolina Ballads. Cambridge, Mass.: Harvard University Press, 1928.

Stout, Earl J., Folklore from Iowa (Memoirs of the American Folklore Society, Vol. 29). New York: 1936.

Sturgis, Edith B., and Robert Hughes, Songs from the Hills of Vermont. New York, G. Schirmer, Inc., 1919.

Sulzer, Elmer G., Twenty-five Kentucky Folk Ballads. Lexington, Ky.: Transylvania Printing Co., 1946.

Thomas, Jean, Ballad Makin' in the Mountains of Kentucky. New York: Holt, Rinehart & Winston, Inc., 1939.

———, Devil's Ditties. Chicago: W. W. Hatfield Co., 1931.

———, and Joseph A. Leeder, The Singin' Gatherin'. Morristown, N.J.: Silver Burdett Company, 1939.

Thompson, Harold W., Body, Boots and Britches. Philadelphia: J. B. Lippincott Co., 1940.

Thompson, Harold W., and Edith E. Cutting, A Pioneer Songster: Texts from the Stevens-Douglas Manuscript of Western New York, 1841–1856. Ithaca: Cornell University, 1958.

Thorp, N. Howard, Songs of the Cowboys. Revised and enlarged. Boston and New York: Houghton Mifflin Company, 1921.

Van Wey, Adelaide, and Donald Lee Moore, *Smoky Mountain Ballads*. New York: G. Schirmer, Inc., 1949.

Wetmore, Susannah, *Mountain Songs of North Carolina*. New York: G. Schirmer, Inc., 1926.

Wheeler, Mary, *Kentucky Mountain Folk-Songs*. Boston: Boston Music Co., 1937.

———, *Steamboatin' Days*. Baton Rouge: Louisiana State University, 1944.

Wolford, Leah Jackson, *The Play-Party in Indiana*. Indianapolis: Indianapolis Historical Society, 1959.

Wyman, Loraine, and Howard Brockway, *Lonesome Tunes*. New York: H. W. Gray Co., 1916.

———, *Twenty Kentucky Mountain Songs*. Boston: Oliver Ditson Co., 1920.

DISCOGRAPHY

(A partial list of commercial recordings with materials pertinent to the subject of this study.)

CAMPUS 201: *Green Fields of Illinois.*

COLUMBIA LK 211: *Canadian Folk Songs.* Columbia World Library of Folk and Primitive Music, Vol. 8, eds. Marius Barbeau and Alan Lomax.

ELEKTRA EKL 125: *Kentucky Mountain Songs.* Sung by Jean Ritchie.

FOLK LEGACY FSA 1: *Frank Proffitt of Reese, North Carolina.*

FOLK LEGACY FSA 2: *Joseph Able Trivett of Butler, Tennessee.*

FOLK LEGACY FSA 3: *Edna Ritchie of Viper, Kentucky.*

FOLK LEGACY FSA 10: *Tom Brandon of Peterborough, Ontario.*

FOLK LEGACY FSA 11: *Max Hunter of Springfield, Missouri.*

FOLK LEGACY FSA 15: *Lawrence Older of Middle Grove, New York.*

FOLK LEGACY FSA 17: *Hobart Smith.*

FOLK LEGACY FSA 22 and 23: *The Traditional Music of Beech Mountain, North Carolina,* Vols. I and II.

FOLK LEGACY FSA 24: *Carolina Tar Heels.*

FOLKWAYS 2036: *L. M. Hilton—Mormon Folk Songs.*

FOLKWAYS 2309: *Old Love Songs and Ballads from the Big Laurel, North Carolina.* Recorded by Peter Gott and John Cohen.

FOLKWAYS 2314: *American Banjo, "Scruggs Style."*

FOLKWAYS 2316: *Ritchie Family of Kentucky.*

FOLKWAYS 2317: *Mountain Music of Kentucky.* Collected by John Cohen.

FOLKWAYS 2350: *Clarence Ashley and Tex Isley.*

FOLKWAYS 2351: *Dock Boggs.*

FOLKWAYS 2354: *Songs of a New York Lumberjack.* Sung by Ellen Stekert.

FOLKWAYS 2355: *Old-Time Music at Ashley's.*

231

FOLKWAYS 2356: *Old Harp Singers.*

FOLKWAYS 2359: *Clarence Ashley—Old-time Music.*

FOLKWAYS 2360: *Frank Proffitt Sings Folk Songs.*

FOLKWAYS 2362: *Horton Barker, Traditional Singer.*

FOLKWAYS 2363: *Holcomb and Ward—Ky. and Va. Traditions.*

FOLKWAYS 2365: *Mountain Music, Autoharp.*

FOLKWAYS 2368: *Roscoe Holcomb.*

FOLKWAYS 2392: *Dock Boggs, Vol. 2*, Mike Seeger.

FOLKWAYS 2434: *Old-Time Fiddlers, Union Grove, N.C.*

FOLKWAYS 2951: *Anthology of American Folk Music*, ed. Harry Smith.

FOLKWAYS 3810: *Buell H. Kazee—Songs and Music.*

FOLKWAYS 3828: *Pete Steele—Banjo Tunes.*

FOLKWAYS 4001: *Wolf River Songs.*

FOLKWAYS 4005: *Folk Songs of Ontario.*

FOLKWAYS 4018: *Songs of the Great Lakes.*

FOLKWAYS 4051: *Irish and British Songs from the Ottawa Valley.* Sung by O. J. Abbott.

FOLKWAYS 4052: *Lumbering Songs from the Ontario Shanties.*

FOLKWAYS 4307: *Maritime Folk Songs.*

FOLKWAYS 4312: *Folksongs of Saskatchewan.*

FOLKWAYS 5324: *Loman Canser—Missouri Songs.*

FOLKWAYS 5458: *Dock Boggs—Interview—M. Seeger.*

LIBRARY OF CONGRESS AAFS L1: *Anglo-American Ballads,* ed. Alan Lomax.

LIBRARY OF CONGRESS AAFS L7: *Anglo-American Ballads,* ed. B. A. Botkin.

LIBRARY OF CONGRESS AAFS L14: *Anglo-American Songs and Ballads,* ed. Duncan B. M. Emrich.

LIBRARY OF CONGRESS AAFS L21: *Anglo-American Songs and Ballads,* ed. Duncan B. M. Emrich.

LIBRARY OF CONGRESS AAFS L51–L53: *The Ballad Hunter.* Illus. lectures by John A. Lomax.

LIBRARY OF CONGRESS AAFS L54: *Versions and Variants of "Barbara Allen,"* ed. Charles Seeger.

LIBRARY OF CONGRESS AAFS L57 & L58: *Child Ballads Traditional in the United States,* ed. Bertrand H. Bronson.

OLD-TIMEY 100: *Old-Time Southern Dance.*

PRESTIGE 14030: *Old Time Fiddling at Union Grove.*

PRESTIGE/INTERNATIONAL 25003: *Ballads and Breakdowns from the Southern Mountains.* Southern Journey 3.

PRESTIGE/INTERNATIONAL 25006: *Folk Songs from the Ozarks.* Southern Journey 6.

TRADITION 1007: *Southern Appalachians Instrumental Music.*

VANGUARD VRS 9158: *Almeda Riddle: Songs and Ballads of the Ozarks.*

INDEX

"Across the Blue Mountain," 87, 179
Action, in folksongs, 38, 78 (*see also* Ballads)
  symbolic, 7, 9
Addison, Joseph, 6
Adultery, in folksongs, 94
Alteration, in folksongs, 138–139
Ambrosian modes, 154
Analyzing folksongs, 210–224
Art, of folksong, 4–11
Auden, W. H., 5
Authority roles, in folksongs, 97, 101

"Babes in the Woods, The," 121
Bach, Johann Sebastian, 5
"Bachelor's Hall," 90, 120
"Baggage Coach Ahead, The," 121
"Bailiff's Daughter of Islington, The," 93 n., 95, 101, 114
Balance, in folk poetry, 61
Ballad meter, 62, 140
Ballads, 37–60, 78–83
  action in, 38–42, 48–49, 58–59
  blues ballads, 83–85
  broadside ballads, 6, 35, 48, 63, 64, 81–83, 114, 178
  changing styles of, 48
  Child ballads, 48, 83, 92–110
  "come-all-ye" ballads, 48, 65, 126
  coronachs, 48, 83–85
  decay in, 13
  dialog technique in, 41, 45, 57

Ballads (cont.)
  laws of, 81
  legendary songs, 89
  lyric elements in, 24
  occupational ballads, 126–131
  and oral change, 48–60
  as story-song, 37–47
  street ballads, 82–83
  understatement in, 7
Ballet books, 36
"Bangum and the Boar, 34, 59, 93 n.
Banjo, 148
Banjo songs, 85
"Banks of the Ohio, The," 116
"Barbara Allen," 93 n., 94, 104, 170, 171
Bartók, Béla, 5, 224
Belles lettres:
  and folk art, 4–11, 37
  poetic meter in, 133
Binary pattern, in folksongs, 62
Blake, William, 142
Blues ballads, 83–85
"Bold Soldier, The," 111
"Bonny Barbara Allen," 93 n., 94, 104, 170, 171
"Bonny Earl of Murray, The," 83
Borrowing, of folk tunes, 180–185
Botkin, Ben A., 187
Brahms, Johannes, 5
"Bramble Briar, The," 112
Broadside ballads, 6, 35, 48, 63, 64, 81–83, 114, 178
Burdens, in folksongs, 58, 63, 66, 166
Burns, Robert, 5

Caesura, in folksongs, 62
"Cambric Shirt, The," 92 n.
"Captain Kidd," 64
"Captain Wedderburn's Courtship," 53, 86, 179
"Careless Love," 169
Carter Family, 68
"Casey Jones," 34
Causal chain, in folksongs, 70
Change, in folksongs (see Oral transmission)
Chanson d'aventure, 87
Chant, 134 n., 141, 141 n.
"Cherry Tree Carol, The," 93 n., 171
"Chevy Chase," 42, 93
Child, Francis James, 48
Child ballads, 48, 83, 92–110
Children:
    death of, in folksongs, 121–122
    songs of, 186–187
Choruses, in folksongs, 66–69
Chromaticism, in folksongs, 153, 159, 159 n., 211
Church modes, 154–155, 154 n.
Circular repetition, 70
Circular tunes, 158
Classifying folksong, 210–224
Closing, law of, 81
Coffin, Tristram P., 13, 20, 28, 84
Coleridge, Samuel Taylor, 5
Collecting folklore, 203–205
Collins, Floyd, 34
"Come-all-ye" ballads, 48, 65, 126
Commonplaces, in folksongs, 32
Composition, of folksongs, 33–35
Compression of action, in ballads, 58–59
Contour, in folk tunes, 160–164
    classification by, 210, 218–220
Conventionalization, in folksongs, 7, 9, 18–19, 57
    elements of, 31–33
Copland, Aaron, 5
Coronachs, 48, 83–85
Country-music style, 148–149, 187–188
Couplets, 62
Courting songs, 118–120
Cowboy songs, 128
"Cripple Creek," 187
"Cruel Brother, The," 28
"Cruel Mother, The," 93 n., 94, 97
"Cumberland Gap," 187
Cumulative chain, in folksongs, 73–75

Dance tunes, songs set to, 147–148
Dancing, social, 5
Death, in folksongs, 92–126

"Death of Queen Jane, The," 29, 56
Degenerative change, in folksongs, 13, 17–18
"Derby Ram, The," 90
Devil, in folksongs, 25, 99–101
"Devil and the Farmer's Wife, The," 99
"Devil's Nine Questions, The," 86
Dialog songs, 38–39, 69, 85–87, 116–117
Diatonicism, in folksongs, 153, 159, 211
Dipods, 62, 134, 140
Dooley (Dula), Tom, song about, 84
Drunkards, in folklore, 110
"Drunkard's Courtship, The," 180
Dula (Dooley), Tom, song about, 84
Dulcimer, 148

"Earl Brand," 7, 9, 78, 93 n.
"Edward," 85, 93 n., 184
"Elfin Knight, The," 92 n.
Emasculation, in folksongs, 97, 104, 108
Emotional core, in folksongs, 20–24, 31
"Empty Cot in the Bunkhouse Tonight, An," 128
English and Scottish Popular Ballads, The (Child), 48
Erotic love, in folksongs, 104
Expression, folk, 7–11

"Fair and Tender Ladies," 178
"Fair Florella," 29, 34, 116
"Fair Margaret and Sweet William," 93 n., 180
"False Knight Upon the Road," 92 n.
"Farmer's Curst Wife, The," 93 n.
Fathers, in folksongs, 97, 101, 110–114
Faulkner, William, 5
Feminine rhyme, 63
Fiddle, 148
Fidelity, in folksongs, 117–118
Final tone, of folk tunes, 157–158
"Five Nights Drunk," 93 n., 186
Five-tone scales, 155 n., 158–159, 211, 213–218
"Floyd Collins," 34
Folk art, 5–6
Folk expression, characteristics of, 7–11
Folk narrative, laws of, 81
Folk poetry, regularity and balance in, 61
Folk tunes (see also Folksongs):
    borrowing of, 180–185
    common characteristics in, 153
    contour in, 160–164, 210, 218–220
    final tone of, 157–158
    inflection in, 159, 211

Folk tunes (cont.)
  melodic progression in, 159
  melody in, 152
  monophonic, 153
  multiple use of, 177–185
  nature of, 151–164
  octave in, 157, 158, 159, 211, 212
  phrases (see Musical phrases)
  polyphonic, 153
  range in, 157, 212
  scales in, 153–159, 210–224, (tables) 214, 216
  stability in, 170–172
  and story families, 172–176
  and text, interdependence of, 139–140
  tune families, 164, 171–172
Folklore:
  collecting of, 203–205
  drunkards in, 110
  and illiteracy, 35–36
Folksongs:
  action in, 7, 9, 38, 78
  adultery in, 94
  alteration in, 138–139
  analyzing and classifying of, 210–224
  art of, 4–11
  authority roles in, 97, 101
  ballads (see Ballads)
  banjo songs, 85
  binary pattern in, 62
  burdens in, 58, 63, 66, 166
  caesura in, 62
  causal chain in, 70
  choruses in, 66–69
  chromaticism in, 153, 159, 159 n., 211
  collecting of, 203–205
  commonplaces in, 32
  composition of, 33–35
  conventionalization in, 7, 9, 18–19, 31–33, 57
  country-music style, 148–149, 187–188
  courting songs, 118–120
  cowboy songs, 128
  cumulative chain in, 73–75
  death in, 92–126
  death of children in, 121–122
  degenerative change in, 13, 17–18
  devil in, 25, 99–101
  dialog songs, 38–39, 69, 85–87, 116–117
  diatonicism in, 153, 159, 211
  emasculation in, 97, 104, 108
  emotional core in, 20–24, 31
  erotic love in, 104
  fathers in, 97, 101, 110–114
  fidelity in, 117–118
  form in, 61–76, 165–185, 220

Folksongs (cont.)
  formula in, 33, 56–58, 69–76
  framing device in, 33
  ghosts in, 27
  gibberish in, 18
  girl-dressed-as-boy songs, 114
  hillbilly songs, 35
  humorous songs, 145–146
  imitation in, 34
  improvisation in, 12
  incest theme in, 28
  isochronic arrangement in, 62, 134
  laments, 48, 83–85
  last-goodnight songs, 84
  legendary songs, 89
  localization in, 29–31
  love in, 92–126
  lumberjack songs, 126
  lyric songs, 38, 87–89, 116
  magic in, 25
  melody of (see Folk tunes)
  metaphor in, 38
  metrical aspect of, 132–150
  mothers in, 97, 104
  motion songs, 149–150
  motivation in, 78
  murder in, 94
  Negro, 57–58, 159 n., 169 n.
  obscenity in, 76, 186
  opposition to lovers in, 110–114
  oral transmission of (see Oral transmission)
  ornamentation in, 144
  parodies, 34
  predictability in, 69
  pregnancy in, 114
  progressive chain in, 73
  punishment in, 93–94
  railroading songs, 130
  rationalization in, 18–19
  recomposition of, 33–35
  recording of, 35–36
  refrains in, 58, 66, 166
  religious songs, 125, 188–189
  repetition in (see Repetition)
  revenants in, 25, 27
  reworking of, 34, 178
  rhyming in, 62–65, 161
  rhythm in, 132–133, 149–150, 152
  riddles in, 53–55
  role-reversal in, 96
  sadness of, 131
  scene in, 78
  in Scotland, 35
  sentimental songs, 121, 126
  separation of lovers in, 110–120
  sex in, 104

Folksongs (cont.)
  singability of, 159
  Southern Appalachian, 144
  story-songs, 37–47, 78–83, 142–148
    (see also Ballads)
  style or organization of meaning, 77–91
  supernatural in, 25–27
  suspended chain in, 76
  symbols in, 7, 9, 90
  syncopation in, 138–139
  traditional shapes of content, 61–76
  transcribing of, 206–209
  tunes of (see Folk tunes)
  universalization in, 29–31
  wooing in, 95–96
Forget-Me-Not Songster, 113
Forgetting, as cause of change, 19–20, 24–29, 29–31
Form, in folksongs, 61–76, 165–185, 220
Formula, in folksongs, 33, 56–58, 69–76
"Found a Peanut," 69
Four-tone scales, 211, 215, 217
Framing device, in folksongs, 33

"Geordie," 93 n., 94
"George Collins," 93 n.
Gerould, Gordon Hall, 133–134, 139
Ghosts, in folksongs, 27
Gibberish, in folksongs, 18
"Giles Collins, " 93 n.
Girl-dressed-as-boy songs, 114
"Girl Volunteer, The," 114
Glareanus, 154 n.
"Golden Vanity, The," 66, 79, 93 n., 95, 101, 103, 112
"Green Grass Grows All Around, The," 73
Gregorian modes, 154
Guitar, 148
"Gypsy Laddie, The," 65, 93 n., 94, 181

"Hangman, The," 93 n.
"Hangman's Tree, The," 93 n.
"Happy Birthday," 152
"Henry Martyn," 93 n.
Heptachordal scale, 156–157
Hexatonic scale, 156
Hillbilly songs, 35
Hodgart, M. J. C., 93
Hoedown, 187
"House Carpenter, The," 25, 93 n., 94, 162
Humorous songs, 145–146
Hyman, Stanley Edgar, 25
Hyperbole, in folk expression, 8

"I Wish I Was a Single Girl Again," 119
"I Wish I Was Single Again," 119
Iamb foot, 134 n.
"Ida Red," 187
Illiteracy, and folklore, 35–36
Imitation, in folksongs, 34
Improvisation, in folksongs, 12
Incest theme, in folksongs, 28
Incremental repetition, 33, 66, 69
Indy, Vincent d', 155
Inflection, in folk tunes, 159, 211
Instruments, influence of, 148–149
"Irish Washerwoman, The," 148
Isochronic arrangement, in folksongs, 62, 134
Ives, Edward, 188

"Jack and Joe," 116
"Jack Monroe," 114
"Jackie's Gone a-Sailing," 82
Jackson, George Pullen, 189
"Jam on Gerry's Rocks, The," 126
"James Harris or The Daemon Lover," 25, 93 n.
Jenkins, Rev. Andrew, 188
"Jennie Jenkins," 85
"Jesse James," 89
"Joe Bowers," 116
"John Henry," 89
"John of Hazelgreen," 93 n.
"John Reilly," 117

Keats, John, 5

"Lady Alice," 93 n., 95
"Lady Gay, The," 27, 93 n., 94
"Lady Isabel and the Elf Knight," 92 n.
Laments, 48, 83–85
"Lamkin," 93 n., 94, 97
"Lass of Loch Royal, The," 52
Last-goodnight songs, 84
Laws, G. Malcolm, 116
Laws, of folk narrative, 81
Leaping-and-lingering technique, 78
Legendary songs, 89
"Letter Edged in Black, The," 121
Literacy, and folklore, 35–36
"Little Joe, the Wrangler," 128
"Little Mattie Groves," 32, 93 n., 94
"Little Mohee," 177, 178
"Little Musgrave and Lady Barnard," 93 n.
"Little Rosewood Casket, The," 121
"Little Sparrow," 88, 114

"Lizzie Wan," 28
Localization, in folksongs, 29–31
"Locks and Bolts," 111
"Lord Bateman," 83, 93 n., 95, 101
"Lord Lovel," 34, 93 n., 170
"Lord Randall," 85, 93 n., 104
"Lord Thomas and Fair Ellender [or Eleanor]," 32, 45, 93 n.
"Lost Jimmie Whalan," 27
Love, in folksongs, 92–126
    opposition to lovers, 110–114
    separation of lovers, 110–120
"Love Henry," 93 n., 97
Lumberjack songs, 126
Lyric expression, and ballads, 24, 37–60
Lyric songs, 38, 87–89, 116

Magic, in folksongs, 25
"Maid Freed from the Gallows, The," 93 n., 96, 101
Mandolin, 148
"Mantle So Green, The," 117
"Mary Hamilton," 29, 49
"Mattie Groves," 32, 93 n., 94
Meaning, organization of, 77–91
Melodic progression, 159
Melody, of folksongs, 66, 152 (see also Folk tunes)
Memory, and oral transmission, 12, 19–29
"Mermaid, The," 93 n.
Metaphor, in folksongs, 38
Meter, in folksongs, 132–150
    ballad meter, 62, 140
    influence of instruments on, 148–149
    metrical rigidity, 140–142
    in motion songs, 149–150
    and rhythm, 132–133
    in story-songs, 142–148
    in traditional music, 134–139
    in traditional verse and song, 133–134
Mid-cadence tone, 161, 172
Mishearing, as cause of change, 17–18
Misunderstanding, as cause of change, 17–18
Modal systems, 154–155, 154 n.
Monody, 155
    monophonic folk tunes, 153
Morality modes, 93–97
Mothers, in folksongs, 97, 104
Motion songs, 149–150
Motivation, in folksongs, 78
Murder, in folksongs, 94
Musical phrases, 151
    analysis by, 165
    contour of, 160–164

Musical phrases (cont.)
    finals and openings, 160–162, 171–172, 218–220
    relationship between, 220
    stability of, 171–172

Narrative, folk, laws of, 81
Negro folk music:
    chromaticism in, 159 n.
    repetition in, 57–58, 169 n.
Negative tropisms, 25–29
"New River Shore, The," 111
"Nottalin Town," 8

Obscenity, in folksongs, 76, 186
Occupational ballads, 126–131
Octave, in folk tunes, 157, 158, 159, 211, 212
"Old Joe Clark," 89, 150, 187
Olrik, Axel, 81
"Omie Wise," 116
"On Top of Old Smoky," 88
Opening, law of, 81
Opposition to lovers, in folksong, 110–114
Oral transmission, of folksongs, 9, 12–36
    and ballads, 48–60
    change through, 13–18, 48–60
    and composition and recomposition, 33–35
    and conventionalization, 18–19, 31–33
    and emotional core, 19–24
    and forgetting, 19–29
    and literacy, 35–36
    and localization, 29–31
    and musical stability, 170–172
    and negative tropisms, 24–29
    and rationalization, 18–19
    and recording of repertoire, 35–36
    and story-songs, 142–143
    and universalization, 29–31
Ornamentation, in folksinging, 144
"Our Goodman," 93 n., 108
Overstatement, in folk expression, 7, 8
"Oxford Girl, The," 29, 115

"Paper of Pins," 85
Parental separation of lovers, 110–114
Parodies, 34
"Pearl Bryan," 29, 30, 34, 116
Pentatonic scales, 155 n., 158–159, 213–218, (tables) 214, 216
"Peri Meri Dixie Dominie," 55
Phonograph, and country music, 148–149

Phrase finals and openings, 160–162, 171–172, 218–220 (*see also* Musical phrases)
Plainsong, 134 n., 135 n.
Play-party games, 187
Polyphony, 155
    polyphonic folk tunes, 153
Popular art, 5–6
Predictability, in folksongs, 69
Pregnancy, in folksongs, 114
"Pretty Fair Miss All in the Garden, A," 85, 87, 117
"Pretty Polly," 169 n.
Primary relationship, of scale groups, 215
Private expression, 7–11
Progressive chain, in folksongs, 73
Progressive recitation, 71–72
Public expression, 7–11
Public symbol, 7, 9
Punishment, in folksongs, 93–94

Radio, and country music, 148–149
"Railroad Bill," 89
Railroading songs, 130
Range, in folk tunes, 212
    difficulties caused by, 157
Rationalization, in folksongs, 18–19
Recomposition, of folksongs, 33–35
Recording, of folksongs, 35–36
"Red Herring, The," 90
Reflective techniques, 10
Reflexive techniques, 10
Refrains, in folksongs, 58, 66, 166
Regularity, in folk poetry, 61
Reilly, William, songs about, 113
Religious folksongs, 125, 188–189
Repetition, in folksongs, 7, 9, 63, 169 n.
    and form, 65–69, 165
    formulaic repetition, 56–58, 69–70
    incremental repetition, 33
    law of, 81
Revenants, in folksongs, 25, 27
Reworking, of folksongs, 34, 178
Rhyming, in folksongs, 62–65, 161
Rhythm:
    and melody, 152
    and meter, 132–133
    work-rhythms, 149–150
Richmond, W. Edson, 36
"Riddle Song, The," 55, 179
Riddles, in folksongs, 53–55
"Riddles Wisely Expounded," 92 n.
Rigidity, metrical, 140–142
Ritchie, Jean, 188
Role-reversal, in folksongs, 96

Romance modes, 93–97
"Rose Connley," 116

Sadness, of folksongs, 131
"Sam Bass," 89
"Sam Hall," 64
Sandburg, Carl, 5
Scales, in folk tunes, 153–159
    classification by, 210–224, (tables) 214, 216
Schinhan, Jan P., 212, 224
"Sea Crab, The," 186
Secondary relationship, of scale groups, 215
Scene, in folksongs, 78
Scotland, folksongs in, 35
Sentimental songs, 121, 126
Separation of lovers, in folksongs, 110–120
Seven-tone scales, 211, 215, (tables) 214, 216
Sex, in folksongs, 104
Shakespeare, William, 5
Sharp, Cecil, 158
Sharpe, Charles Kilpatrick, 49
"Ship that Never Returned, The," 34
Simple repetition, 69
Singability, of folksongs, 159
"Sir Andrew Barton," 93 n., 94
"Sir Hugh or the Jew's Daughter," 93 n., 94, 97
"Sir Lionel," 59, 93 n.
Six-tone scales, 156, 159, 211, 215, 217, (tables) 214, 216
Smith, Reed, 18
Social dancing, 5
Sophisticated art, 5–6
Southern Appalachian folksongs, 144
"Sow Took the Measles, The," 90
"Springfield Mountain," 34, 84, 146, 176
Square dance, 187
Stability, in folk tunes, 170–172
Stanzaic form, 62–65, 139
Stichic composition, 12
"Storms Are On the Ocean," 68
Story-songs, 37–47, 78–83, 142–148 (*see also* Ballads)
Street ballads, 82–83
Stress-slack patterns, 134, 140–142
String bass, 148
Strophic composition, 12
Style, and organization of meaning, 77–91
Supernatural, in folksongs, 25–27
Suspended chain, in folksongs, 76

"Sweet Betsy from Pike," 178
"Sweet Trinity," 93 n.
Symbolic action, 7, 9
Symbols:
  in folksong, 90
  public, 7, 9
Syncopation, in folksongs, 138–139

"Ten Thousand Miles," 68
Tension and repose, pattern of, 160–161
Tertiary relationship, of scale groups, 217
Text and tune, interdependence of, 139–140
"There's a Hole in the Bottom of the Sea," 90
"There's More Pretty Girls Than One," 178
Thomas, Jean, 188
Thomson, Virgil, 5
"Three Crows, The," 176
"Three Nights Drunk," 93 n.
"Three Ravens, The," 29, 34, 93 n., 172, 176
Three-tone scales, 211, 215
Tonal center, concept of, 155
Tonic, ending on, 157–158
"Tragic Romance, The," 29
Transcribing folksongs, 206–209
Transitional phrases, 172
Transmission of folksongs (see Oral Transmission)
Tri-tones, 215, 216
Tschaikowsky, Peter I., 5
Tunes (see Folk tunes)
"Twa Corbies, The," 34, 172, 176
"Twelve Days of Christmas, The," 73
"Two Brothers, The," 28, 93 n.
"Two Sisters, The," 20, 25, 58, 63, 64, 66, 93 n., 94, 148, 170–171

Two to a scene, law of, 81
Two-tone scales, 215

Ultimate repose, point of, 157–158
Understatement, in folk expression, 7
Universalization, in folksongs, 29–31
"Unquiet Grave, The," 40
"Utah Carroll," 128

Variety of contour, in folk tunes, 162–164
Verse:
  forms of, 62–65
  meter of, 133–134, 140
Verse-chorus alternation, 66–69
"Villikens and His Dinah," 177

"Wagoner's Lad, The," 177, 178
"Wayfaring Stranger," 178
"When the Work's All Done This Fall," 128
Whispering Down the Lane (game), 13–14
"Who Killed Cock Robin?" 90
"Who's Gonna Shoe Your Pretty Little Feet?" 68–69, 116
"Wife of Usher's Well, The," 27, 93 n.
"Wife Wrapt in Wether's Skin," 93 n., 94, 110
Wilgus, D. K., 84, 188
"Will the Weaver," 110
"Wondrous Love," 64
Wooing, in folksongs, 95–96
Word-rhythms, distortion of, 149–150

"Young Beichan," 93 n.
"Young Hunting," 93 n.

INDEX OF
TITLES AND FIRST LINES

(Titles given in capital letters)

ACROSS THE BLUE MOUNTAIN, 14
ARCH AND GORDON, 84
As I cam' by yon auld house end, 175
As I went down to fair Nottalin Town, 8
As slowly I roamed by the banks of the river, 28
BABES IN THE WOODS, 122
BACHELOR'S HALL, 120
BIRD SONG, 90
CHARMING BEAUTY BRIGHT, 112
CHEVY CHASE, 43
Come all of you bold shanty boys, 125
Come all ye gee-wee-wents, 142
Come all you maids and pretty fair maidens, 88
DANDOO, 167
Darlin' you can't love one, 73
Deep, deep in a lonesome valley, 29
THE DEVIL AND THE FARMER'S WIFE, 99
THE DEVIL'S NINE QUESTIONS, 86
Down in the lovely meadow, 29
THE DYING NUN, 124
EARL BRAND, 7
FAIR FLORELLA, 29
First night that I came home, 108
FOOLISH BOY, 71
FOUR (FIVE) NIGHTS DRUNK, 108
God prosper long our noble king, 43

240

GOLDEN WILLOW TREE (VANITY), 79
Good morning, good morning, good morning in May, 14
GREEN GROW THE RUSHES, O, 74
GYPSY LADDIE, 183
HANGMAN, 41
Hangman, hangman, hold your rope, 41
THE HOUSE CARPENTER, 25
Hug me closer, Mother, closer, 122
I am a poor girl, my fortune is sad, 40
If you can't answer my questions nine, 86
I'll sing you one, ho, 74
I'm just a poor wayfaring stranger, 125
It was a day and a high old day, 105
It was late in the night when the captain came home, 182
JACK AND JOE, 67
JACKIE'S GONE A-SAILING, 82
JAMES HARRIS OR THE DAEMON LOVER, 25
THE JAM ON GERRY'S ROCKS, 127
JESSE JAMES, 130
JOHN OF HAZELGREEN, 95
Lady Marg'ret was a-goin' to her bed one night, 97
LASS OF LOCH ROYAL, 52
Last night I dreamed of my true love, 111
Let the air blow in upon me, 124
LITTLE BESSIE, 122
Little did my mother think, 51
Little girl you turned me down, 178
LITTLE MUSGRAVE AND LORD BARNARD'S WIFE, 105
LITTLE SPARROW, 88
Living in Missouri was a brave bold man, 130
LOCKS AND BOLTS, 111
LORD BATEMAN, 101
Lord Bateman was a noble lord, 101
LORD THOMAS AND FAIR ANNET (ELEANOR), 46
Lord Thomas, he was a bold keeper, 46
LOST JIMMY WHALAN, 27
LOVE HENRY, 97
THE MAID FREED FROM THE GALLOWS, 41
MARY HAMILTON, 51
MATHA GROVES, 105
Monday morning I married me a wife, 72
NOTTALIN TOWN, 8
Oh, don't you remember a long time ago, 122
Oh, time draws near my dearest dear, 52
Oh, when I was a 'prentice boy, 115
Oh, who killed Cock Robin?, 70
The old Devil came to our field, 99

OLD JOE CLARK, 90
An old knight rode one summer's day, 95
Once I courted a fair and beauty bright, 112
One morning, one morning, one morning in May, 16
On Springfield Mountain where we all do dwell, 146
OUR GOODMAN, 108
THE OXFORD GIRL, 115
PEARL BRYAN, 29
A PRETTY FAIR MISS ALL IN THE GARDEN, 117
A pretty fair miss all in the garden, 117
RAINBOW WILLOW, 111
Rise ye up, rise up my seven sons bold, 7
Says the robin as he run, 90
THE SCOLDING WIFE, 72
SPRINGFIELD MOUNTAIN, 146
There been falling drops of dew, sweetheart, 40
THERE'S MORE PRETTY GIRLS THAN ONE, 178
There was a little ship that sailed upon the sea, 79
There was an old man who lived in the West, 167
There lived an old lord by the Northern Sea, 20
There was a wealthy merchant, in London he did dwell, 82
There was three crows on yonder's tree, 176
There were three rauens sat on a tree, 173
THE THREE CROWS, 175
THE THREE RAVENS, 173
Three years ago both Jack and Joe, 67
TIME DRAWS NEAR, 52
'Tis the lowly Lamb of God, 178
THE TRAGIC ROMANCE, 29
THE TWA CORBIES, 173
THE TWA SISTERS, 23
Two loving sisters was a-walking side by side, 23
THE UNQUIET GRAVE, 40
UTAH CARROLL, 128
WAGONNER'S LAD, 40
WAYFARING STRANGER, 125
When Archie went to Louisville, 84
When young men goes courtin' they'll dress up so fine, 120
WHO KILLED COCK ROBIN?, 69
THE WIFE WRAPT IN WETHER'S SKIN, 167
Word's gane to the kitchen, 49
Yes sir, the Gypsies in the North, 183
You ask me why my little friend, 128
Young Gypsy Davey came merrily by, 181
YOUNG HUNTING, 97